D1433039

Helping Families
Through Divorce

Ellen B. Bogolub, MSW, PhD, is Assistant Professor, School of Social Work, Adelphi University, Garden City, New York. She has worked extensively with families of divorce in social agencies and in private practice, and has taught and written in the area of divorce for many years.

Helping Families Through Divorce

An Eclectic Approach

Ellen B. Bogolub, MSW, PhD

SPRINGER PUBLISHING COMPANY

Springer Publishing Company, Inc.
536 Broadway
New York, NY 10012-3955

Cover design by Tom Yabut
Production Editor: Joyce Noulas

95 96 97 98 99 / 5 4 3 2 1

Library of Congress Cataloging-in-Publication Data

Bogolub, Ellen, B.
   Helping families through divorce: an eclectic approach / Ellen Bogolub.
      p.   cm.
   Includes bibliographical references and index.
   ISBN 0-8261-9060-X
   1. Divorce therapy.   2. Divorce—Psychological aspects.
3. Children of divorced parents—Mental health.   I. Title.
RC488.6.B64   1995
616.89'156—dc2O   95-18572
                                                              CIP
                                                              REV

Printed in the United States of America

For my parents
Lillian and William Bogolub

Contents

Acknowledgments

I would like to acknowledge the assistance of the many people who contributed to the development of this book.

A major debt is owed to five esteemed colleagues who generously and carefully read the entire manuscript and offered perceptive and valuable ideas: Joel Blau (School of Social Welfare, State University of New York at Stony Brook), Roberta Sands (School of Social Work, University of Pennsylvania), Lawrence Shulman (School of Social Work, Boston University), Mary Van Hook (School of Social Work, University of Michigan), and Dean Janice Wood Wetzel (School of Social Work, Adelphi University). An equal debt is owed to Armand Lauffer (School of Social Work, University of Michigan), who provided incisive ideas that contributed in a major way to the organization of the manuscript. Ruth Brandwein and Abe Lurie—both of the School of Social Welfare, State University of New York at Stony Brook—also contributed thoughtfully.

Many people provided in-depth interviews that greatly increased my knowledge about divorce or ethnicity. In particular, I extend appreciation to Regina Arrata, Barbara Fritz, Tom Maligno, and Ettie Teichman of Nassau–Suffolk (NY) Law Services; Pinchas Berger of the Jewish Board of Family and Childrens' Services (New York, NY); Ruth Gutmaker and Michael Murphy of the Suffolk County (NY) Department of Social Services; Gladys Serrano of the Hispanic Counseling Center (Hempstead, NY); Paulette Moore Hines and Nydia Garcia Preto of the UM-DNJ Community Mental Health Center (Piscataway, NJ); Harriette McAdoo of the Michigan State University Department of Family and Child Ecology; Luz Melecio of the Puerto Rican Family Institute (New York, NY); Roni Berger of the School of Social Work, Adelphi University; and Mona Barsky, Elana Schondorf, and Dana Van Buskirk.

Excellent advice that kept me on track during particular periods in the book's development was given by Herb Strean, Professor Emeritus, School of Social Work, Rutgers University; and by Rebecca Loew, School of Social Work, Adelphi University.

Most important of all was the assistance of my husband Neil ("Nick") Friedman, whom I had the good fortune to meet and the courage to marry while writing a book on divorce. His editorial comments, encouragement, and love were invaluable in the completion of this volume.

Part I

INTRODUCTION

Chapter 1

Divorce in America: An Overview

"My parents are divorced." "Tom? Oh, I guess I haven't seen you for a while. We split up about a year ago." "I've been too embarrassed to tell anyone except my best friends, but my daughter Sue and her husband just decided to call it quits." Forty years ago comments like this in ordinary conversation were rare. Today they are common.

"I knew I had to leave him, but now I'm having a terrible time getting ends to meet for the kids and me." "I want to see my son and daughter, but my ex-wife is so mad at me, she makes it almost impossible." "I'm 50 years old, devoted myself to the kids and the house, and I've never held a paying job. Who on earth will hire me now?" Forty years ago problems like these were rare in the offices of mental health practitioners. Today they are common. Both the casual personal exchanges and the requests for professional help reflect something that most Americans know, either from their own experience or that of friends, family, neighbors, and colleagues: Marital separation and divorce in America have increased dramatically since 1960 (Furstenberg & Cherlin, 1991; Guttmann, 1993; Marshall, 1991; Spitze, Logan, Deane, & Zerger, 1994).

WHY ANOTHER BOOK ON DIVORCE?

As divorce has become a fact of life for many Americans, popular literature on the topic has burgeoned. Professional literature, while less abundant, has also appeared. So why do we need one more book about divorce?

Unfortunately, the literature on marital rupture generally has not spoken to the experience of the vast majority of ordinary divorced people. For example, early mass-market writing on the topic frequently extolled the virtues of divorce as an opportunity for personal growth, and the exploration of individual freedom (e.g., Johnson, 1977; Krantzler, 1974). As Hetherington notes, for a time, the myth of romantic divorce replaced the myth of the romantic marriage (Hetherington, Cox, & Cox, 1978). This trend may have provided valid encouragement for the psychologically oriented among the upper income divorced population to develop new friendships, new sexual relationships, and new hobbies. However, it offered little comfort to blue-collar housewives facing male noncompliance with court-ordered child support, and the crushing new responsibility of supporting young children alone.

Although empirical research on the impact of divorce is well developed, more practical literature for mental health professionals is somewhat scanty. Early how-to-help articles (e.g., Kelly & Wallerstein, 1977; Kenemore & Wineberg, 1984; Thweatt, 1980; Wallerstein & Kelly, 1977) paid attention to the necessities of assisting parents and children with emotions and relationships. However, they usually had less to say about therapeutic challenges such as helping clients negotiate the red tape of public assistance applications, and choose carefully as consumers of legal assistance; such practical issues were generally seen as mere manifestations of more ''real'' psychological conflicts (e.g., Kressel & Deutsch, 1977). The divorce treatment literature in the eighties and nineties, while still not abundant, has been somewhat more likely to promote combining clinical sensitivity with hands-on involvement (e.g., Constantino, 1981; Counts & Sacks, 1985; Haffey & Cohen, 1992; Hulewat & Levine, 1994), drawing attention to external, as well as internal (or psychological), reality. However, with a few exceptions (e.g., Kaslow & Schwartz, 1987; Yu, 1993), recent literature has skirted sociological and economic issues such as ethnicity as an influence on the divorce experience, the recent upswing in midlife and late-life divorce, and postdivorce financial decline.

Such gaps in the literature are the reason for one more book on divorce, one that attempts to portray the internal and external struggles of real people of varied age, gender, ethnicity, and income as they face the dissolution of their marriages. As a how-to-help book for mental health practitioners, it will build on this portrayal to put forth a comprehensive approach to assisting clients throughout the divorce process. The chapters that follow present professional mental health practices that take into account all aspects of clients's lives—financial, legal, and vocational, as well as emotional and social. Client issues and practitioner approaches for each step of the divorce process (the preseparation phase, the divorce transition, and the postdivorce phase) are specified. Before we can focus on practice, though, an overview of facts, findings, and ideas about divorce in America is necessary.

DIVORCE: FACTS AND FIGURES

In the postwar 1950s, there was widespread agreement on the importance of the nuclear family and a closely knit domestic life (Furstenberg & Cherlin, 1991); the United States divorce rate in 1958 was a low 2.1 divorces per 1,000 people (Glick & Lin, 1986). The divorce rate then jumped to 2.5 per 1,000 by 1965, and to a record 5.3 per 1,000 in 1979 (Glick & Lin, 1986)—more than 2 1/2 times the 1958 rate. It reached this same record again in 1981 (Scott, 1990). After dipping slightly, to 4.8 per 1,000 in 1988 and 4.7 per 1,000 in both 1989 (Scott, 1990) and 1990 (Darnton, 1992), the divorce rate stabilized during the early 1990s (Cooney, 1994; Teachman & Paasch, 1993). Fear of contracting AIDS in postdivorce relationships and the prohibitive costs of supporting a family in two housing units rather than one may account for this stabilization (Scott, 1990). Another possibility is that today's young married adults, who frequently experienced their parents' divorces, will work hard to avoid the pain of severed relationships (Darnton, 1992).

About half of all marriages still end in divorce (National Center for Health Statistics, cited in Bray & Depner, 1993) with the divorce rate slightly higher for second marriages (Furstenberg & Cherlin, 1991; Ganong & Coleman, 1994). The recent stabilization of the divorce rate should not blind us to the fact that the United States divorce rate is still much higher in the 1990s than it was several decades ago (Ahlburg & DeVita, 1992; Guttmann, 1993), with divorce a majority experience among both children and adults (Bray & Depner, 1993; Bumpass, Martin, & Sweet, 1991). With its continued presence, of course, goes the need to refine our skills in working with the troubled in the divorced population.

The Divorced Population

Who gets divorced? Although the Trumps make headlines, they are not representative of divorcing couples. Divorce correlates with low income

(Bumpass, Martin, & Sweet, 1989, 1991; Ganong & Coleman, 1994; Guttmann, 1993; Pear, 1993), low educational level (Bumpass et al., 1989, 1991; Guttmann, 1993; White, 1990), young age at marriage (Bumpass et al., 1989, 1991; Guttmann, 1993; Kitson, 1992) and—for Whites more than for Blacks—premarital birth (Guttman, 1993). In other words, it is under-30, poorly educated couples with limited earnings and job options who form the core of the divorced population. The risk for divorce increases with premarital sex (Kahn & London, 1991) and premarital cohabitation (Bumpass et al., 1989, 1991; Thomson & Colella, 1992). The most common explanation for the correlation with premarital cohabitation is that the people who rebel against society's norms by living together unmarried extend their rebellion by refusing to take marital commitment seriously either (Kahn & London, 1991; Thomson & Colella, 1992). Among married couples with children, those with daughters are more likely to divorce than those with sons (Morgan, Lye, & Condran, 1988; Mott, 1994), perhaps because fathers are more involved in raising their sons than their daughters (Katzev, Warner, & Acock, 1994; Morgan et al., 1988; Seltzer & Brandreth, 1994).

Most divorces occur early in marriage (Ahlburg & DeVita, 1992), with fully half taking place within the first 7 years (Bee, 1994; Germain, 1991). Although the risk for divorce is highest for couples in their late teens and early twenties (Bumpass et al., 1991) there has been a recent increase in divorce among midlife and late-life couples (Cooney, 1994; Jones & Jones, 1993; Yu, 1993). The United States National Center for Health Statistics estimates that 20% of all divorces involve women over 40, with this percentage on the rise (Canter, 1990). Since most people who marry do so in their twenties, this means an increase in the rupture of marriages that have lasted not 3 or 4 years, but 15 or 20. Usually, the woman is the partner who initiates divorce proceedings (Masheter, 1991; Mitchell-Flynn & Hutchinson, 1993)—in 61.5% of cases, to be precise (Canter, 1990).

Divorce and Ethnicity

Divorce rates vary dramatically with regard to ethnicity. There is widespread consensus that divorce is much more common among Blacks than among Whites (Bumpass et al., 1989, 1991; Heaton & Jacobson, 1994; Moore & Schwebel, 1993; Williams, Takeuchi, & Adair, 1992). This Black/White differential is longstanding, first noted in Goode's 1956 *After Divorce*, one of the early empirical studies on the topic. Additionally, compared to Whites, Blacks are less inclined to marry at all (Bulcroft & Bulcroft, 1993; Cherlin, 1992; Taylor, Chatters, Tucker, & Lewis, 1990; Williams et al., 1992), or to remarry after marital dissolution (Del Carmen & Virgo, 1993; Williams et al., 1992). The rate of marriage is declining among Black Americans (D. L. Franklin, 1992), and African American* marriages are, on the average, shorter than other marriages (Sidel, 1990).

The divorce rate for Hispanics is similar to that of non-Hispanic Whites (Family and household structure, 1992). The divorce rate for Puerto Ricans is much higher than that of other Hispanic subgroups (Chillman, 1993), and the overall Hispanic divorce rate appears to be growing (Family and household structure, 1992; Vega, 1990). Since most Hispanics are Catholic, their rate of marital dissolution becomes particularly interesting in the face of the Catholic prohibition against divorce (Del Carmen & Virgo, 1993; N. G. Preto, personal communication, December 14, 1990). In fact, the divorce rate among Catholics in general is slightly greater than that among Protestants (Bumpass et al., 1989, 1991).

Jewish divorce rates are relatively low (Guttmann, 1993). Currently, at least one in four, and possibly closer to one in three Jewish couples married within the last 10 years will divorce (Friedman, 1994); we recall that in comparison, approximately one in two marriages in the United States overall ends in divorce (National Center for Health Statistics, cited in Bray & Depner, 1993). Jewish divorce rates are even lower among those affiliated with synagogues (Bayme, 1990), and lower still among those who observe Orthodoxy (Bayme, 1994), the branch of Judaism in which divorce must be granted in a rabbinical court at the initiative of a male (Breitowitz, 1994). However, the divorce rate is higher among younger Jews than among older Jews (Bayme, 1990), indicating that Jewish divorce rates may rise along with assimilation into the broader culture.

Clearly, African Americans, Hispanics, and Jews do not represent the full ethnic spectrum in the United States. However, subsequent references to these three groups will suggest the wide ethnic variety in the American divorce experience. As well as providing information, these references will hopefully heighten readers' sensitivity to diverse experiences among divorcing or divorced clients of ethnic backgrounds that are not covered in this volume, for example, Asian, European, or Native American.

---

*Throughout this volume, in accordance with common current usage, the terms *African American* and *Black* will be used interchangeably.

As is the case among most ethnic groups (Mirande, 1991), there are subcultures among African Americans, Hispanics, and Jews. Since there is a need for study in the area of subculture and divorce (Fine, McKenry, & Chung, 1992) this volume will, as a beginning, provide examples of divorce experiences in three Jewish subcultures (Orthodox Jews, mainstream American Jews, and Soviet Jewish emigrants). Divorce among Blacks and Hispanics are discussed from the viewpoint of each group's common base (Castex, 1994; Del Carmen & Virgo, 1993). I hope that future authors will pursue ethnicity, subculture (e.g., African Americans of West Indian descent, Puerto Ricans) and divorce in greater depth.

DIVORCE: THE REASONS

Ask people why they get divorced, and they will mention infidelity, alcoholism, drug addiction, physical abuse, emotional abuse, incompatibility, lack of affection, lack of communication, lack of sex, unemployment, partner's unwillingness to help with household tasks, and many other problems (Gelles & Cornell, 1990; Greif & DeMaris, 1990; Hochschild, 1989; Kitson, 1992; Moore & Schwebel, 1993; Yu, 1993). However, all of these subjectively experienced problems existed before the 1960s, when the divorce rate jumped. So to understand why ordinary people now reject what they previously endured, we most move from the realm of individual experience to the realm of economics and sociology. Mental health practitioners must learn to think in terms of these disciplines, if we are to have a comprehensive perspective on our clients. In the following discussion on the objective basis for divorce—as well as subsequent topics in this chapter—I point out some of the implications for mental health practice, while saving more developed ideas on intervention for subsequent chapters.

Women's Labor Force Participation

The main reason for the increased divorce rate in the United States is, of course, the entry into the labor market during the last several decades of large numbers of women, whose economic dependence on men has been lessened (Cherlin, 1992; Furstenberg & Cherlin, 1991; Guttmann, 1993; White, 1990). Currently, women's labor force participation is accelerating while men's is declining, and women are expected to comprise 47.3% of the labor force by the year 2000 (Marshall, 1991). In

1991, more than half of mothers in the United States with children under age 6 were employed outside the home, about two thirds of these full time, and the proportion of employed women in this group is increasing steadily (Ahlburg & DeVita, 1992). Money, rather than personal fulfillment, appears to be the primary motivation for women who work (Marshall, 1991; Morgan, 1991).

But, is women's paid employment always the key to the capacity to divorce and then survive economically? Greenstein (1990) points out that work outside the home is not a simple matter of female freedom gained. Drawing on an analysis of census data, he indicates that the number of hours a married woman currently works create an "independence effect," increasing the risk of divorce. However, the same study also indicates that a married woman's high earnings may alternatively produce an "income effect," creating the possibility of marriage-specific capital. In other words, for high income wives, working may actually decrease the possibility of divorce, while the "women at the greatest risk of marital disruption are low-income wives who work 35–40 hours per week" (Greenstein, 1990, p. 674).

Suzette, a former battered wife with five children, is an example of the independence effect. When asked what gave her the final push to leave a man who had physically abused her for several years, she replied, "I got a clerical job with the IRS and started my own bank account." An increase in self-esteem as well as in financial independence was obvious as she spoke.

While paid employment galvanized Suzette's long-overdue departure, we should not romanticize its effects. Her own savings allowed her to set up an apartment, and tided her over for a couple of months, but Suzette could not support herself and her five children on a clerk's salary, even with the addition of court-mandated child support. She went through a stint on public assistance, which she described as "degrading," before two of her children left home and two more became old enough to share the financial burden. Still, she doubts if she would have left without money of her own.

Divorced Women, Their Children, and Their Standard of Living.

As it was for Suzette, the standard of living for most working women and their children is greatly diminished by divorce (Acock & Demo, 1994; Cherlin, 1992; Marshall, 1991). Women tend to work either in low-paying sex-segregated fields or to receive less pay for work comparable to men's when they work in fields that are not sex-segregated. The result is the "gender wage gap": women earn less than men, even when education, experience, and other human capital factors are controlled (Kissman & Allen, 1993; Morgan, 1991). Also, as more women, including those with young children, enter the labor force while married, the possibility of improving income by going to work postdivorce is increasingly foreclosed, and divorced women find themselves pedalling harder and harder to stay in a financial place that is generally behind the one they occupied while married (Morgan, 1991). Finally, child support from a noncustodial father, when available, does not compensate for the loss of a complete second salary.

The Limited Contribution of Child Support to Quality of Life for Divorced Women and Their Children.

The contribution of child support is limited even today, when the federal Family Support Act of 1988 mandates child support award amounts that are standardized and regularly updated by states (Fine & Fine, 1994; Garfinkel & McLanahan, 1990; Garfinkel, Meyer, & Sandefur, 1992), causing substantial dollar increases over the judicial discretion awards of past years (Garfinkel et al., 1992; Glass, 1990). There are several reasons that even with a climate of increased government attention to child support, women still cannot rely extensively on it to bolster a subsistence earned postdivorce income. First, awards are not granted automatically, and some divorcing women, who fear assault or even murder (Peterson & Nord, 1990), or simply want nothing to do with the former spouse ("I don't want your money; I just want you out of my life"; Kamerman & Kahn, 1988), do not request an award. Clinical experience suggests that reluctance to engage in more spousal conflict, or intimidation by legal processes may also be causal factors here. Second, although approximately 80% of divorced women do obtain an award (Meyer & Garasky, 1993), men are more likely to pay when economically well off and steadily employed (Arditti & Keith, 1993; Ihinger-Tallman, Pasley, & Buehler, 1993), so that the families in the greatest need of child support benefit the least. Third, among women who do have a support award, only about half actually receive the full amount, while about one quarter receive part, and about one quarter receive nothing (Ahlburg & DeVita, 1992; Cherlin, 1993).

Why is awarded child support not always received? Although the 1988 Family Support Act promotes tightened collection procedures such as tax refund intercepts for delinquent fathers, and, as of 1994, mandatory withholding of all child support payments from obligors' paychecks (Cherlin, 1993; Fine & Fine, 1994), many fathers cross state lines to avoid paying, or conceal income (Glass, 1990). This concealed income generally means "off-the-books" employment among blue-collar and working poor men, and income tax maneuvers among men in the middle and upper income brackets, particularly the self-employed. In the end, the mother, who is the custodial parent for 90% of children living in single-parent families (Guttmann, 1993; Mott, 1994) is frequently without the father's support payments. It is her earnings which are the main source of a diminished postdivorce income for herself and her family (Ahlburg & DeVita, 1992; Cherlin, 1992; Teachman & Paasch, 1993).

Of course there is a minority of highly publicized, highly educated divorced women earning large salaries, and another minority of women old enough to be free of the care of very young children, young enough to escape age-based employment discrimination (Rayman, 1987), and motivated to train or retrain for high-paying careers. But they are exceptions.

Clinical Implications of Women's Labor Force Participation.

Today's mental health clinician must pay careful attention to issues of income adequacy, particularly when it comes to divorced women and children. Our role must include helping women seek child support awards—even though the task may seem overwhelming to the newly separated—and helping women pursue these awards when they go unpaid. More important, because a divorced woman's earnings are her major source of income unless she receives public assistance (Ahlburg & DeVita, 1992; Cherlin, 1992; Teachman & Paasch, 1993), therapists must be alert to complications presented by finding and/or maintaining a job. For example, developing well thought-out referrals for education and job training, overcoming fear of competition with younger women also seeking employment, and working through anxiety about "leaving the baby with strangers," are as worthy of treatment attention as the identification of self-destructive patterns in choice of marital partner.

Feminist Ideas

The widespread availability of birth control, liberalized attitudes towards sex outside of marriage, and the rise of feminism, which promotes the value and social acceptability of women regardless of marital status, are also thought to contribute to the upswing in divorce (Ahrons & Rodgers, 1987; Cherlin, 1992; Guttmann, 1993). Divorcing women affected by these trends can look forward not just to postdivorce bare-bones economic survival as independent beings, but also to some improvement in life quality, with "single" a status to be enjoyed rather than shunned.

However, such liberal, feminist thinking may be most common among high-income and educated people, and a push toward hasty and sometimes inappropriate remarriage—for money and rescue from overwhelming family responsibilities as well as for self-esteem and a sense of meaning—is a problem familiar to most professionals working with the divorced. Tom Maligno, Executive Director of Nassau-Suffolk Law Services, which provides lawyers to low-income clients on New York's Long Island, feels that a "backlash against feminism" has developed among some women his organization serves, with earning a living seen as foreign and undesirable (T. Maligno, personal communication, August 16, 1990); a staff attorney for Nassau-Suffolk states that many of her female clients are drawn to "typical gender roles" (B. Fritz, personal communication, November 2, 1990). And Hispanics raised according to Roman Catholicism, Orthodox Jews, and other people influenced by traditional religious views may view sex outside marriage as simply wrong. Thus, it appears that feminism is an influence in some divorces (mostly in the middle and upper income brackets) but not others; we should not automatically ascribe liberal views or a strong desire to be independent and/or "free" to the divorcing and divorced women we see in either private practice or mental health clinics.

Women's Labor Force Participation Revisited: The Impact on Divorce Among Men

Returning to the issue of the increase of women in the paid labor force as the major divorce catalyst, Furstenberg and Cherlin (1991) point out that this trend may also have promoted a tendency for men to disrupt marriages. That is, with the increasingly androgynous household roles caused by wives being out of the house from nine to five, men have experienced a change in previously common arrangements, under which wives did the cooking, cleaning, and laundry. Although Hochschild, in her well-known 1989 study of California couples, found that many wives in two-job families do a "second shift" of housework from which husbands exempt themselves, she also emphasized the stress entailed for these "two-shift" women. Therefore, one might conclude that some men are not taken care of the way they were in the fifties, while the others are no longer cared for with enthusiasm and extra touches. Either way, motivation for men to stay married in order to receive payment in kind for earning a living has waned. Women's increased labor force participation may have promoted men's divorce initiation in another way, too: Men who do not have an exclusive breadwinning responsibility for their children may have fewer qualms about leaving or even abandoning them than their counterparts in a more traditional era (Furstenberg, cited in Marshall, 1991).

High Black Divorce Rates: Three Reasons

To understand the particularly high divorce rate among Black Americans, we must again look to economics rather than ideology. First, although most Black men view the traditional provider role as an important part of being a husband (Bowman, 1993; Tucker & Taylor, 1989), constraints such as low educational attainment, joblessness, and underemployment frequently make it difficult for them to fulfill this role (Bulcroft & Bulcroft, 1993; W. J. Wilson, cited in Cherlin, 1992; Tucker & Taylor, 1989). These constraints on Black men may stem, in turn, from inferior public school educations (McAdoo, 1990), or from the stereotyping and discrimination that Black men often encounter as they look for jobs or attempt to advance their careers (Boyd-Franklin, 1989; A. J. Franklin, 1992; McAdoo, 1990). The net result can be an earnings deficit, marital tension, and, ultimately divorce.

This trend gains strength when the wife, because of a higher educational level, is able to sustain steadier and/or more gainful work than her husband. Both Nancy Boyd-Franklin (1989) and Harriette McAdoo (1990), experts on the Black experience in America, indicate that Black women tend to exceed Black men in educational attainment, while Bumpass et al. (1991) found that "compared to couples in the same educational category, . . . marital disruption rates are . . . 29% higher if the wife has more education than her husband" (p. 34). It is important to note that in contrast to Black couples that experience problems such as low male earnings or a husband-wife earnings differential, middle-class Black couples among whom husbands transcend the numerous biases against their earning a living in this society have the same divorce rates as middle class Whites (H. P. McAdoo, personal communication, December 10, 1990). Likewise, reviewing several studies, Chan and Heaton (1989) found that when income and unemployment are statistically controlled, racial divorce rate differences diminish greatly. In other words, one reason there is more divorce among African Americans is that there is more experience of prejudice, financial strain, and material poverty.

A second reason for the high divorce rate among Blacks is the skewed sex ratio in the Black community (Bulcroft & Bulcroft, 1993; Cherlin, 1992; Fossett & Kiecolt, 1993; Hines, 1990). In some urban areas, the ratio of women to men is as high as 7 to 1 (Hines, 1990). The roots of this skew lie in (a) the exit of Black men from the community to both prisons and the military, and (b) the frequent early deaths of Black men due to drugs and street violence (Bulcroft & Bulcroft, 1993; Hines, 1990; McGoldrick, Preto, Hines, & Lee, 1991). Outnumbered by women and socialized to "succeed" with multiple women in a society where other expressions of potency are systematically denied (Boyd-Franklin, 1989), available Black men may shun commitment to marriage (Taylor et al., 1990), and readily consider dissolution as a response to marital problems. Awareness of the low male/female ratio in the African American community will clearly shape the work of any mental health practitioner who helps a Black woman face life after her divorce; the possibility of remarriage is much slimmer than for a White woman (Del Carmen & Virgo, 1993; Sidel, 1990).

Finally, research suggests that marriage may be less central as a value among Blacks than among other groups (Bulcroft & Bulcroft, 1993; Cherlin, 1992; Fine et al., 1992). That is, the widespread economic independence of Black women and the tradition of supportive extended family combine to provide financial and emotional benefits that deplete marriage of some of its importance as a basis for family life. When marriage is less necessary, divorce follows more readily.

DIVORCE: THE EFFECTS ON CHILDREN

How Destructive is Marital Rupture?

Will divorce destroy my kids? This question undoubtedly plagues many parents as they separate, wondering if they are creating irreversible psychological damage to their offspring. If they separated in the 1980s or 1990s, the work of Judith Wallerstein (e.g., Wallerstein, 1993, 1994; Wallerstein & Kelly, 1980; Wallerstein & Blakeslee, 1989) may have convinced them that they are. Wallerstein has written for the popular (Wallerstein, 1989) as well as the scholarly press, and has appeared on television, so her views are widely known. Although conceding that some offspring of divorce arrive at adulthood "compassionate, courageous, and competent" (Wallerstein & Blakeslee, 1989, p. 298), her work emphasizes what she sees as divorce's lasting scars. Briefly, Wallerstein believes that many people who experience divorce as children have trouble establishing satisfying lives and stable relationships as adults. According to Wallerstein, this is because children of divorce are frequently depleted rather than nurtured by their upbringing. Wallerstein bases this conclusion on a longitudinal study of 60 families, largely White and middle-class, from Marin County, California who answered advertisements for a free divorce-related counselling service (Wallerstein & Blakeslee, 1989; Wallerstein & Kelly, 1980).

Wallerstein's writings may be quite useful for clinicians helping White, middle-class families facing difficult divorces. However, numerous authors (e.g., Cherlin, 1992; Chess, Thomas, Korn, Mittleman & Cohen, 1983; Furstenberg & Cherlin, 1991; Kitson, 1992; Riessman, 1990; Tavris, 1989) have criticized her research methods. For example, Wallerstein did not study any families who did not feel they needed professional help, which may have skewed the findings from her help-seeking sample toward pathology. She also did not compare the families in her sample with a control group of intact families. Thus, divorce was never isolated as the only possible source of any psychological malfunctioning in her respondents. Finally, her failure to require research staff to tape-record interviews with respondents leaves rampant possibilities for bias in the gathering and evaluation of data. For such reasons, there has been much challenge to the relevance of Wallerstein's bleak conclusions to children of divorce in general.

The Actual Toll of Marital Rupture on Children

For a more accurate response to the question of long-term effects of divorce on children, we must look at the findings of other, unfortunately lesser known, researchers. Clearly, divorce does take its toll on children—but generally on a temporary basis. Youngsters whose parents physically separate and legally divorce are usually subjected to a transition period of intense upheaval involving—at a minimum—the physical loss of the noncustodial parent on a daily basis and financial decline. Other divorce-related life changes over which children have absolutely no control may include a household move, loss of friends, a new school, and a strange, sometimes poorer, more dangerous neighborhood. Perhaps most important, during this period children may experience self-absorbed or even rejecting mothers and fathers whose capacity to provide affection, attention, and discipline is diminished by the drain of their own problems (Amato, 1993; Cherlin, 1992; Guttmann, 1993; Wallerstein & Kelly, 1980). The divorce transition period is generally thought to last between 2 and 5 years (Amato, 1993; Brown, 1989; Chase-Lansdale & Hetherington, 1990; Olson & Haynes, 1993).

As one would expect, children who experience their parents' marital rupture often have a hard time, and hundreds of studies have examined the effect of divorce on children. As Kitson (1992) notes, some of these studies parallel Wallerstein's in their unfortunate reliance on divorced people who sought professional help; although these people are relatively accessible to researchers, they may be more likely than the general divorced population to be troubled. Thus, the results of these studies about the effects of divorce on children should be taken with some caution.

However, other studies of children and divorce rely on nonclinical samples, have more accurate measurement of emotions and behavior than Wallerstein's, and utilize control groups of intact families as a basis of comparison to divorced families. Reviewing studies with varying degrees of methodological rigor, meta-analysts conclude that divorce often increases children's antisocial and delinquent behavior (Emery, 1988; Guttmann, 1993) and the likelihood of their referral for mental health help (Emery, 1988; Grych & Fincham, 1992), while it decreases children's academic performance (Amato & Keith, 1991b; Guttmann, 1993) and their ability to cope with stress (Krantz, 1988).

Among children of divorce who experience negative impact, particularly affected are only children, because they are deprived of sibling support (Johnston, Gonzales, & Campbell, cited in Tschann, Johnston, Kline, & Wallerstein, 1990), and boys (Bee, 1994; Demo & Acock, 1988; Hetherington & Clingempeel, 1992), who may have more difficulty because they are more likely than girls to live with the opposite-sex parent (Furstenberg & Cherlin, 1991). The more subtle, internal problems that may develop in girls (Chase-Lansdale & Hetherington, 1990; Tschann et al., 1990) have unfortunately received less scholarly attention than the hard-to-miss acting-out of boys.

The existence of children troubled by parental divorce is undoubtedly corroborated by the practice wisdom of the average mental health clinician and the simple observations of the average sensitive adult. Both could undoubtedly report numerous vignettes of depressed, wild, or confused children reacting to their parents' split.

However, it appears the consequences of divorce for offspring are not as severe as researchers initially thought (Barber & Eccles, 1992; Kitson, 1992); differences between children from divorced families and children from intact families are small (Amato & Keith, 1991b), and differences within each of these two groups are generally much larger than differences between them (Barber & Eccles, 1992). Additionally, divorce can actually benefit some children, when it involves the departure of a particularly dysfunctional parent (Barber & Eccles, 1992; Guttmann, 1993). Admittedly, there are slight enduring differences (e.g., in the area of educational attainment) between people who experienced parental divorce and those who did not (Amato & Keith, 1991a), but in general, negative reactions to divorce pass with time (Bee, 1994; Cherlin, 1992; Walsh, 1991). For example, Emery (1988) found that in the long run, children of divorce are at no greater risk for adult depression than are other people. Although Amato and Keith (1991b) take issue, meta-analysts Barber & Eccles (1992), Furstenberg and Cherlin (1991), Kurdek (1989), Lowery (1989), and Soldano (1990) similarly conclude that the long term development of most children is not impeded by divorce.

The Impact of Diminished Postdivorce Contact with Fathers

This trend is particularly striking when juxtaposed with the finding that most children have little contact with their fathers after parental separation (Ahlburg & DeVita, 1992; Booth & Amato, 1994; Furstenberg, Morgan, & Allison, 1987; Seltzer, 1991). For example, Seltzer (1991) found that among children of divorce, more than half saw their fathers several times per year or less, while only about one quarter saw their fathers once a week or more. The missing empirical link is that many investigators (e.g., Furstenberg et al., 1987; Ihinger-Tallman et al., 1993; King, 1994; Maccoby & Mnookin, 1992) have found little relationship between frequency of child/nonresidential parent contact and child's postdivorce adjustment. The many children who desperately miss their absent fathers (Wallerstein & Kelly, 1980), and the currently fashionable idea that children need both parents to develop properly (Furstenberg & Cherlin, 1991) do not erase the fact that even without fathers' participation, children of divorce can arrive at adulthood psychologically intact. In fact, most recent research indicates that a strong relationship with just one parent, which would be a custodial mother in most cases, is a strong buffer against lasting divorce-engendered offspring damage (Furstenberg & Cherlin, 1991).

The Parental Conflict Factor

One exception to the trend of the eventual similarity of those who experienced their parents' marital dissolution and those who did not is in the area of the intergenerational transmission of divorce. Both early (e.g., Pope & Mueller, 1976) and recent (e.g., Kitson, 1992; McLanahan & Bumpass, 1988) researchers indicate that divorce is slightly more prevalent among those whose parents dissolved their own marriage. Even here, though, research casts doubt on the supposed long shadow of the childhood experience of parental divorce. For example, Furstenberg and Teitler (1994) indicate that a focus on divorce per se as causal may be misguided; processes (e.g., parental conflict) that often result in divorce may hurt children whether or not parents actually separate. In a like vein, Booth and Edwards (1989) found that the adult children of those who remained in unhappy marriages suffered more pervasive adverse effects (e.g., problems with children, marital disagreements) as adults than the adult children of those who ended marriages, even though the latter group was more likely to divorce.

Consistent with these findings, many authors suggesting therapeutic approaches for the divorced family (e.g., Ahrons & Rodgers, 1987; Grych & Fincham, 1992; Kalter, 1990; Kaslow & Schwartz, 1987; Lowery, 1989) assert that the eventual positive adjustment of children is best ensured if former spouses contain their own conflicts, and make attempts not to let these conflicts interfere with the work of raising children. Likewise, meta-analysts of studies on children and divorce (e.g., Allen, 1993; Amato, 1993; Krantz, 1988) conclude that it is interparental conflict—and postdivorce financial decline—rather than an absent father or a "broken home" that is the cause of any subsequent problems.

The findings about interparental conflict and poverty rather than divorce per se causing any lasting problems for offspring are not new. The first empirical studies of divorce (Despert, 1953; Goode, 1956) cite uncontrolled postdivorce arguments as a major preventable stressor for children, and an early but still-cited and classic meta-analysis (Herzog & Sudia, 1973) indicates that poverty rather than father absence may account for high rates of delinquency and other behavior problems in children following divorce.

The Persistence of the Myth of Inevitable Divorce-Engendered Damage

Yet, the "myth of the inevitable damage" caused by divorce (Lowery, 1989, p. 227) persists in the face of such evidence that damage to children is in fact (a) usually temporary, and (b) best attributed to two factors (interparental conflict and financial decline) that are at least partially modifiable through intervention by helping professionals and other, informal, helping networks. Perhaps the persistence of this myth reflects the widespread impact of the religious idea that it is somehow wrong to put asunder what God has joined together. This position was promoted until recently by now-overturned fault-based divorce laws; there was an assumption that marriages should last and divorce should be difficult to obtain (Fine & Fine, 1994).

Another possible reason for the persistence of the myth of inevitable damage is the influence of traditional psychoanalytic thinking, which suggests that trees grow as twigs are bent, and a childhood disruption will most likely have an adult outcome. Adherents of such traditional views are likely to assume, for example, that divorce that occurs early in childhood is the most damaging (e.g., Gardner, 1990), since it occurs at the beginning of the "formative" years. However, there is no consistent evidence for this assertion (Amato, 1993; Furstenberg & Teitler, 1994; Hetherington & Clingempeel, 1992), and the whole linear child-rearing-as-cause-adult-personality-as-effect way of thinking has recently been called into question. First, we are beginning to realize that family status is only one of many early-life variables influencing eventual adult adjustment (Furstenberg & Teitler, 1994). Innate temperament, for example, is now being recognized as an important modulator of divorce impact: Some children are simply more sensitive to potentially traumatic events than other children (Bee, 1994; Grych & Fincham, 1992; Kalter, 1990; Tschann, Johnston, Kline, & Wallerstein, 1989). Second, there is debate over whether all childhood experiences—even major ones—influence adult personality (Birns & Ben-Ner, 1988; Kagan, 1984). Kagan (1984), for example, questions the whole idea of all childhood traits persisting into adulthood. He raises the possibility that some personality characteristics prevalent in childhood may simply disappear by adulthood and be replaced by new qualities that emerge later, in response to subsequent life experience.

None of this new thinking negates a child's pain as she experiences the dismantling of her parents' relationship, or the relevance of mental health professionals to divorces that are overwhelming to the parents or children involved. It simply removes the invisible label of "pathogenic" from the parents we treat.

Of course, the fact that most children are not severely harmed by divorce should not blind us to the fact that a minority may be effected in more than a transitory way (Furstenberg & Cherlin, 1991). In fact, as clinicians, we need to help these people. Sometimes, lifetimes of bitterness, insecurity, or inability to trust do ensue. In this sense, Wallerstein's moving portrayals of young adults adrift (Wallerstein & Blakeslee, 1989) may inform some clinical practice. Perspective cannot be lost, though, on the relatively small numbers entailed.

Findings about Children and Divorce: Clinical Implications

The findings on the generally short-term nature of divorce's effect on children are of more than academic significance. If, as clinicians, we are aware that parental divorce is something that most offspring can surmount, we can communicate genuine therapeutic optimism in our efforts to educate parents about how to handle divorce with offspring. We can also bypass both the pseudo-necessity of delivering bad news when asked "What is this going to do to my kids?" and the potentially damaging countertransference toward our parent clients as destroyers of offsprings' lives. We can even share research findings with selected parents about the lack of correlation between parental divorce during childhood and subsequent adult emotional problems (Emery, 1988). Our work with younger, adolescent, and young adult children of divorce is affected too. We can encourage clients to reach for "silver linings" of the experience of parental divorce (e.g., an end to domestic violence). We can draw out personal strengths as well as pain, without worry that we are being "superficial" or "colluding with denial."

In the first part of this overview we have higlighted (a) the tremendous rise in marital disruption over the last 30 years in the United States, particularly among those with limited financial resources, education, and job options, (b) married women's labor force participation and the societally imposed marginal economic position of many Black men as major catalysts of the high divorce rate, and (c) research that portrays the overall long-term positive adjustment most children make to parental divorce and that pinpoints parents' behavior rather than marital rupture per se as the source of any ill effects that do occur. Our attention will now move to (d) the nature of the severed marital tie, and (e) postdivorce financial decline. In these two areas, we will see that divorce has gradually—and correctly, in my estimation—come to be recognized not as simply an event or a process, but as a way of life.

DIVORCE: THE SEVERED MARITAL TIE

From a social science (as opposed to a legal) point of view, the loss of one's spouse through divorce was originally conceptualized as a stressful life event. In 1967, Holmes and Rahe rated divorce second on their classic, still-cited (e.g., Amato, 1993) scale of 43 events that require major personal readjustment. Only death of a spouse was rated as more serious than divorce, while major physical injury, going to jail, and being fired were all rated as less serious. As an event that happened to a person, divorce was thought to be relatively straightforward and circumscribed; little attention was given to nuance or change in the divorced person's experience over time.

Thinking About Divorce: From Event to Process

Subsequent thinking on divorce was more developed. Wiseman's seminal article (1975) drew attention to its psychological complexity, characterizing divorce as a mourning process typically encompassing the various grief stages outlined by Kubler-Ross (1969): denial, loss and depression, anger and ambivalence, reorientation of lifestyle and identity, acceptance and new level of functioning. Wiseman's article set the stage for many later references linking divorce and mourning (e.g., Guttmann, 1993; Kaslow & Schwartz, 1987; Kitson, 1992; Sprenkle, 1989). In a related vein, a still-cited (e.g., Kitson, 1992) 1970 article by Bohannon drew attention to various facets of divorce (emotional, legal, economic, coparental, community, and psychic). Bohannon highlighted the relationships between the divorced person and the ex-spouse, children, old and new social contacts, and lawyer; he also highlighted possible postdivorce changes in the financial situation. Bohannon and Wiseman concurred that divorce was a long and complicated journey that ultimately ended after various psychological, social, and financial problems had been mastered. At this early stage of thought about divorce, from a clinical point of view, marital disruption implied a short-term challenge to a person's coping skills. Treatment was designed to promote individual mastery, which, in turn, would lead to a regaining of equilibrium, with trauma successfully mourned and the past relinquished (Kressel & Deutsch, 1977; Wiseman, 1975).

The Lasting Nature of Spousal Ties

Later authors asked whether every divorce actually reaches such a closure. Jacobson (1983) indicates that when one's ex-spouse is alive, the mourning process can be endlessly complicated by attempts at rapprochement or new anger based on current behavior; neither of these is possible when the object of grief is dead. The persistence of attachment to one's ex-spouse, even in the face of the erosion of love (Weiss, 1975) is another force that often prevents spouses from ever "cutting the cord." This may be particularly true for those who have lived many years together, or who are very dependent.

In a grimmer and more concrete vein, we note the persistent ties that may plague battered ex-wives. Some have ex-husbands who do not want to let them go, and continue to harass, threaten, intrude upon, or assault them (Koff, 1989; Rather, 1994). Even when these ex-wives obtain orders of protection or similar restraining orders, police often fail to arrest the men (Koff, 1989; Rather, 1994), so that women are not assisted in breaking the destructive connection. Other battered women may feel an ambivalent emotional connection to the men they are leaving, and sporadically seek reconciliation; abuse leads to low self-esteem, which in turn may cause a woman to doubt the correctness of leaving (Dutton & Painter, 1993; Johnson, 1992; Lawson, 1992). Similarly, despite the maltreatment, the abusers sometimes fulfill powerful needs the women have for attention, security, and closeness (Dutton & Painter, 1993; Zastrow & Kirst-Ashman, 1990).

Benefits as well as drawbacks of the ongoing spousal tie have come to light. For example, Ahrons and Rodgers (1987) conceptualize the divorced "bi-nuclear family" as it exists in two households, with two (potentially) responsible parents. Ideally, these parents are able to put aside adult conflicts and plan for children in a cooperative, coparental way. Of course, coparenting is impossible when one parent literally disappears from contact. Previously cited findings (Ahlburg & DeVita, 1992; Booth & Amato, 1994; Furstenberg et al., 1987; Seltzer, 1991) indicate that such disappearance is, unfortunately, quite common. Further, recent research indicates that among fathers who do remain in contact with their noncustodial children, *parallel parenting*, without co-operation between former spouses, is far more common than coparenting (Furstenberg & Cherlin, 1991; Maccoby & Mnookin, 1992), because most adults who could not get along when married also cannot get along when divorced (Furstenberg & Cherlin, 1991). Still, Ahrons' work implies that ongoing coparental contact, when available, can sometimes ease the burden on an overloaded divorced mother, as can parallel parenting, to a lesser degree. (Some exceptions to the pattern of ongoing ties between former spouses lie among partners exiting childless marriages of short duration; such marriages are not a focus of this volume, which will emphasize families with children.)

Former Spousal Ties, Extended Family Ties: Areas of Overlap.

The child's need for contact with both sets of grandparents may engender extra contact, cordial or conflicted, with a former spouse. This is particularly so in Black and Hispanic families that sanction the care of offspring by extended family, and are generally not guided by the cultural norms of noninterference in children's concerns that are more common in White families (Bogolub, 1989; Boyd-Franklin, 1989). In some Black families, even when the father has disappeared, a child's contact with the father's family can partially satisfy a longing for missing family (Boyd-Franklin, 1989; McGoldrick et al., 1991).

Current Treatment Approaches:
Emphasize Former Spouses and Extended Family.

The recognition of lasting spousal and extended family ties—both detrimental and beneficial—has led to treatment approaches emphasizing attention to these relationships before, during, and after marital separation. Contrasted to earlier, individually oriented approaches, current strategies do not assume it is always desirable or possible to sever longstanding ties. As will be detailed throughout this volume, current literature emphasizes clinical work with former spouses present together in sessions (Peck & Manocherian, 1989; Sprenkle, 1989), in-session confrontations regarding fathers' unmet financial obligations (Myers, 1989), and outreach to grandparents (Bogolub, 1989; Sprenkle, 1989) and elusive noncustodial fathers (Walsh, 1991).

As clinicians, we should clearly avail ourselves of these tactics when possible; Furstenberg and Cherlin (1991) indicate that whatever increases support for custodial mothers or decreases interparental conflict will benefit children of divorce. However, we should also recognize that despite the "cult of fatherhood" recently promoted by the popular press (Furstenberg & Cherlin, 1991; Johnson, 1993), fathers are frequently unavailable for treatment because they want nothing to do with their ex-wives and children; this is particularly so when fathers have remarried (Furstenberg & Cherlin, 1991). The exceptions to the general pattern of either nonexistent fathering or parallel parenting are likely to be highly educated divorced couples of upper middle- or upper-class socioeconomic status (Furstenberg & Cherlin, 1991). Mental health practitioners however, should not be discouraged from reaching out to fathers who seem, on the surface, to lack interest in their children; in fact, the details of such intervention are described in chapter 8. But therapists should expect paternal resistance to such efforts as a matter of course, and get used to a low "batting average" for heightened postdivorce coparental cooperation and increased father-child contact as therapeutic outcomes.

DIVORCE: FINANCIAL DECLINE

The impact of the severed relationship with the former spouse—whether this relationship be friendly, embittered, or indifferent—is felt perhaps most strongly in the area of postdivorce financial decline. As previously indicated, two households cost more to maintain than one, and some fathers either are not legally obligated to pay child support, or do not pay it if they are. The net result is long-term—not temporary—financial decline for most women and children after marital rupture (Acock & Demo, 1994; Amato, 1993; Cherlin, 1992; Guttmann, 1993).

Divorce, Economic Descent, and Social Class

Upper Middle- and Middle-Class Families.

Even though fathers in the higher socioeconomic brackets are somewhat more likely to pay child support (Arditti & Keith, 1993; Ihinger-Tallman et al., 1993; Morgan, 1991), getting by on less is a problem for almost all women and children after marital rupture. The financial problems facing upper middle- and middle-class families that disrupt have been described by both Weitzman (1988) and Wallerstein (Wallerstein, 1986; Wallerstein & Blakeslee, 1989; Wallerstein & Kelly, 1980). Compared to families from contrasting socioeconomic classes, these families actually experience the greatest proportional drop in income, and the sense of loss is frequently devastating (Furstenberg & Cherlin, 1991; Marshall, 1991; Morgan, 1991). Weitzman and more recent authors (e.g., Fine & Fine, 1994) detail court-ordered marital property distributions among these families that often grossly favor husbands; since 90% of the children in families of divorce reside with their mothers (Emery, 1988; Guttmann, 1993; Mott, 1994), these distributions—of possessions, savings, and the like—work against children as well as wives. It is true that the amenities and advantages at stake, such as extra or better-than-basic cars, are foreign to the vast majority of American families, intact or single-parent. So is disposable wealth for vacations, home computers, state-of-the-art athletic equipment, and cultural and sports events. However, the change to a more modest lifestyle can be both depressing and anxiety-producing for previously financially fortunate mothers who try to lift their children's spirits, as well as their own, in the aftermath of marital rupture. These losses can also cripple efforts to save face in a subculture in which "keeping up with the Joneses" matters, especially when divorce has already dealt a humiliating blow.

In addition to unfair distributions of possessions and money, Weitzman (1988) also describes the forced selling of the family home to free assets for division, even when the sale creates a traumatic, unwanted move for the wife and school-age children who reside in the home. In a like vein, Wallerstein (1986) portrays the devastation of former upper middle-class housewives who must work for a living when they never thought they would have to, and noncustodial fathers who change their minds about private college tuition for shocked children with whom they no longer reside.

Blue-Collar Families.

While these examples demonstrate the pain caused to people of means by a drastic, divorce-engendered shift in finances, they do not speak to the far more common financial problems of divorced families who have no savings to divide, no house to sell, and no commitments to higher education. With the blue-collar divorced family, the issue is distributing paychecks and child support checks for food, clothing, and shelter; usually, these checks are simply too small to go around. Even though women frequently increase their earning power during the first 3 years following divorce—either by moving from unemployment to employment, by upgrading a previous position to a more lucrative one, or by increasing work hours—net household income generally stays lower than pre-divorce because of the noncustodial father's decreased contribution (Peterson, 1989); the notion that divorced women experience a financial "dip and recovery" during the first few years after marital rupture is comforting but false (Morgan, 1991). This financial decline is only heightened if the nonresidential, paying parent (generally the father) faces additional monetary pressures because of remarriage. Another common problem for working-class divorced families is that employed adolescents and young adults residing with their divorced mothers may feel guilty about age-appropriate attempts to establish their own apartments, because their mothers depend on offspring income (Bogolub, 1991).

Poor Families.

Finally, because of divorce, the poor family often becomes more poor (Mauldin, 1991; H. P. McAdoo, personal communication, December 10, 1990). When the marital disruption of a poor family entails a split into two separate households both requiring ongoing maintenance, the result may be substandard housing, public assistance, fear of letting children play outside in dangerous neighborhoods, and the cheapest, least nutritious foods. When the marital disruption entails the temporary or lasting return of custodial parent and children to grandparents or other extended family, as is often the case in Black and Hispanic families, it can mean overcrowded quarters, and new tensions to resolve, as well as much-needed material and emotional support (Boyd-Franklin, 1989). Although less frequently portrayed in the literature, the material descent of the poor parent postdivorce is just as traumatic as that of the suburban housewife-turned-salesclerk, or the waitress who must work more hours when she would rather work fewer because her 19-year-old son wants to move out.

On the other hand, Mauldin (1991) and Morgan (1991) note that a minority of poor divorcing women and their children actually experience some financial improvement upon marital rupture. The exit of an intermittently unemployed male can bring financial relief: one less mouth to feed, or less money siphoned into drugs, gambling, and other illegal activities. In these families, when the man leaves, income remains constant, and poverty declines slightly (Morgan, 1991). However, these families, with husbands gone, are still poor, and their slight elevation in standard of living to a less brutal form of poverty should not blind us to the fact of permanent financial decline for the vast majority of women and children postdivorce.

The Impact of Remarriage and Alimony
on Women's Financial Status

It is true that most White divorced women eventually remarry (Cherlin, 1992), but even then women do not usually catch up to their predivorce financial status (Morgan, 1991). Black women remarry much less frequently than White women (Cherlin, 1992; Del Carmen & Virgo, 1993). Also, the remarriage rate for divorced people is dropping (Ganong & Coleman, 1994; Guttmann, 1993); 50% of children entering a single-parent home because of parental divorce remain there until they reach adulthood (Bumpass et al., 1991). Furthermore, second marriages are more likely to disrupt than first marriages (Furstenberg & Cherlin, 1991; Ganong & Coleman, 1994), and widowhood is more likely in second than in first marriages. For these reasons, it is incorrect to assume that remarriage will eventually solve a struggling mother's financial problems, although it generally does improve the financial situation of women and children somewhat (Morgan, 1991).

Alimony, too, is a relatively minor consideration. It is received by only about 15% of women (Fine & Fine, 1994; Zastrow & Kirst-Ashman, 1990), generally those over 40 and originally of middle or upper income status (Hewlett, cited in Walsh, 1991). A recent trend has been for increasingly small and short-term "rehabilitative" alimony (Fine & Fine, 1994; Guttmann, 1993). The rehabilitation idea has its roots in the "no-fault" divorce laws currently operant in all states (Fine & Fine, 1994; Guttmann, 1993); these laws do away with the distinction between victimizer and victim prevalent under formerly operant fault-based laws requiring grounds for divorce. Current laws suggest that since men and women are equal, women should be able to earn postdivorce incomes commensurate with men's if they are strongly motivated (Bogolub, 1991; Guttmann, 1993). Although women tend to use such rehabilitative alimony for its intended purpose (Kitson, 1992), there appears to be no evidence for significant elevation of standard of living via vocational rehabilitation.

Men and Money After Divorce

But what of *men* and money? Many researchers indicate that while the standard of living for women and children generally diminishes after divorce, the standard of living for men improves (Bee, 1994; Kitson, 1992; Maccoby & Mnookin, 1992; Teachman & Paasch, 1993; Weitzman, 1988). Although men's household income tends to show a postdivorce decrease (but not as great as women's; Ross, Mirowsky, & Goldsteen, 1990), the male financial situation improves because the demands on male income decrease. Child support, even when paid, does not approach the bite on the father's salary that occurred while he was living with wife and children.

Clinical and Practical Implications of Divorce-Engendered Financial Descent

In light of a postdivorce diminished standard of living for women and children, the clinician, on the most basic level, must take clients' financial problems seriously. This includes listening to expressions of the ongoing pain of doing without, helping with plans to obtain jobs, child support payments, and other benefits when indicated, and generally dignifying day-to-day survival with the same concentration that therapists formerly reserved for dreams and childhood memories. If the client is ashamed of financial problems, it may be necessary for the therapist to aggressively raise the issue of money.

With regard to the male role in bringing more money into the family, Weitzman (1988) suggests that fathers pay more to mothers and children, both at the time of the divorce settlement and afterwards, in ongoing child support. Payment at the time of the divorce settlement is of greatest concern to middle-class and upper middle-class families; as previously indicated, other families have little to distribute. Currently, under the equitable distribution laws operant in most states, judges generally award the woman approximately half of the marital property (Weitzman, 1988), or less (Koff, 1989), even though the woman's household, in most cases, includes children, and thus constitutes much more than half of the former family. The rationale for the equitable distribution laws is an assumed equal capacity for self-support postdivorce among men and women (Guttmann, 1993; Weitzman, 1988); as is the case in the rationale for diminished alimony, women are wrongly thought to be able to go to work and provide for the children to the same extent that their ex-husbands are. Because the reality is usually a male-female earning power discrepancy, and because the woman is frequently either a custodial parent or an older woman with limited marketable skills, judges ought to consider different proportions in their divisions to men and women (Weitzman, 1988). Recently expanded definitions of marital property that include, for example, pension funds, and health insurance (Noble, 1994a), are a help to women experiencing current so-called equitable distributions, but do not fully remedy the problem.

As indicated, any alterations in property distribution would have their greatest effect on divorcing families with homes, savings, and the like. Specifically, it would help the many divorcing families who want to avoid the emotional drain and monetary expense of litigation by settling out of court. A pattern of court-ordered equitable distribution that is more advantageous to women and children would provide divorcing wives with some leverage with which to extract more fair out-of-court settlements. However, as mental health practitioners working with people from all walks of life, we need to remember that most divorcing couples have little property to divide (Seltzer & Garfinkel, 1990).

For most families, then, child support is a far more salient issue. As previously indicated, there has been some recent increase in child support payments because of the Family Support Act of 1988, which requires states to standardize support amounts and tightens collection procedures for delinquent fathers. When actually paid, child support does represent significant income for mothers and children from all walks of life. For example, among formerly middle-class and blue-collar families, child support payments can keep a working mother off public assistance. It can also prevent teenaged offspring of divorced parents who make appropriate contributions to household expenses via part-time employment from working so many hours per week that their academic and social activities are hampered. However, common sense warns against expecting miracles. Child support payments cannot, for example, lift the divorced mother and children from a previously intact working-class two-breadwinner family to the middle class when the split family now has greater expenses because it occupies two households. Only improved earnings for the mother can do that.

In light of the amount of income improvement that child support can provide, a few authors feel that coercive measures for noncompliant fathers are counterproductive. For example, Chambers (cited in Arditti, 1991) designates child support payments as "taxation without representation" (p. 108). Haskins (cited in Arditti, 1991) points out that divorced fathers sometimes do not pay child support because they suspect their ex-wives rather than their children would benefit. Arditti (1991) suggests, therefore, that increased joint custody may be preferable to tightened collection procedures, because joint custody would promote voluntary increases in support payments. The views of these academics are echoed in the current "fathers' rights" movement, which consists of divorced men who feel current child support policies infringe on their rights (Bertoia & Dakich, 1993).

While such views are minority, they draw attention to the need to avoid making fathers the divorce scenario villains. It is possible to promote strict enforcement on a legislative level, and simultaneously, in the treatment process, to view nonpaying fathers as people to be helped rather than criminals to be rejected. For example, as chapter 8 explains, fathers may abandon families because they do not recognize their own importance, or cannot face the pain of being reminded of children they miss. Overall, as will be seen in detail throughout this volume, the clinician working with the divorced family on issues of money must strike a balance between helping families increase income through both mother's and father's contributions insofar as possible, while also enabling female clients and their children to express feelings about and adjust to an almost always permanently reduced financial status.

Added to our sense of who gets divorced, why they do so, and the eventual positive adjustment of most children, then, has come a sense of the lasting residues of divorce for children and adults. First, emotional bonds forged in the original intact family are not easily broken, though they change after divorce. Second, a lifetime of reduced income and practical problems is a given for most divorced women and their children, although the nature of the these dilemmas varies according to socioeconomic class.

CLINICAL ASSESSMENT AND TREATMENT OF THE DIVORCED FAMILY

Perhaps because mental health professionals have traditionally stressed assistance to the intact family (Price & McKenry, 1988), writing about assessment and treatment of the divorced is somewhat sparse (Sprenkle, 1989; Grych & Fincham, 1992). Within the clinical literature, Ahrons and Rodgers (1987), and Kaslow and Schwartz (1987) have been perhaps the most attentive to treatment implications of issues outlined in the preceding review. For example, Ahrons and Rodgers (1987) give ample attention to midlife divorce and the general relevance of age to the divorce experience, as do Kaslow and Schwartz (1987), who also focus on some financial and legal issues facing divorced women. With few exceptions, however, (e.g., Bogolub, 1991), the contributions of other authors have not been informed by the same understanding of age and gender. This volume will approach divorce treatment guided by the work of Ahrons and Rodgers, and Kaslow and Schwartz. It will also open up the almost entirely uncharted area (Moore & Schwebel, 1993) of divorce treatment and ethnicity.

Guidelines for Practice with the Divorced

The Sociological Perspective.

The preceding review suggests several guidelines underlying the more specific practice suggestions in the ensuing chapters. First, clinicians must employ a sociological as well as a psychological perspective. This implies attention to gender, age, ethnicity, income, and any divorce-induced income change. The informed therapist will not just jot a few lines about these sociodemographic variables, but will take time to reflect on their meaning for clients' lives. With regard to these variables, divorce has been sometimes portrayed in a comparative manner—harder for women than for men (Chiriboga, Catron, et al., 1991; Riessman, 1990), harder for White women than for Black women (Gove & Shin, 1989; Kitson, 1992), harder for older people than younger people (Bee, 1994; Jones & Jones, 1993). These comparisons may be valid. But perhaps more important than telling us whose difficulties are worse, these comparisons alert us to the overlapping yet different stresses divorce creates for different groups.

The "Stage-of-Divorce" Perspective.

Second, to make hypotheses about issues likely to be salient for particular divorcing and divorced clients, and to conduct correctly paced and correctly focussed treatment sessions with these clients, the clinician must employ a "stage" perspective. Organization of subsequent chapters around a three-stage model of divorce (preseparation period; divorce transition period; postdivorce period) reflects acceptance of the utility of a widely used paradigm (e.g., Everett & Volgy, 1991; Guttmann, 1993; Kaslow & Schwartz, 1987; Sprenkle, 1989). To an extent, as will be detailed in subsequent chapters, each stage generates its own issues. For example, ambivalence about a decision is usually most intense predivorce, while feelings of loss are usually most intense during the divorce transition. Therapists who are unaware of stage-specific issues may not be able to make optimal use of their "third ear" in understanding and helping the divorced.

Of course, divorce stages overlap, individuals vary in their experience of them (Sprenkle, 1989), and some issues (e.g., financial decline) are present in more than one stage. Other issues (e.g., loss) disappear from awareness in one stage if they are too painful to experience, and then reappear in another, when time has passed, external stress has partially abated, and integration is more likely. Even if the stages defy precise definition (as does any model of a particular human experience), this paradigm generally helps therapists organize thinking about their clients, who may seek professional help at any stage.

The Psychological Perspective.

Third, clinicians must assess each client's ego strengths, ego weaknesses, and coping skills. As part of this assessment, clinicians ought to evaluate whether any deficits in ego functioning (e.g., diffuse anger or hypersensitivity in object relationships, suicidal gestures or other forms of poor impulse control) or any deficits in coping skills (e.g., impaired concentration on the job, inattention or inconsistency as a parent) are chronic or, alternately, divorce specific. Such an assessment will help the therapist identify the strengths that can be supported, the deficits that can be remedied, and the deficits that must be tolerated. The necessity of an ego assessment may seem obvious to the intelligent reader. However, as Myers (1989) points out, in our efforts to be accepting of divorce as a normal occurrence, we often err on the side of underdiagnosis. Boyd-Franklin (1989) and Devore and London (1993) point out that the same mistake—insignificant attention to pathology—can stem from a desire to be tolerant of cultural diversity.

An Eclectic, Goal-Oriented Approach

Because of the variety divorced clients present, there is no one approach that works with every case. An upper-income man reveals after 2 months of treatment that he is not once but twice divorced; he needs a psychodynamic understanding of his ill-fated choice of marital partners, to avoid wreaking further havoc on himself and his children. A low-income battered wife who wants to leave home needs information on public assistance and orders of protection before introspection about how her predicament arose makes sense. An 8-year-old boy misses the father who abandoned him and cannot concentrate on his homework; he needs individual treatment if his mother is too preoccupied to pay attention to him, but would benefit more from family treatment strengthening the mother-son bond. In any case, the therapist, or, preferably, the mother encouraged by the therapist, needs to meet with the boy's teacher. And so on. As will be seen in the following chapters, the careful assessment of sociodemographic, divorce-specific, and psychological parameters in each case will lead to varied and sometimes interdisciplinary interventions. Given the diversity of the population, adherence to one approach (e.g., crisis intervention, psychodynamic treatment, structural family therapy) is most likely a detriment; the therapist working with the divorced must be eclectic.

Not all readers of this book will share my eclectic point of view; readers' clinical orientations may vary considerably. For example, some therapists are oriented to brief or crisis therapies that tend to focus on the presenting problem (in this case, marital), and emphasize cognitive and behavioral approaches, although not exclusively. In contrast, psychoanalytically oriented therapists tend to view any here-and-now concern, such as divorce, as a tip of the iceberg. From this point of view, although divorce related matters must be addressed, their real clinical utility is as entry points to therapist-client dialogue on the client's enduring personality traits, and typical patterns of relating to other people. It is hoped that practitioners of various schools will be able to selectively utilize some of the suggestions in the ensuing chapters, weaving them into the orientations and practices to which they generally adhere.

Eclectic, however, does not mean that anything goes; therapeutic intervention is by definition geared to goals. For example, as detailed in chapter 3, during the first, or preseparation phase of the divorce process, the goal is to facilitate a decision about maintaining or ending the marriage. Likewise, as detailed in chapter 6, treatment during the divorce transition has multiple goals (e.g., improving support for the custodial parent, decreasing interparental conflict).

When working with the divorced, limited achievement of therapeutic goals is sometimes the best possible outcome, as will be seen in the ensuing chapters. For example, given the inequities in the labor market and the numerous problems obtaining child support, few women can dramatically improve their finances. Likewise, for adults who could not get along while married, decrease rather than elimination of spousal conflict after divorce is an accomplishment.

The Therapist's Personal Involvement

No matter whether a therapist is eclectic or a proponent of one school of thought, if she or he is working with the separating, divorcing, and divorced population, the clinical material encountered is often highly charged, emotionally. For this reason, the feelings of the therapist frequently come into play, and the consideration of countertransference will be discussed throughout the following chapters. The possibility of feeling judgmental toward adults whom one erroneously believes to be destroying offspring has already been identified. Other conflicts that the divorced can evoke in clinicians will be noted, along with suggestions for containing or utilizing these reactions in the treatment process.

It is hoped that after reading this book, therapists working with the divorced can experience a contrasting, nonconflictual feeling: therapeutic optimism. Although the long-term financial consequences of divorce are not happy, women do have options, and most children can weather their parents' divorces successfully. If the therapist believes this, the client will sense it, and the positive mood will enhance the therapy.

Part II

HELPING CLIENTS PREDIVORCE

Chapter 2

Adults, Children, and Adolescents in the Predivorce Stage

Joe's 45 now, and he's been a changed person for three months—from Dr. Jekyll to Mr. Hyde. First of all, he's never home for dinner. His excuse is that the kids are getting older and they don't need him any more. He always gave them a lot of attention, so this is not like him. He's getting interested in running, too. He comes home from work, puts on his jogging clothes, and leaves. Lately I wonder if running is really where he goes. Basically, he wants nothing to do with me at all, including in bed. Even though he barely speaks to me, we put on an act for his family. We see them once a month or so, and we just pretend everything is fine. First I ignored the change in him. I figured all marriages have their ups and downs. When I finally brought it up to him two weeks ago, how much he's changed, he said I was making a big deal out of nothing. I hope we can straighten this out, but he doesn't even admit anything is wrong. I don't know if I can keep living like this.

Jane—highlights of initial
psychotherapy sessions at a
community mental health clinic

I didn't tell anyone I made this appointment, not even my sister or my mother. The problem is that Juan gets crazy sometimes, and I can't take

37

it. Ever since we are married, he hits me for no reason. I'm 29. Once he gave me a black eye. It was in the summer, so I wore sunglasses when I went to the store, and nobody knew. He doesn't hit the kids, but sometimes he hits me in *front* of them. The little one doesn't understand, but the two big ones cry. I think the fighting scares them. That's why I finally came to this place. Myself, that's one thing, but I don't want my kids to get messed up from all this. Maybe it's my fault. I let the house get messy, and Juan does have a right to get upset. Maybe I can learn how to act different, and calm him down. But he's so excitable, it seems like nothing might work, and my oldest is getting very nervous. I don't think I want my kids growing up in this type of atmosphere.

Maria—highlights of initial
sessions at a community
service for battered women

Jane, who suspects infidelity, and Maria, a victim of domestic violence, are both in the initial phase of the divorce process. In each case, a married couple is still under one roof, but at least one party is deeply troubled, and beginning to think about severing the marital tie. Part II covers the initial phase of the divorce process. Here, in chapter 2, we identify some issues clinicians frequently see in adults, children, and adolescents who live with the possibility of divorce. Recalling the comprehensive assessment techniques suggested in chapter 1, the concerns of adults, children, and adolescents will be viewed in the context of psychological makeup (e.g., ego strengths and weaknesses) and sociological reality (e.g., age, gender, ethnicity, and income). Relevant practice techniques for adults making a decision about divorce—and for their offspring—will be presented in chapters 3 and 4.

The deliberate presentation of two women in the examples above reflects the fact that, as previously noted, most divorces are initiated by women (Masheter, 1991; Mitchell-Flynn & Hutchinson, 1993). It also reflects that women form the majority of people seeking professional mental health help, both in general (Meth & Passick, 1990) and in divorce-related situations (Cohen & Lowenberg, 1994; Myers, 1989). However, in this book as a whole, the male divorce experience and clinical work with divorcing and divorced men will also be addressed.

THE PRESEPARATION PHASE: ISSUES OF ADULTS

The Beginning: From Denial to Ambivalence

What can we learn about the beginning of the divorce process from Jane and Maria? In both cases, we observe a psychological transition from complete denial of a problem (suspected infidelity for Jane, and domestic violence for Maria), to ambivalence about facing it (Everett & Volgy, 1991). In this sense, the literature on divorce as a mourning process beginning with denial (e.g., Guttmann, 1993; Kaslow & Schwartz, 1987; Kitson, 1992; Wiseman, 1975) retains its utility. The duration of denial is an individual matter: Jane's lasted a few months, and Maria's lasted a few years. Eventually, something precipitates conscious, although not constant, awareness of a marital problem. In Maria's case, it was her children's terror of violence; when they cried in reaction to Juan's brutality, she could no longer pretend the brutality did not exist. In the ambivalence marking the first phase of the divorce process, the conscious awareness that something is wrong alternates with avoidance and/or rationalization of problems. Thus, Jane describes aberrant behavior at length, only to stop short of asking the obvious question ("Where is he going?"), while Maria seeks help from a feminist organization, yet still blames herself for the abuse she experiences. The attempts both women make to hide their problems from extended family members also signify the difficulty in admitting a problem that often marks the beginning of the divorce experience.

For people who are very dependent, emotionally or financially, this ambivalence about acknowledging unhappiness can last years, or even becomes a way of life. For people with greater psychological or material resources, though, ambivalence about acknowledging a problem eventually turns to ambivalence about the marriage itself. At this point, consideration of marital separation begins. Since the consideration of separation, as opposed to its enactment, is essentially a private matter (Ahrons & Rodgers, 1987), another issue of the initial stage of divorce can be social isolation, with disclosures limited to dearest friends, and a face-saving but false impression presented to acquaintances, neighbors, and colleagues.

Two Major Preseparation Fears:
Starting Anew and Damage to Offspring

Although neither woman could verbalize it during initial treatment interviews, fear of starting anew, another typical initial phase issue, often underlies the ambivalence about leaving the marriage. The thought of being single again terrifies many married people, and can cause impaired work performance, difficulty sleeping, somatic symptoms, increased drinking, and increased smoking (Kitson, 1992). This is because married people of all ages, even when they are not happily married, have a social status and a shared life that can provide security and comfort. Married women—particularly older married women—frequently have financial advantages that they will never be able to recover should they divorce. Anticipation of the loss of such a social and economic arrangement, even for independent, mature people, can evoke extreme anxiety, or even panic.

In addition, as noted in chapter 1, many parents contemplating divorce fear, usually incorrectly, that they will create permanent psychological damage in their children. Such parents may be plagued by visions of long-range decreased school performance, lifelong inability to form satisfying personal relationships, and the like. Parents may also fear, correctly, that the material standard of their children's lives (as well as their own) will be permanently lowered. Overall, fear about hurting children can compound panic about being alone, and can sometimes create an almost unbearable emotional pressure. If people do not cope well with stress, or lack social support, these fears, as well as their behavioral manifestations, tend to be intensified.

Additional Preseparation Fears: The Impact of Age, Ethnicity, and Gender

Being alone and damaging offspring are fears that most people experience when considering marital separation. Some people have additional fears. Younger women with children, like Maria, also fear the emotional and physical drain of raising children alone. They wonder about jobs, and day care, and, sometimes, the indignities of public assistance. They may also wonder who would marry them only to take on the burden of a new family. Middle-aged women like Jane fear lack of opportunities for remarriage because of waning sexual attractiveness and the shrinking pool of available men. They also fear age discrimination in hiring if they intend to improve their financial situation (Bogolub, 1991). Older women who are no longer employable may wonder, quite understandably, how they will manage alone on fixed incomes, or what they will do if their health deteriorates.

Fear of what life will be like after separation may be particularly strong among Hispanic women like Maria. Maternal self-sacrifice for family unity is central to Hispanic feminine identity (McGoldrick et al., 1991; Neff & Schluter, 1993; Wagner, 1993; N. G. Preto, personal communication, December 14, 1990). As a result, the Hispanic woman is more likely than other women to anticipate withdrawal of social support if she initiates marital separation, thereby asserting rather than sacrificing her own needs (Hines, Preto, McGoldrick, Almeida, & Weltman, 1992; N. G. Preto, personal communication, December 14, 1990). A similar sense of being "damaged goods" may be experienced by Orthodox Jewish women, who are often socialized to experience raising a family as their sole reason for being. For Black women, on the other hand, there is a long tradition of self-support and survival (Hines, 1990; Neff & Schluter, 1993) and marriage is not normative (Sidel, 1990; Williams et al., 1992), so fear and stigma may be minimized.

A man's fears about marital separation may revolve, in part, around loneliness and difficulty in managing domestically (Riessman, 1990). Cooking, laundry, and bed making may loom ahead as unmanageable or demeaning. More important, if a man has strong bonds with his children, he will fear the loss of daily parent-child connection (Hetherington & Tryon, 1989). Despite conventional wisdom about "Daddy's little girl," men are generally more involved in rearing their sons than their daughters (Katzev et al., 1994; Seltzer & Brandreth, 1994). Men actually leave homes where they are raising sons less frequently (Morgan et al., 1988; Mott, 1994), but when they are considering such a move, the anxiety may be intense. The anticipation of hearing about what happened in school not in person, but over the phone—especially from a son—may be extremely painful. A caring father contemplating divorce may also agonize about the decreased standard of living in store for his children. Finally, he may also wonder if his children will come to love their mother more than they do him, or if they will forget about him altogether.

Guilt During the Preseparation Phase

Divorce is rarely mutual; even when conflict is acknowledged by both spouses, there is usually an initiator and an assenter (Ahrons & Rodgers, 1987; Guttmann, 1993; Kitson, 1992). Guilt is another emotion that initiators may experience at this time (Guttmann, 1993; Kitson, 1992). Jane and Maria both have husbands whose behavior is flagrantly unacceptable; the guilt of these women about anticipated separation may be confined to thoughts that the upheaval they fear inflicting on their children cannot be helped. But for people who leave marriages for less socially sanctioned reasons, (e.g., their own finally-acknowledged homosexuality or a feeling that one married a decent but incompatible spouse chosen by parents, not self), the guilt about pain inflicted on spouse, children and other family members can be intense.

Home Life During the Preseparation Phase

What is life at home like at this time? In Jane's, the atmosphere was tense and too quiet, and the air could be cut with a knife; in Maria's, the conflict was open, violent, and physical. In other homes, there may be a combination, with aloofness alternating with battles, verbal and/or physical. Overall, unhappy families vary, but all probably express themselves with some combination of emotional distance, arguments, and/or violence. If both parents are working outside the home, as is true in many intact families today, or if the marital problems are less serious than Jane's or Maria's, spouses may not be inclined to directly express their unhappiness daily. In such cases, problems may go underground, only to resurface a few days or a few weeks later. Still, during the preseparation phase, which can last months or years, such discord persists, sometimes in an open way, and sometimes more subtly.

THE PRESEPARATION PHASE: ISSUES OF CHILDREN AND ADOLESCENTS

Marital Discord: The Impact on Children

It is widely recognized that marital discord takes it toll on children (Amato, 1993; Guttmann, 1993; Krantz, 1988), and may be, in fact, more destructive for them than divorce, as previously noted (Booth & Edwards, 1989; Furstenberg & Teitler, 1994). Children in unhappy homes typically experience preoccupied parents, inconsistent discipline, decreased affection, and role models of destructive behavior. They may be exposed to crying, drinking, physical fights, stony silences, or avoidance-based frenzy. Predictable routines, so important to children (Kalter, 1990; Kaslow & Schwartz, 1987) may be interrupted by such events as late-night arrivals of parents expected home for dinner. Children may be embarrassed to invite friends to visit, and they may receive attention when parents need to diffuse their own problems, rather than when it is truly desired.

Wallerstein and Kelly (1980) observe that a minority of adults can be fine parents even when involved in miserable marriages. For these parents, a close, nurturing relationship with one or more children is treasured because it counteracts marital unhappiness. Because these parents are exceptions and because this book emphasizes clinical attention to troubled people, emphasis here will be on children experiencing the more usual predivorce scenario showing parental deficit.

Unlike adults, who, as noted, are frequently ambivalent about ending marriages, children tend not to be ambivalent at all. Both Caplan (1990) and Cherlin (1992), for example, assert that most children in divorcing families do not want the divorce. This is because children, especially young children, do not want their worlds disrupted. They are attached to their parents, imperfect though they are, cannot envision improvement stemming from parental separation, and fear the unknown (Caplan, 1990). Riessman (1990) has noted that divorce has distinct "his" and "her" versions; it may be that divorce has a parents' version (divorce as ambivalent, both desired and feared) and a children's version (divorce as undesirable) as well.

How Offspring of Different Ages React to Marital Discord

Preschool age children like Maria's (ages 3, 2, and 1) are highly vulnerable to marital discord, although they are too young to realize that divorce is being considered. Little children who have quarrellng or violent parents may cling, throw toys, cry easily, and regress in toilet and eating habits. Unlike older children, they are almost totally dependent on adults, react strongly to any disruption of nurturance, and are not old enough to withdraw from stress into homework, activities and peer relationships (Kalter, 1990; Wallerstein & Kelly, 1980).

Even though older children have a greater capacity to separate themselves from their parents' problems, offspring of all ages react to marital discord. Recent literature (Beal & Hochman, 1991; Bonkowski, 1989: Cain, 1989; Cooney, 1994; Holdnack, 1992; Kaufmann, 1988) indicates that reactions to parental divorce extend not just through adolescence, but also into young adulthood; it is reasonable to assume that reactions to the threat of divorce extend similarly. Offspring in these older age groups may be sensitive to muted marital tensions that very young children do not notice. Whether parents' problems are blatant or subtle, school-age, adolescent, and young adult children may be pervasively anxious, or if less defended, specifically fearful that their homes, perhaps like those of their friends, are about to disrupt, embarking on emotional chaos and financial descent. Manifestations may include both externalizing problems (e.g., aggression toward peers, substance abuse) and internalizing problems (e.g., depression, inability to concentrate on schoolwork). On the positive side, though, these older offspring are sometimes able to maintain a self-protective distance from their parents' problems, with both externalizing and internalizing problems minimized or avoided.

Forces that Modulate the Impact of Marital Discord on Children

As previously indicated, certain variables intervene between parental discord and children's reactions. One variable that may account for different levels of well-being among siblings in the same family is temperament, or an individual's level of innate vulnerability to external events (Bee, 1994; Kalter, 1990). Therapists cannot change a child's sensitive temperament, but once aware of it, they can help develop means to compensate for it; some children need particularly large parental doses of reassurance that they are still loved, no matter what, while others need a definite plan (e.g., listen to popular music) to follow when parents fight.

If a girl or boy is disturbed rather than simply sensitive, the situation is worse. Whether offspring are preschool, school-age, or adolescent, the demands of parenting a disturbed child can not be met by most adults distracted by marital discord, so serious child deterioration may ensue when a marriage begins to unravel. Children with serious externalizing or internalizing problems may require individual therapy, special attention in school, or even residential placement.

On the other hand, children's experience of parental discord can be buffered by other family members. Siblings, when present, can validate each others' reality testing regarding a new, ugly, or puzzling home situation. Such confirmation offsets fears or parental accusations that one is "imagining things" or "exaggerating," and maintains a child's confidence in the ability to understand the world around her. Siblings can also refocus attention to conflict-free and enjoyable arenas, listen to each other, and assist each other with concrete tasks. Although they cannot really "parent" each other, they can sometimes partially compensate for a parental deficit (Combrinck-Graham, 1988; Farmer & Galaris, 1993; Kaplan, Hennon, & Ade-Ridder, 1993).

We should not assume, however, that siblings are always a blessing for children when parents are at odds. Children below age 4 or 5 are too young to offer emotional or tangible assistance, extremely rivalrous or distant siblings will not automatically transform into close allies, and self-destructive acting-out can be contagious. Also, siblings in low-income families may find their unconscious or deliberate efforts to create a separate and nurturing family subsystem hampered; in cramped quarters, it is sometimes impossible to shut out upsetting sights and sounds.

Extended family is another potential source of support for children of parents in troubled marriages. In Black families, grandparents are frequently highly involved in raising their grandchildren (Boyd-Franklin, 1989), as are godparents in Hispanic families (Longres, 1990). Since Black and Hispanic families tend to regard children as belonging to an entire extended family rather than to biological parents (Fulmer, 1989), these grandparents and godparents can do far more than visit occasionally and bring presents; they may carry out real work in parenting domains such as affection, guidance, discipline, and housework, partially compensating for the void left by preoccupied mothers and fathers. Although they are central, grandparents and godparents are not the only relatives who participate in childrearing in Black and Hispanic families; others may assist as well (Chillman, 1993; Del Carmen & Virgo, 1993; Hatchett & Jackson, 1993).

As with siblings, this involvement is not to be romanticized. Boyd-Franklin (1989) points out that African American grandparents and parents sometimes disagree about the upbringing of children to whom both lay claim, while Timberlake and Chipungu (1992) describe the role overload of employed Black grandmothers. Chillman (1993) and McGoldrick et al. (1991) note that among recently emigrated Hispanics, extended family may not be nearby. Still, extended family, can, to an extent, mitigate the decreased parental participation of troubled spouses.

Chapter 3

The Mental Health Professional's Role: Predivorce Emotional Concerns

This chapter and chapter 4 describe some techniques useful in assisting those contemplating marital separation. The present chapter focusses on help for major emotional concerns; the following one on help for major practical concerns, and also on the implementation of the actual separation decision. As do subsequent chapters describing professional activity, chapters 3 and 4 attempt to present treatment ideas with reference to clients' psychological makeup, and in a sociological context rather than in a vacuum. As with subsequent chapters describing professional activity, the presentation of techniques is not meant to be exhaustive, but rather to cover basic skills, which are applicable to a broad range of clients and situations. Likewise, the description of circumscribed approaches is for discussion purposes only; in actual practice, the therapist combines or shuttles flexibly between them according to the needs of the client or clients in a given session.

Some of the approaches described in this chapter and the next may, on occasion, be relevant in later phases of the divorce cycle. Likewise, some approaches described as appropriate for middle and later phases of the divorce cycle may apply, on occasion, to the preseparation phase counselling discussed here and in chapter 4.

PREDIVORCE THERAPY:
CONTEMPLATING SEPARATION

One concern transcending the specification of techniques is that not all clients focus exclusively on marital issues during the preseparation phase of the divorce cycle. Clients may haltingly work up to introducing the highly charged topic of marital dissatisfaction, after a period of focus on a presenting problem which in retrospect emerges as a smokescreen for the more threatening couple concerns. Likewise, throughout the preseparation phase of treatment, discussion of the dysfunctional marriage may be interspersed with other topics. Sometimes these other topics are valid in their own right, and sometimes they demonstrate avoidance as a necessary and adaptive defense mechanism against the tremendous anxiety stirred up by the possibility of marital rupture; sometimes a combined meaning operates regarding these nonmarital concerns.

The upshot is that the therapist needs to treat the topic of marital dissatisfaction like a big fish, respecting the client's need to alternately approach and avoid it, in order to help the client develop increased tolerance for in-depth discussion over time. This caveat may be less relevant to the middle phase of the divorce cycle, when separation has just occurred, emotional and practical concerns are often blatant, and avoidance and denial, although possible, are less likely. Also important during the preseparation phase of the divorce cycle is the therapist's reassurance that talking about separation does not necessarily lead to separation; a long, hard look at the issues may lead to the decision that maintaining the marriage is preferable to ending it (Haffey & Cohen, 1992). With these cautions about the pace of therapeutic work in mind, let us turn, then, to some techniques particularly relevant to the preseparation phase of divorce treatment. Overall, the goal will be to precipitate an informed decision about maintaining or leaving the marriage.

PRESEPARATION TREATMENT TECHNIQUES

Exploring Client Ambivalence

Bob, a 50-year-old lawyer, is thinking of leaving Sue, his wife of 20 years, for Karen, a 30-year-old attorney who began working 2 years ago at the firm where Bob is employed. Bob and Karen have been involved for a year, and Bob says that Karen makes him feel "more alive than I have in years." Bob has recently begun seeing Roy, a therapist in part time private practice. Roy also works part-time at a community mental health clinic, where he sees Maria, described above. We recall that Maria is torn between leaving her abusive husband, and trying to change her behavior, which she thinks might stop the abuse.

As he starts his work, Roy considers some of the countertransference issues that are potentially entailed in helping both Bob and Maria. Roy has been doing therapy for more than a decade, and reflects to himself that he has grown. As a beginner, he would have wanted to help Bob give up Karen, and stay with Sue. He also would have wanted to help Maria leave Juan. At this point, though, Roy has abandoned fantasies of rescuing clients, and does not think he knows how other people should live their lives. He simply wants to help them make up their own minds (Haffey & Cohen, 1992; Kaslow & Schwartz, 1987).

To convey his wish to help clients choose their own paths, Roy takes two steps. First, realizing that any troubled spouse is likely to be exquisitely sensitive to the therapist's possible promotion of either separating or staying (Marek, 1989), Roy explicitly declares his neutrality on the topic of divorce. He is also careful to back up this declaration nonverbally. Roy knows, though, that no matter how scrupulous his attention to neutrality, the feared encouragement to separate or stay may be projected onto him when it is not in fact present, and that no matter what he does, some anxious clients may disappear from treatment prematurely.

Second, if Roy's clients do not bolt, and demonstrate an ability to tolerate sustained attention to marital problems, he proceeds to explore all aspects of ambivalent clients' conflicted realities. That is, he finds out about both the positive and negative feelings toward the current spouse, and the anticipated positive and negative aspects of the potential separation. For example, if Roy focusses solely on guilt Bob might feel 5 years into a relationship with Karen, after the sexual excitement has faded (negative aspect of separation), and does not respect the possibility that Bob has in fact met someone who is better suited to him than his wife is (positive aspect of separation), he is listening to only part of the story. Bob may then feel Roy is pressuring him to stay with Sue, and flee treatment. Likewise, if Bob only asks about what happens when Juan hits Maria (negative aspect of spouse), Maria may end up defending Juan, because she feels her choice of spouse has been attacked. But, if Roy also asks what Maria likes about Juan (positive aspect of spouse), she may feel freer to question what she is doing with him. Eventually, after Maria has explored all sides of her ambivalence, she will make up her own mind.

In cases like Maria's, where the threat of violence inhibits her from speaking freely in front of her husband, exploration of ambivalence is best accomplished in individual sessions (Mack, 1989). In Bob's case, there is no such threat. So, if Bob or a similar client is ready to discuss his affair openly, his mixed feelings should be explored in couple as well as individual sessions (Everett & Volgy, 1991; Marek, 1989). In fact, feedback from his wife Sue (e.g., about an unenacted but deeply felt sexual restlessness paralleling her husband's) may help either or both parties decide whether to stay or leave. The possibility of extreme displays of emotion in these couple sessions should not deter the therapist, who may want to remember that the emotion is expressed, not created in the treatment.

Whether they are seen in couples or individual treatment, spouses who are contemplating separation and have the ego capacity for insight may sometimes increase understanding of their ambivalent feelings toward each other via focussed attention on selected family of origin issues (Heitler, 1990). These include displacement of anger at a parent onto a spouse (Marek, 1989), or unrealistic expectations that a spouse will compensate for parental deficits experienced during childhood (Kersten, 1990). Sometimes, when a spouse is psychologically relieved of such responsibility, the balance of feelings in the ambivalence shifts, and positive feelings about the marriage begin to predominate. For example, an adult daughter of an alcoholic father is initially unaware that she is governed by childhood longings for a caring and consistent male; through treatment, she realizes that her husband's attentiveness, which she initially perceived as insufficient, is to be valued. She then loses interest in the possibility of ending the marriage.

Understanding the Impact of Client Ethnicity
on Preseparation Ambivalence.

For a therapist to fully appreciate a client's ambivalence about a marriage, deepened knowledge of other cultures is sometimes necessary. For example, McGoldrick, Preto, Hines, and Lee (1989) point out that on occasion, the Black woman tolerates abuse from the Black man. One reason is that she may well understand his rage against an unjust society, rage for which she can be the target (McGoldrick et al., 1989); the shared experience of racism mutes her anger. Knowing this, a therapist may transcend a countertransferential urge to move prematurely to "rescue" a battered Black female client. Rather, the therapist will reach both for the client's anger, and for compassion engendered by the woman's awareness of the pressures besetting her husband (see Note 1).

At the same time, the therapist must be sensitive to the Black cultural orientation to doing, as opposed to thinking, feeling, or discussing (Mc-Goldrick et al., 1991). Thus, the Black woman's in-session discussion of marital ambivalence would likely be less emotional and discursive than that of the Jewish woman, who tends to be more verbal and therapy oriented (Hines et al., 1992). Another variable that will condense discussion of ambivalence is the likelihood that the Black woman client values the maternal role above all others, and may be uncomfortable with protracted discussion of her own wishes (Hines, 1990); the effect of wife battering on offspring may be a more acceptable topic than the effect of battering on the woman herself.

The experience of recent female Hispanic emigrants provides another example of how ethnicity can shape women's ambivalence about facing male abuse. In contrast to Black culture, Hispanic culture has historically stressed the importance of woman as homemaker and man as breadwinner (Del Carmen & Virgo, 1993; Hines et al., 1992); accordingly, empirical studies of Hispanic families tend to demonstrate a negative relationship between wives' employment and marital satisfaction (Ross et al., 1990). However, in recent years, female Hispanic emigrants—like female emigrants from many countries (Drachman & Shen-Ryan, 1991)—have often surpassed their male counterparts in vocational success. Newly arrived Hispanic women obtain work in domestic, service, and menial jobs that are off limits to Hispanic men, in part because of the rigid male roles in Hispanic culture (McGoldrick et al., 1989).

When Hispanic wives support their families, unemployed husbands sometimes experience a decrease in self-esteem, which can lead to domestic violence (Facundo, 1991). On the one hand, when a Hispanic woman is earning money and freed to see marriage—at least intellectually—as a choice rather than a mandate, she is better able to acknowledge the violence. On the other hand, Hispanic culture emphasizes unquestioning respect for male authority (Facundo, 1991; McGoldrick et al., 1991), and upholds a norm of lasting marriage more binding than the marital norms affecting non-Hispanic women (Del Carmen and Virgo, 1993). These traditions may make it difficult for a Hispanic woman, even when employed, to recognize abuse, or to give serious consideration to marital separation. So does the anticipation of the social stigma facing the separated or divorced Hispanic woman. When working with abused Hispanic homemakers like Maria, ample therapeutic attention to the value a woman places on her marriage is required.

It is interesting to note that for recently emigrated Soviet Jewish women, who also tend to surpass male counterparts in vocational success, there is less cultural emphasis on the traditional feminine role (Belozersky, 1990; Castex, 1992). Among this population, the concept of marital separation may cause less ambivalence; with a female population often capable of self-support, divorce is comparatively common (Belozersky, 1990; P. Berger, personal communication, January 4, 1991).

On the other hand, among American Jewish women, ambivalence about facing domestic violence is generated by the notion that "Jewish men don't do things like that" (Axelrod, 1994; Jacobs & Dimarsky, 1991/2; Kaye/Kantrowitz, 1991). Feeling that "it can't happen here," American Jewish women may—for a time—blind themselves to abuse. Most American Jews are middle class or upper middle class (DeFrain, LeMasters, & Schroff, 1991; Soifer, 1991), largely because of the financial support of Jewish husbands, and there is an erroneous tendency to think that such men would not beat their wives.

Although it appears that Jewish families may experience less wife abuse than the United States population at large (Axelrod, 1994; Guterman, 1993), there is no evidence for the myth that ability to earn a living rules out a violent temper. In fact, among Jewish families, it is possible that high socioeconomic status may increase the risk for family violence (Guterman, 1993). Jewish therapists are not immune to the myth, and must take pains to make sure that they explore abuse among Jewish clients with the same diligence that they exercise with other clients.

Among Jewish women with religious background, this myth-based ambivalence about facing male violence may be compounded by female self-blame; a religious belief that peace in the home is the woman's responsibility (Jacobs & Dimarsky, 1991/2) can transform the experience of male violence into the experience of "I must be doing something wrong to cause this." When working with Jewish women, therapists need to raise such religiously engendered self-blame as a possibility if it does not arise spontaneously in session. A clinician should not make assumptions about a client's religious background from a current lifestyle; although people may become less religiously observant as adults, they are often still influenced by beliefs inculcated during a traditional upbringing.

The Therapist's Stance with Clients Ambivalent About Separation.

Whether exploration of marital ambivalence is individual or conjoint, tied to a client's history or framed exclusively in the here and now, linked to culturally determined attitudes or not, the topic is almost always excruciatingly tense. This is particularly so if one partner is more invested in the marriage than the other. When clients are so edgy that they only yell, interrupt, repeat, and accuse, the therapist can create a rational tone (Baucom & Epstein, 1990) via modelling, and if necessary, by setting ground rules for controlling voice volume, letting the other person finish, etc..

The therapist must recognize that despite skillful attempts to help clients verbalize their ambivalent feelings during individual or couple sessions, behavioral expressions of these feelings, sometimes volatile, may occur outside the treatment sessions. This is particularly true among clients who generally tend to externalize or act out their emotions rather than discuss them. Specifically, externalizations of marital ambivalence may include dramatic at-home "flip-flops" in behavior, such as alternation of passionate sex, and one partner sleeping on the couch. Adherence to cherished couple rituals and an individual spouse's evenings out alone with no questions asked may alternate too.

In the face of such externalization, the key is therapist humility. A number of authors (e.g., Rice & Rice, 1986a, 1986b) suggest that some clients can avoid a fair amount of acting-out of ambivalence if their therapists endorse a structured, trial separation, and help clients carefully plan behavior outside sessions (e.g., number and type of in-person contacts per week). I believe that very dependent clients are perhaps most likely to respond to this approach. In general, though, during the early stages of the contemplation of separation, people experiencing serious marital distress are so upset that they may not adhere to or even remember agreements to structure their seemingly exhausting behavior. They are in the grip of powerful ambivalent feelings about contact with each other, feelings that they may need to express in a variety of verbal and nonverbal ways, depending on their characteristic styles of discharging emotion.

Exploring Fear and Its Manifestations

As fear of the future often underlies ambivalence about leaving a marriage, it is also important to be very specific about a client's thoughts about striking out on her own. Although a therapist does not always know what topics will arise in which session, in general anticipation of "going it alone" is best covered in individual sessions, so that the reality of independence is experienced while it is being discussed. Sometimes the client speaks only of anticipated gains, such as freedom from marital strife, and does not volunteer any fears in response to open-ended questions such as "At those times when you think you might leave, what goes through your mind?" Although excitement and optimism are not to be discounted, and in fact are valid and deserve support, it is also necessary to ask more focussed questions, such as "Are you ever afraid?" Sometimes, such a question still elicits "no." Then, the therapist herself may have to broach the sometimes frightening challenges of life alone. Depending on the age, gender, ethnicity, or economic status of the client, these challenges might include balancing the work and child-care responsibilities of single parenthood, discrimination against the middle-aged job seeker, social stigma, loss of income, loneliness, difficulty in finding a remarriage partner, or loss of contact with children.

Awareness of cultural variety may help a therapist to reach out to probe fears that lie below a client's surface presentation, or to be sensitive to fears that might otherwise seem unfounded. For example, therapists working with Orthodox Jewish women need to understand the realistic fear of actually obtaining a divorce; in Orthodox Judaism, only a man can grant a divorce, and a husband scorned may not cooperate in doing so (Breitowitz, 1994). Knowing this, a therapist working with a young, employable, childless, Orthodox Jewish woman would avoid the temptation of sending out a message (either verbal or nonverbal) that the client "has her whole life in front of her," and is relatively lucky as far as those contemplating divorce go. Rather, the therapist would be empathic with the client's fears of protracted spousal conflict.

When working with those contemplating marital separation, it is also important to find out how any of these fears may be acted out. "How does the fearfulness effect you?" "Who do you find yourself gravitating towards these days?" "Do you ever need a drink to take the edge off your fear?" "Do you ever need any drugs to take the edge off your fear?" and "Do you have any concerns about your driving?" are relevant questions. Although male clients, in particular, may initially present an "I can handle this" bravado to their therapists (Myers, 1989), most clients find it a relief to be asked questions like these. Contrary to what inexperienced therapists sometimes think, inquiry about any dangerous deterioration in functioning is not generally viewed as accusatory or intrusive. Rather, it demonstrates care about important matters that even close friends generally skirt. Again, the thought of breaking up a marriage can be terrifying, and the therapist needs to be aware of any and all acting out that this leads to, including substance abuse.

Further questions (e.g., "Any other drugs that you try?" "How often do you go in for this? "Is it ever more often?") are particularly important for clients with suggestive histories, such as inpatient detoxification or psychiatric hospitalization. Depending on the answers, the therapist may have to help the client control herself (e.g., insist that Alcoholics Anonymous attendance operate simultaneously with therapy). Later in the treatment process, problem solving in relation to the psychological and practical stresses engendering fear occurs. However, the first step is to get specific fears out in the open, and any dangerous acting out under control.

Exploring the Possibility of Suicide

Suicidal risk must be monitored in a similarly specific fashion. The thought of marital separation, especially when one is not the initiator, can catalyze suicidal ideation, threats, gestures, and even attempts. Both verbal cues (e.g., "Sometimes I wonder what the point of all this discussion is," "Life alone seems hopeless") and nonverbal cues (e.g., deterioration in physical appearance, noticeable weight gain or loss, slouched body position in chair, monotone voice) need to be taken seriously. Some of the key questions here are: "When you get depressed, how depressed do you get?" "Do you ever feel you might harm yourself?" "What specifically have you thought about?" and "What has stopped you so far?" Discussion will often overlap with exploration of substance abuse, as legal and illegal drugs can both be ingested in lethal doses.

Suicidal threats and gestures are generally manipulations by assenters to invoke guilt in initiators, and prevent their departure. In these cases, the client can be made aware of the impact of the action ("What effect does it actually seem to have on Doris when you tell her you are going to slit your wrists if she leaves?" "How do you feel about living like this?"), and alternate routes of expressing anger can be explored. Also, the side of the client that does want to live, as opposed to the suicidal side, needs to be elicited ("Are there times that you do *not* feel this upset?"). In this way, the client gains control over depressive urges that are but a part of her total life experience at a very anxiety-provoking point.

Sometimes a client contemplating marital separation is beyond threats or gestures. The client's wish is to die, rather than to manipulate a spouse. There is no ability to envision a life worth living, but there is a plan to kill oneself, and nothing, including cowardice or anticipated effects on children, seems to be an impediment. The feeling of being hopeless, helpless, and alone is overwhelming. In these cases, to prevent self-inflicted injury, psychiatric consultation for medication and/or hospitalization may be warranted (Heitler, 1990), and are usually experienced (correctly) by the client as a protective mechanism.

Spouses contemplating separation are likely to differ in their degree of commitment to each other (Guttmann, 1993; Kitson, 1992). Thus, it may be difficult to enlist a more stable but relatively uncommitted spouse in the care of a spouse endangering herself with substance abuse or suicidal risk, although a soon-to-depart spouse will sometimes help care for children who cannot count on a deteriorated parent for physical or psychological sustenance. In the absence of a committed spouse, a therapist may need to help a client reach out for extended family, or even personally call such relatives. In general, when possible, it is best for clients to hold off on actual physical separation until dangerous behavior is controlled, or at the very least, adequately monitored.

Involving Spouse and Children in Treatment

Therapeutic Options for Spouses:
Individual Treatment and Couple Treatment.

When one spouse arrives for the initial interview and describes a marital concern, the therapist may struggle over whom to involve in subsequent sessions. There is no cookbook answer. Generally, though, as suggested in the case of Bob and Sue above, if a nonviolent problem is described, it is diagnostically useful to see the originally absent spouse (Marek, 1989). Distortions of this person as described to the therapist can be corrected, and the therapist quickly gains access to contributions of both spouses to marital problems. Although the "two-way street" can usually be elicited in individual sessions via skilled questioning (e.g., "You say he doesn't lift a finger to do housework, and you both work full time. I wonder if there's anything going on below the surface, that he would want to give you such a hard time."), the individual route takes longer, and is not always as successful.

Reaching out for the originally absent spouse for diagnostic purposes does not mean that ongoing couple sessions will continue, although they may. Sometimes levels of distress differ so markedly that only the person suffering continues to be seen. The work, though, is rendered more effective by the knowledge the therapist obtained by meeting the other partner. In a like vein, a partner's refusal to attend even one session may indicate low commitment to the marriage, and is worthy of discussion in subsequent sessions with the help-seeking spouse.

Some clients, in contrast, desire "couples work" which initially feels like a dead end to the therapist. Most frequently, a woman with a violent husband hopes to salvage her marriage. For several reasons, the therapist must respect the woman's hope and begin counselling the couple (see Note 2). First, the emotional tie in violent couple relationships can be powerful (Douglas, 1991; Dutton & Painter, 1993; Johnson, 1992; Lawson, 1992); the principle of "starting where the client is" requires that the husband not be excluded. Second, men who batter can sometimes be helped to control, diminish, or change their abusive behavior (Douglas, 1991; Sakai, 1991; Tolman & Bennett, 1992). Third, in a brutally realistic vein, some women with limited employability and economic resources will ultimately choose to make the best of an abusive situation because the standard of living outside the marriage would likely be much lower than in it (Johnson, 1992); such women need to learn to cope with their relationships if they do not leave them. Fourth, on occasion, a battered woman needs to experience an abortive counselling attempt to salvage a violent marriage, before she shifts to an orientation to life on her own. (The vast majority of spousal violence is perpetrated by men against women [Brody, 1992]; therapists are likely to encounter men with violent wives much less frequently, if ever.)

Inherent in counselling volatile people are uncertainties around attendance and around the ability to integrate treatment gains. Thus, these client-initiated couple sessions may not continue long. Whether the client-initiated conjoint treatment is of shorter or longer duration, clinicians must take *both* husband and wife in the couples sessions *seriously*. A common mistake is to go through the motions with the abusing spouse (usually the man) and work harder with the abused spouse (usually the woman); even the most experienced therapist sometimes needs to manage a countertransferential tendency to take sides and try to rescue the woman.

On the other hand, if a woman like Maria requests individual help in thinking about leaving someone who has thrown her against walls, punched her, or perpetrated marital rape, a dogmatic family therapist's knee-jerk attempts to help her approach her husband about counselling may cause her, correctly, to bolt therapy. Here a contrasting countertransference ("family therapy for all occasions") must be overcome. The woman's experience of an unworkable situation must be respected, and forcing a couples approach on someone who does not want it implies a superior, nonempathic attitude (Davis & Hagen, 1992).

The Therapist's Responsibility to Clients' Children.

Usually, children should be seen early in treatment (with one or both parents) when the presenting problem is marital. The reason is that highly stressed parents are not always reliable raters of their children's well- being. Sometimes parents are so preoccupied with their own problems that they minimize children's symptoms or miss them altogether (Kalter, 1990; Kitson, 1992; Walsh, 1991). Alternately, because they fear an anticipated separation may psychologically destroy their children, parents may pathologize healthy responses to parental distress (e.g., a 9-year-old boy who was previously lackadaisical regarding school suddenly becomes very involved in homework) or have extreme reactions to children's troubling but transient responses to parental tension (e.g., a 15-year-old girl announces she wants to eat all meals in her bedroom). If the therapist senses that parents are either minimizing or exaggerating their children's troubles, it is the responsibility of the therapist to raise the subject.

If parents exaggerate, it is generally not difficult to simply invite them to bring the children about whom they are so concerned to a session. If parents are self-absorbed, or involved in reaction formation against fear of harming children, it may be more difficult to involve them. True, when the client seeks help to discuss a troubled marriage, this motive must be respected. But, at some point the therapist can initiate a subject change by saying something like, "I'm going to shift gears now. How is all this for Joey?" If the client is annoyed about the loss of attention to her own concerns, or reluctant to open up yet another anxiety-provoking subject ("Maybe I'm not a good parent; the therapist thinks I'm ruining my child's life"), the therapist should address these resistances.

If reluctance to bring offspring to treatment persists, the therapist should use her authority and say something like "I know you're here because you need to sort out what's going on between you and Ray, and we'll be devoting a lot of our work together to that. But at this clinic [or, in my practice] we are always concerned about how children react to rough times in a marriage. That doesn't mean we want to make a patient out of your kid. From what you describe, he may be doing very well. Or, if he's having any kind of reaction that's been missed, it might be that you can help him yourself, if only we spend some time talking about it here. It's just usually a good idea to spend a little time with a child in person." While validating the client's stated request for help, the therapist also educates the client about other areas where therapy can help, and gently challenges her to move beyond divorce-induced narcissism. The therapist's sensitivity to children applies to client families from all income and ethnic groups, including those where divorce is most common; with regard to children, there appear to be no findings that where divorce is more common, it is less painful. (For a comment on the need to look below the surface of the finding that divorce may be less painful for Black adults than for White adults, see chapter 11.)

In one family a couple that was considering marital separation was grateful for the opportunity to bring their 11-year-old son, Tony, to a mental health clinic for evaluation. Although the marriage, not Tony, was the presenting problem, his parents welcomed the therapist's questions about their son. They knew deep down that they were minimizing Tony's pain, and seemed to experience child-oriented questions as getting them back on track as parents. Tony was described as beginning to overeat, and as sullen and provocative, for example, constantly "forgetting" to do chores and homework. In a "one-shot" family session, Tony said he knew his parents were "sticking to the marriage partly because I don't want to live in a broken home." The parents said they were "too worn out to insist that Tony do his homework and take out the garbage."

Subsequent marital sessions, while pertaining largely to the parents' conflicts, also were partially devoted to the need to decrease Tony's excessive power in the family. Although the parents had a troubled marriage, they were not highly disturbed individuals, and were quickly able to realize that they were minimizing some important concerns: Tony should not feel in charge of the future of his parents' relationship, or experience any gap in discipline. The therapist discussed Tony in future sessions, and saw him once more, 2 months after the first meeting. Tony had lost weight, and confirmed that his parents had reinvolved themselves with expectations of him: "I can't get away with anything any more."

Disturbed Parents, Disturbed Children: What to do.

Other parents, more disturbed, may not be able to respond to a troubled child this quickly or this well. In such cases, the therapist may suggest separate therapy sessions for a child who is not able to distance herself from parents' problems. This could be because of sensitive temperament, lack of support from siblings or extended family, or other reasons. The purpose of the sessions would be to help the child faced with parents' marital problems to express reactions, such as fear and anxiety, in the presence of a caring and validating adult. In this way, the feeling of being overwhelmed is counteracted, and children (from preschool age through adolescence) are encouraged to verbalize rather than externalize their emotional burdens. Another purpose of the sessions is to promote involvement in age appropriate activities, and connection to extended family members and other concerned adults. Through such connections, the impact of parents' marital problems may be buffered or diminished.

Sometimes, particularly when offspring feelings include severe depression and/or emotional isolation, externalization may include a wide range of self-destructive behavior, including substance abuse and suicide attempts. In these cases, specific discussion of how to control self-destructive impulses is clearly warranted. So is outreach to even the most self-absorbed parents, as they must be helped to see that their parental responsibilities (particularly to children and adolescents living at home) do not end when marital problems develop or deepen.

NOTES

1. Here, as in many subsequent examples, ideas about treatment involve generalizations about an ethnic group. The reader must bear in mind that such generalizations may or may not apply to a given client. While ethnicity is a central fact of any client's life, members of any group are diverse. ideas about treatment that are based on what is generally known about a particular group will apply in varying degree—or not at all—depending on tbe client at hand.

2. Tolman and Bennett (1992), presenting a model for group work for men who batter, state that "conjoint sessions are dangerous if undertaken prior to a man successfully stopping his violent behavior" (p. 207). These authors contend that use of conjoint sessions implies that women's efforts can modify male violence. The point that responsibility for male violence rests with men and is not shared by women is well taken. However, I believe that individual or group treatment of violent men can, on occasion, be profitably combined with conjoint treatment, particularly when the woman feels deeply involved in the marriage.

Chapter 4

The Mental Health Professional's Role: Predivorce Practical Concerns

In addition to help with their feelings and their children, clients thinking about leaving marriages need help with practical matters. Information and education, although important, are not enough. For information and education to be assimilated, they must be presented clinically, with due respect for clients' psychological makeup and sociological reality, and with due respect for the therapeutic process. This chapter describes some practical matters important to clients considering marital separation, as well as clinical skills for presenting information and education about these matters. It also identifies skills for helping clients finalize and implement their decisions about their troubled marriages.

THREE MAJOR PRACTICAL MATTERS: SAFETY, SHELTER, AND INCOME

Safety, shelter, and income are basic practical issues for any separating family. In some separations (e.g., those involving non–acting-out, securely employed spouses), safety, shelter and income are not jeopardized, and the therapist need not dwell on them. However, when any one of these may be threatened by a marital split, it is *the* priority in clinical sessions. Sometimes, clients are ashamed to raise these issues, particularly if there is a cultural mandate against "airing dirty linen in front of strangers." In these cases, therapists must listen for hints and omissions, and, if necessary, gently take the initiative in asking questions.

Protecting Abused Women

Sometimes a client must face the fact that her departure from the marriage may create the risk of physical danger, usually caused by an enraged spouse. Consider Maria, the battered client whose description of her husband's brutality introduced chapter 2. In chapter 3, we developed some ideas for helping her with her ambivalence about marital separation and her fear of the future as a single woman. As she contemplates separation, Maria rightfully fears for her safety, anticipating harassment or worse from Juan should she leave.

Maria's therapist should inform Maria that an order of protection (obtained in many states through family or criminal court) will render Juan's approaches illegal, and enable Maria to summon police to enforce this directive if necessary. Unfortunately, Maria also needs to learn that police enforcement sometimes amounts to little more than a slap on the wrists (Koff, 1989; Rather, 1994), and that there is no foolproof method of keeping Juan away.

The therapist's use of the technique of education is based on the premise that information can decrease powerlessness, on both feeling and reality levels. To be truly effective, though, education about safety needs to be combined with other clinical techniques, such as exploration, and resolution of any conflicts Maria may have about obtaining and using an order of protection. For example, such an order may be foreign to a Hispanic woman raised to defer to men (McGoldrick et al., 1991), and Maria may ultimately reject the option. The therapist cannot force an action on a client, no matter how correct it seems to the therapist. On the other hand, if Maria's decision is to pursue the order of protection, and she happens to be a recent immigrant who lacks coping skills for negotiating external reality, the therapist's use of in-session rehearsal of Maria's court visit may further ensure that the order of protection gets beyond the drawing board stage. If Maria (or her Russian counterpart) does not speak English, a bilingual therapist may choose to make the necessary phone calls in the client's presence, and even to accompany her to court. Therapists should discuss other practical resources for ensuring safety (e.g., public programs that fund doorlock changes for endangered separating spouses) in a similar way. That is, providing multiple vantage points—informational, psychological, and cultural—increases the possibility that clients will actually use available services.

Sheltering Poor Clients with No Place to Go

Sometimes, a client realizes that because she is poor, she will literally have no place to go if she initiates marital rupture. If the separation is her idea, the burden of moving will frequently be on her, but often she has no savings, no job, and no relatives able to provide transitional housing—or financial assistance to secure transitional housing. In some states, while she is still residing with her husband, she cannot initiate the public assistance application that would enable her to set up an independent household. For these reasons, such a client sometimes cannot begin planning effectively for a move, and may encounter what seems to be a major impediment to divorce. In such cases, the therapist's job is to present options.

If a woman is being physically abused, battered women's shelters comprise one such option. Although nationwide there are far too few shelters to accommodate the women who want to use them (Brody, 1992), their numbers have increased in recent years (Gelles & Cornell, 1990). The therapist's knowledge about length of stay allowed, children's access to local schools, room arrangements, secret location to protect women from infuriated husbands, and other details can all help. Recently emigrated battered wives who are registered aliens married to United States citizens, but not citizens themselves, may benefit from learning that they too can make use of shelters, and that their spouses' common threats of deportation are hollow (Howe, 1991). In fact, if so inclined, these noncitizens can also take steps to separate, divorce, and seek citizenship, although they are not eligible for public assistance (Howe, 1991).

Therapists should be prepared to face other professionals whose opinions may diverge on matters such as shelters. For example, a male psychiatrist encountered in a community mental health setting as a consultant, stated his belief that an impoverished wife preparing to leave an abusive husband should sign herself into a psychiatric hospital to obtain a roof over her head. Had the woman's therapist implemented the psychiatrist's idea, the therapist would have denied the client knowledge that could enable her to take charge of her life, and would have conveyed the message that a physical move away from an abusive husband was not a topic important enough for a therapist to research. She would have further diminished the client by implying that a strength, the desire to separate, was a form of psychopathology warranting hospitalization. However, the therapist obtained another opinion. She then decided to tell the client about her shelter options, explore her feelings about them, and treat her wish to separate as worthy of thorough and knowledgeable consideration. A potentially demeaning treatment was avoided.

If a woman without funds or employment is not experiencing domestic violence and is thinking about separation, her therapist may need to inform her about shelters for the homeless. Again, facts (as opposed to myths) on location, physical plant, and type of resident likely to be encountered will generally prove invaluable. While in a transitional location, a woman will be able to seek employment, or (in some states) apply for public assistance if necessary. Ultimately, she will be able to move into her own apartment.

Cultural factors are also relevant when considering temporary shelter for poor or near-poor separating clients. For example, in the choice between moving in with extended family, or going to a shelter, views often diverge along racial lines. Black clients generally accept it as usual (though not necessarily problem-free) to move in with extended family, while White clients generally prefer to live near but not with extended family (Walsh, 1991). Therapists need to be aware of such cultural mandates when helping clients contemplating divorce think through their postseparation housing options and other practical matters facing them.

Facilitating the Search for New Quarters

Clients who are contemplating marital separation and have incomes sufficiently above the poverty level will most likely be thinking about the possibility of moving, rather than finding a funded shelter or living with relatives. Among these clients, some are better at negotiating the business world than the interpersonal world, and need to remind themselves of this coping strength—something they *have*—when facing the possible loss of spouse and social status, as well as diminished income and material circumstances. By focussing on their capacity to find a new place to live, these clients can boost the faltering sense of competence that sometimes plagues those who experience divorce as a personal failure. This is true even if they know the new apartment or house is likely to be smaller, plainer, or in a less desirable neighborhood than the old one. Such a client would be insulted if her therapist asked her how she planned to go about seeking a new affordable apartment for self and children. The implication that she needed help in planning would be resented. In contrast, other clients, basically capable but feeling tentative at a time of stress, need to explore the ideas they have about moving with a therapist, but do not need information or direction. Still other clients, either because of their limited ability to negotiate the business world, status as recent immigrant, or limited literacy, may need information, suggestions, and the chance to literally rehearse discussions with potential landlords in their clinical sessions.

Helping Clients Cope with Income Problems and Gender Inequity

Most men contemplating marital separation do not face the severe income problems that most women do. Because of the gender wage gap (i.e., when men and women do the same work, women are paid less; Kissman & Allen, 1993), and their greater likelihood of continuous employment history, men generally earn more than women. They are also far less likely than women to become the custodial parent, who bears the day-to-day financial responsibility for offspring (Guttmann, 1993). When there is property to divide, the husband usually gets as much or more than the wife and children combined. If men skip child support payments, as they often do, there are few immediate consequences except a higher disposable income. This may be one reason that in some cases, the standard of living for men goes up after divorce, while that of women and children goes down (Bee, 1994; Kitson, 1992; Maccoby & Mnookin, 1992; Teachman & Paasch, 1993; Weitzman, 1988). The economic stress of responsible separated fathers should not be minimized, but in general, the financial situation for the ex-wife/mother facing the future alone is far more hazardous (Ross et al., 1990; Williams et al., 1992).

Socioeconomic Class, Ethnicity, and Age
Influence Women's Predivorce Attitudes Toward Employment.

Some women considering marital separation are not employed; others, while employed, earn salaries that contribute to a two-wage-earner income base, but are not sufficient to support a new one-wage-earner household, particularly if that new household will include children. For both sets of women, even if they stand to receive full and steady child support payments postdivorce, an improved employment situation is the best case scenario if a decision is made to separate.

During the preseparation phase of the divorce cycle, some women are ready to think about a move from unemployment to employment, an increase in part-time job hours, vocational training, promotion at a current full-time job, or a job switch. This readiness may be most likely among blue-collar women who are accustomed to working; employed, career-oriented middle- and upper middle-class women; and women whose ethnic backgrounds provide them with supports for employment outside the home. For example, Black women and recently emigrated Soviet Jewish women are more likely to find role models and affirmation for vocational success within their own communities than are Hispanic women and Orthodox Jewish women.

For women ready to proceed in improving their work situations, the therapist should be attentive, but not intrusive. Two messages are to be conveyed. First, employment is just as important as emotional matters such as fear of being alone. Second, the therapist is available to delve deeper if need be, but is respectful of the woman's own efforts to increase earnings.

In contrast, some women who are considering separation may not be ready to take steps to achieve improved employment. For one thing, these steps (e.g., return to school, obtaining a part-time job with an eye to eventually increasing hours) suggest an initiator's ideas about separation to the other spouse at a time when the initiator may not yet be ready to share these ideas. Alternately, so much emotional energy may go into making the decision about separation that little energy is left for job interviews, networking, or other tasks. This may be particularly true for middle-aged and older women who correctly fear age-based hiring and wage discrimination, and may have been raised in a pre-feminist era when working for income was considered shameful for middle- and upper-class women. Conflicts about job hunting are also likely among Hispanic and Orthodox Jewish women, who, if employed outside the home, frequently experience added marital tension in the form of wounded male egos, or male retaliation for newfound female independence.

With such conflicted women, the therapist must walk a fine line. On the one hand, it is important to gently point out the benefits of eventual employment, acknowledge the woman's conflicts about working, and be ready to discuss them. On the other hand, the therapist must "stay where the client is," respecting the fact that some women may simply be unable to discuss vocational matters while in the throes of resolving marital ambivalence.

Helping Clients Access Nonemployment Income Sources: AFDC, Private Charity, and Marital Assets.

In situations where nonearning or low-earning women contemplating separation are not ready to face the hurdle of finding or improving employment, therapists need to present an income alternative. The most important of these is Aid to Families with Dependent Children (AFDC), which will provide ongoing income, although at the poverty level.

When AFDC is broached, clients' feelings about seeking government money clearly warrant exploration. Some people, particularly those who thought they would never need it, may feel ashamed and degraded (Brown, 1989; Kaslow & Schwartz, 1987). Others may fear inability to negotiate "red tape." Others may be concerned, understandably, that allotments are not sufficient; as of 1992, grants fell below 80% of the poverty level ($11,280 per year for a family of three) in 33 states (Toner, 1992). If such feelings are not addressed verbally, in session, they may be acted out in unconsciously delayed or sabotaged pursuit of funds. Clients who have received assistance previously may be more matter-of-fact, and have less of a need to discuss their reaction.

AFDC applicants need to be informed that local governments keep most of any child support collected from nonresidential fathers, to recoup "lost" revenue; in all states, only 50 child support dollars per month are passed on to the mother and children as an AFDC supplement (Eckholm, 1992). This AFDC "passthrough" is in marked contrast to the child support payments made to employed, non-AFDC mothers; these payments appreciably increase the standard of living for women and children. The "passthrough" underscores the constricted income situation of any AFDC family, as well as a possible resultant sense of futility and powerlessness. "What good does it do to take my ex to court?" and "Why don't *we* get more of his earnings, when the women who need less help get more?" an AFDC mother might well ask. Ideally, informed therapists help affected clients express and channel their reactions to this double standard, particularly when client emotion interferes with application for financial assistance.

Also important for the divorcing poor is financial aid from churches and other organizations. Such aid is particularly critical for illegal immigrants (e.g., refugees from war-torn Central America) who are not eligible for public assistance. Clinical skills may be required to mobilize eligible clients, as people who are here illegally frequently fear deportation, and are sometimes afraid to ask for anything (McGoldrick et al., 1991).

The therapist's detailed knowledge about government and private assistance is essential. So are informal professional liaisons with employees at relevant agencies (e.g., public assistance center, church council) who can update eligibility information and answer questions about tricky situations. Clinical skills relevant to providing information about public or private financial assistance are similar to those used regarding the matter of moving, or other similar concrete matters. That is, some clients will clearly need to gather information on their own, and will feel patronized if the therapist inappropriately acts for them. At the contrasting extreme, other clients, because of chronic psychological limitations, recent arrival in this country, or divorce-engendered stress, will need just as clearly to be informed directly by their therapists about assistance options.

For clients who are not near the poverty line and have some financial assets, therapists may want to raise the possibility of an angry estranged spouse cleaning out the bank account. Of countertransferential relevance is therapists' comfort with financially explicit discussion. For many mental health practitioners, bedroom details are more comfortable than bankbook details, and savings is a hard subject to broach, particularly for private practitioners who set their own fees. Introspection and/or supervision may be required to see that avoiding this issue when the therapist senses its relevance is to abandon the client. On the other hand, therapists who are meticulous about their own financial issues need to recognize that some clients have little emotional energy available for money matters while contemplating marital separation. A female attorney who meets regularly with women beginning divorce proceedings observed, "They're not thinking about money when they see me" (R. Arrata, personal communication, November 2, 1990).

It is interesting to note that in a previous era, authorities such as child psychiatrist Richard Gardner (1976) exhorted therapists to steer clear of clients' financial concerns. Generally, Gardner and others (e.g., Kressel & Deutsch, 1977) viewed finances as an inappropriate topic for sessions, which were to focus solely on emotion. Money was important only as a symbolic route to deeper issues; for example, women's pursuit of withheld child support was thought to represent a female need to hang onto marital hostility (Gardner, 1976). It is unlikely that many mental health experts today would criticize therapists who treat entitlements, income, and standard of living as important topics in their own right.

LEGAL MATTERS

In addition to grappling with survival issues, clients considering divorce begin to wonder about legalities they may encounter. Timing varies considerably here. People who are very angry, people who defend against pain by being active, and people with money and property generally ask questions about divorce proceedings sooner than those who are depressed or overwhelmed, or those with few material assets.

The key word for the therapist at this juncture is "informed." The client should not be burdened with a therapist unable to discuss divorce law, as inattention to such concrete matters can perpetuate a client's immobilization around decision making (Haffey & Cohen, 1992). Of course, a therapist cannot give legal advice, but she can broadly define basic concepts, and make referrals.

Five Divorce Parameters

Specifically, therapists working with people considering marital separation need a basic grasp of five divorce parameters. Three of these concern children: *custody*, *visitation*, and *support*. Two are relevant only to clients with assets, and incomes above the poverty level: *alimony*, and *property division*.

Custody.

Custody refers to parents' rights and responsibilities regarding minor children. In prior eras, children have been successively seen as their fathers' property, better off with their mothers (the "tender years" doctrine), or better off with just the one parent best able to offer a secure environment (the "best interest of the child" doctrine) (Downey & Powell, 1993; Fine & Fine, 1994; Guttmann, 1993). Today, there is increased interest in the importance of both mother and father, and a presumption of joint legal custody—custody shared by both parents—in approximately half the states (Fine & Fine, 1994; Soldano, 1990). However, joint custody is largely a middle- and upper-class phenomenon, works well only when both parents want it (not when it is imposed as a form of conflict resolution by the court), and requires extensive cooperation (Pearson & Thoennes, 1990; Arditti, 1992). In rare cases, one parent gets along particularly well or poorly with one child in a sibling group, and split custody, in which offspring are divided between parents, may be established (Kaplan et al., 1993; Kaslow & Schwartz, 1987).

Surely, therapists working with those considering divorce need awareness of the theoretical range of custody options (sole paternal, sole maternal, joint, and split). They also need to know how views on custody have shifted over time, so that they will think independently about each case, rather than assuming that the current bias toward joint custody is correct for all clients. However, the major variable affecting therapists who help clients consider custody matters is that most fathers, particularly in the lower income brackets, do not remain involved with their children after divorce (Ahlburg & DeVita, 1992; Booth & Amato, 1994; Furstenberg & Cherlin, 1991; Furstenburg et al., 1987). A mother's sole custody, ultimately operant in 90% of divorced families (Maccoby, Buchanan, Mnookin, & Dornbusch, 1993; Mott, 1994; Walsh, 1991) often seems a foregone conclusion to therapists. Additionally, even joint custody frequently boils down to women assuming the lion's share of responsibility. Specifically, joint custody may be either (a) legal only, or (b) physical. In both joint legal custody and joint physical custody, parents share legal rights and responsibilities. In joint physical custody, children literally divide time between the residences of both parents. When joint custody is legal only and the children reside with the mother, it is in execution not very different from sole maternal custody (Arditti, 1992); although joint custody fathers do tend to be more responsible financially than fathers who do not have joint custody (Arditti, 1992), the day-to-day childrearing responsibility is the mother's. Consequently, with regard to custody, the therapist frequently needs to explain and/or work through the woman's reaction to "the facts of life," in addition to (or rather than) explaining an array of options. Clients who are confused by the custody issue may find it reassuring to learn that as far as child adjustment goes, the postdivorce relationship between the parents is more important than the form of custody itself (Demo, 1992; Maccoby & Mnookin, 1992; Pearson & Thoennes, 1990).

Visitation.

In cases where both parents are involved in and capable of parenting, visitation needs to be predictable for younger children, who are eager for secure routines in the separation upheaval, flexible for preadolescents and adolescents, who often want to plan their free time around peer contact, and revisable, because childrens' needs change over time. When one parent is severely disturbed, or physically or sexually abusive, that parents' visits need to be under court-mandated supervision, so the visiting parent is never alone with offspring.

As parents consider marital separation, therapists sometimes clarify the importance of implementing these goals legally, so that misunderstanding and arguments between divorced parents are minimized. The idea of a formal visitation plan can reassure parents who fear harming their children, as they see a concrete way to promote offspring well-being.

Again, though, because of declining paternal involvement over time (Ahlburg & DeVita, 1992; Booth & Amato, 1994; Furstenberg & Cherlin, 1991), visitation may be a moot point for many families seen in both private practice and community mental health settings today. Helping women and children accept paternal disengagement is not really a preseparation task, as it is not usually clear before separation whether a father will remain involved (Kruk, 1994), but it is a clinical challenge later in the divorce cycle.

Support.

Child support awards most often go from nonresidential fathers to residential mothers. In this arena, as previously noted, there is good news in recent federal legislation that has ensured that award amounts are now generally standardized by states, rather than left to the discretion of individual judges, as they were in the past. As a result, support awards are generally larger than in prior years, and routinely updated in court, to keep pace with inflation and children's changing needs (Fine & Fine, 1994; Garfinkel & McLanahan, 1990; Garfinkel et al., 1992).

However, the bad news is that, as previously noted, about 20% of divorced mothers have no child support award at all (Meyer & Garasky, 1993). And, among women who do have a support award, only about half receive the full amount, while about one quarter receive part, and about one quarter receive nothing (Ahlburg & DeVita, 1992; Cherlin, 1993). Fathers who pay the full amount or close to it tend to have larger incomes than those who do not (Arditti & Keith, 1993; Ihinger-Tallman et al., 1993; Teachman, 1991). Contrary to cherished beliefs (Stack, 1974), fathers who do not pay do not usually provide informally, via gifts or concrete help (Paasch & Teachman, 1991). The upshot is that poor divorcing mothers receive a smaller proportion of smaller child support awards than their middle- and upper-income counterparts; those who need child support most, receive it least.

Therapists should help female clients become aware of the importance of applying for support as soon as they are legally separated; if no application is made, no support will ever accrue. If a woman is discouraged by the relatively small number of fully and promptly paid awards, she needs to know that ever-tightening federal collection procedures (Cherlin, 1993; Fine & Fine, 1994) may cause a woman's support application to yield results eventually, if not immediately. As with other parameters described in this chapter, the therapist attempts to raise a women's consciousness about what lies ahead, while respecting the woman's own pace in acquiring detail, and using the material.

Alimony.

Alimony, or spousal support, is a relatively minor consideration. It is received by only about 15% of women (Fine & Fine, 1994; Zastrow & Kirst-Ashman, 1990), generally those over 40 and originally of middle-

or upper-income status (Hewlett, cited in Walsh 1991). Because many judges erroneously assume that women can earn income commensurate with men's, a recent trend has been for increasingly small and short-term (or so-called rehabilitative) alimony amounts (Fine & Fine, 1994; Guttmann, 1993; Kaslow & Schwartz, 1987). That is, alimony is designed to help a woman "get on her feet" until she improves her money-earning capacity, not to provide long-range income. Female clients anticipating long-term financial relief through alimony may need help in understanding that frequently (and sometimes unfairly) this source of income is not available.

Property Division.

In many states, legal definitions of marital property have recently expanded to include not only homes and bank accounts but also earning power, health insurance, and pensions (Noble, 1994a). This has been of some benefit to women whose ex-husbands would otherwise have benefitted exclusively from such assets. In *community property* states, all property is split fifty-fifty (Fine & Fine, 1994) with the assumption that husband and wife contributed equally to the marriage (Kaslow & Schwartz, 1987). In *equitable distribution* states (more common), courts can equitably divide some or all of the property owned by the spouses at the time of the divorce (Fine & Fine, 1994). In these states, it is usual for approximately one third of marital property to be awarded to the woman, and two thirds to the man, despite the fact that the woman's household often includes minor children, and comprises far more than one half of the original household (Weitzman, 1988). For therapists, the major issues are that (a) most divorcing couples have little property to divide (Seltzer & Garfinkel, 1990), and (b) in equitable distribution states, there is tremendous potential for battle in the minority of divorcing couples who do have significant assets.

For therapists working in community mental health clinics and other sliding scale fee settings, the majority of the low-income clients will most likely have little or nothing to divide, and property division will probably not be a treatment topic at any phase of the divorce cycle. Therapists in private practice face a different situation. During the preseparation phase, when actual property conflict is unlikely, their clients need to develop awareness of the difference between valid disagreements, and lengthy, draining battles encumbered by emotions derived from sources other than the couple's property. Such awareness can sometimes prevent needless haggling in later divorce phases.

Clinical Use of Legal Information: Two Contrasting Cases

Clinical assessment (of both the client's psychological makeup, and of relevant sociological parameters) will dictate if, how, and at what pace legal information is used in the treatment process. One of the most basic client questions facing any therapist working with the population contemplating separation is "Why get a legal divorce at all?" The following two cases illustrate the differential use of legal information in response to this question.

Betty: Client Questions About Legal Matters as an Entry Point for Divorce-Related Emotional Concerns.

Betty M. is 33, the blue-collar mother of two boys, ages 10 and 5. Her husband, George, 37, who had worked for an electronics company, was laid off 2 years ago. Unable to find a new job, George became more and more depressed as his unemployment benefits neared depletion, and began drinking heavily when they ended. Despondent about the receipt of public assistance and his inability to support his family, he has completely stopped seeking employment. For the last year, George has rarely ventured from the house, spends most of his time watching television, and, according to Betty, "just about ignores me and the kids." He refuses counselling and continues to drink. Several months ago, Betty began seeing Joan, a therapist at her local community mental health clinic because "if this is it, then maybe I should think about making a new life for myself and the kids."

> **Betty**: If we split up, do you think I should get divorced? George has no interest in the kids, and no money. If we move in with my parents, he won't bother us. I mean—what would be the point of a divorce? Maybe it's better to let sleeping dogs lie.
> **Therapist**: You don't want to stir up trouble, but you're wondering if a divorce would do you any good. *(The therapist uses reflective techniques to encourage the client to express ambivalent feelings. Although the client requests advice, the therapist does not give it, as advice would foreclose the client's involvement of her total self in the decision about pursuit of legal action.)*
> **Betty**: Yeah.
> **Therapist**: When you think about divorce, what goes through your mind? *(The therapist uses open-ended question to elicit fears and fantasies.)*
> **Betty**: Nothing, well, just a lot of aggravation, I guess.

Therapist: What kind of aggravation? *(Therapist continues to probe for fears and fantasies.)*

Betty: Waiting a long time for a legal services lawyer, and I heard the court is a real zoo.

Therapist: There *are* waits for those lawyers, and the courtrooms *are* crowded; you're certainly right about those things. I wonder if there's anything else about divorce that aggravates you. *(The therapist validates the client's fears, and wonders if even more conflict about divorce lies below surface.)*

Betty: Having a piece of paper instead of a marriage . . . when we used to love each other (she begins to cry). *(Therapist waits silently for a minute, to dignify Betty's tears. Therapist then focusses on helping Betty ventilate fear of loss, which seem to be absorbing most of her emotional energy at this time.)*

Joan senses it is very difficult for Betty to contemplate legal divorce, because she is still somewhat ambivalent about leaving George. Joan decides to use the topic of divorce as a "doorway" to underlying ambivalence and fear, and deliberately refrains from giving concrete information about divorce, even though she is well informed.

Catherine: Therapist Presentation of Legal Information as a Catalyst for Client Action.

Joan has another recently separated woman on her caseload at the clinic: Catherine, who is African American. Like Betty, Catherine functions at a reasonably high level. She is employed, lives alone, and has strong connections to her mother and sisters, who reside within walking distance. Like Betty, Catherine has a history of several jobs held for more than a year, and no background of psychosis. Unlike Betty, who feels that the rug has been pulled out from under her life, Catherine was the initiator of change. She had been physically abused for 5 years, and worked long and hard in treatment before gathering the courage to consider ending her marriage. Catherine finally decided that even though she could understand why her husband John sometimes took the day-to-day frustrations of being a Black man in this society out on her, she could no longer tolerate his inability to control himself.

When Catherine asked Joan for information about divorce, Joan began with open-ended questions similar to those she had used with Betty. While the answers to these questions indicated that Betty's basic emotional state was raw pain, Catherine felt pride in independence, and concern with building a future. Typical of Black women, Catherine experienced some—but not immobilizing—fear around the demise of her marriage. She also felt that "the split was a long time coming, and for the best."

The following excerpt from Joan's session with Catherine illustrates the use of information giving about divorce legalities, which occurs only after the therapist has determined that the client is ready to absorb the information.

> **Therapist**: You know, Catherine, you've been telling me you want to get started with a divorce because you want a clean break, even though right now you think very little about getting married again someday. But there are other reasons for divorce, too.
>
> **Catherine**: Like what?
>
> **Therapist**: For one thing, your daughter. I know that John never had any interest in her. But Susie's only 8, and you never how someone like John will behave. For example, he might get more interested in her when she gets older. It would be good if you had custody, and John had very limited visitation rights, perhaps with a stipulation that he could only see Susie under close supervision. In this way, divorce is kind of an insurance policy, to help you avoid some pretty ugly fighting that you could otherwise run into in the future. *(Therapist gives information in a straightforward, down-to-earth way. Therapist is not afraid to have a point of view, bypassing traditional notions of neutrality.)*
>
> **Catherine**: I didn't know about that.
>
> **Therapist**: There's no reason that you would. But now that you've heard a little bit about custody and visitation, what's your reaction to all this?
>
> **Catherine**: I guess it might be worth the trouble to go after a divorce. I really don't want John to have any claim on Susie. Where am I supposed to go to get this started? I don't have money for a lawyer.

In addition to knowing about custody and visitation, which she has just described to Catherine, Joan also knows about child support laws. Joan realizes that Catherine could probably obtain a child support award. But she also reasons that the likelihood of John paying voluntarily is slim, and that his off-the-books jobs leave no opportunity for an intercepted tax refund to benefit Catherine. So, Joan does not present more information right now; she feels Catherine has absorbed enough new knowledge (i.e., custody, visitation) to help her start her divorce in the near future, and that other legal matters will be dealt with over time. These include not just child support, but also the importance of divorce for Catherine's self-interest. For example, Catherine should become legally single so that she can never be identified as eligible for health insurance and other employment benefits through John.

Divorce Lawyers, Divorce Mediators

To reiterate, legal matters vary in salience for those in the preseparation phase of the divorce cycle. For clients in the throes of resolving ambivalence, discussion of the two major ways of obtaining a divorce (traditional legal methods and mediation) is clearly premature. For clients like Catherine, who are further along in the process, and actively mobilizing for marital rupture, such discussion is clearly indicated. For such clients, the therapist will draw selectively on the following knowledge.

Most divorces are uncontested, and do not result in litigation. In other words, where there is any spousal dispute—whether around custody, visitation, child support, alimony, or property division—it is usually settled out of court. For example, custody battles, a highly publicized, particular case of contested divorce, while typically agonizing for all concerned, occur in only 5% of divorces (Johnson, 1993). However, even without litigation, the legal process needed to arrive at a divorce agreement can consume a good deal of time, energy, and money.

The Two-Tiered Lawyer System: Private Attorneys, Legal Services.

Middle and upper income spouses anticipating property settlements often use private lawyers, and should be careful consumers. With such clients, therapists may discuss checking an attorney's reputation, evaluating an attorney's style of treating clients and answering questions, and finding out exactly how fees are charged and collected. (One client reported that an attorney told her she could pay out legal fees in installments after the actual physical separation, and then charged interest on these payments!)

Predivorce, therapists help clients see that being a careful consumer is easier said than done. For both men and women, divorce can be very draining, precipitating feelings of aloneness that are sometimes overwhelming. It is tempting to lean on an authority figure, such as a lawyer, rather than thinking for one's self about the competence of someone who, in essence, is being hired. Divorcing women may be additionally susceptible to gender-based discomfort when asserting their own needs (Haffey & Cohen, 1992) and take a passive rather than proactive stance when selecting a matrimonial attorney.

Clients who turn to legal services offices may face a different set of concerns (e.g., delays, overworked attorneys), because these organizations sometimes operate with insufficient funding and staff. Such limitations underscore the two-tiered system of law in this country; like the two-tiered system in day care (Zigler & Gilman, 1990), it discriminates against those unable to afford proprietary services. Sometimes, with the help of therapists, legal services clients can assert themselves within this system (e.g., pursuing attention when an application for service "falls between the cracks," clarifying domestic violence as a problem warranting immediate attention), but even the best case scenario will probably be short on consultation time, privacy for interviews, and promptly returned phone calls.

Another concern is that within legal services, family law has long been considered a low-status area (Besharov, 1990), as it has been felt (perhaps incorrectly, in my opinion), that there is less opportunity for reform than in areas such as discrimination, or inadequate government benefits (Besharov, 1990). Therefore, clients involved in divorce-related proceedings may occassionally encounter legal services attorneys who are apathetic, or who are not doing their chosen work. For example, one woman reported that her legal services attorney told her to accept a child support award amount presented by the court, rather than fight for an improvement, because "it's better than nothing." (The incident reportedly occurred prior to the previously mentioned standardization of award amounts.) When a client encounters problems of this type, a therapist can help the client overcome any fear around reporting the incident, and/or requesting a new attorney whose performance is more in line with prevailing standards in legal services.

Divorce Mediation: Nonadversarial, but not for Everyone.

With both private attorneys and legal services, each adult is represented by one attorney, who is concerned with her client's interests, rather than the interests of the family as a whole. An adversarial, spouse versus spouse mentality often prevails. Divorce mediation poses an alternative to the traditional, adversarial approach to divorce. Divorce mediation is a specialized field that blends law and counselling, and is practiced by both lawyers and mental health professionals (Milne, 1992). In contrast to an attorney, one mediator works with a couple or family. The aim is to help a separating couple find agreement about custody, visitation, child support, alimony, and/or property (Kelly, 1993). One advantage of divorce mediation is that the agreements it leads to are less likely to be litigated than agreements developed by two lawyers (Emery, 1988; Grych & Fincham, 1992). Also, mediation contains costs at a time when disposable income is almost always diminished, and promotes a spirit of cooperation (Straus, 1988).

Despite its initial portrayal as a panacea for the divorcing family (Greif, 1992), mediation is only for rational people who are capable of communicating with each other as equals, and there are numerous situations where the traditional, two-lawyer route is preferred. For example, one spouse may be psychotic, violent, a liar, or incapable of responsibly keeping appointments (Kaslow & Schwartz, 1987; Kelly, 1993). Or, one spouse may be markedly depressed and/or dependent to the point of not being able to express or assert herself. Such a spouse—most frequently a woman because of the way women are socialized in this society—needs her own attorney (Grych & Fincham, 1992). Since divorce mediation is not always the better route (Kelly, 1993), therapists need to be equally knowledgeable about lawyers and mediators, and capable of broaching both options. As with most predivorce practical matters, the therapist should be directive about a choice of option or a particular person only when the client is not capable of thinking through the decision herself.

THE FINAL PRESEPARATION ISSUES

Helping Clients Make Up Their Minds

Sometimes, even after emotional, family, practical, and legal issues are aired, hesitation to make a decision remains, and a repetitive or "broken record" quality arises in the sessions. Attention to how clients coped with previous experiences of ambivalence, fear, and guilt may free insightful clients to make a decision. Another possibility is to focus on pervasive lack of confidence in one's own decisions, when this is the suspected cause of the "spinning wheels" (Heitler, 1990).

With more limited clients, though, neither of these approaches may work, and the therapist's patience is taxed. Consciously thinking about any similar excruciating personal choice can help the therapist get in touch with powerful emotions such as fear of change, fear of being alone, and lack of confidence, and will promote empathy. In a session, it is useful to gently point out that the clients are going over and over the same material. Then, they can be encouraged to make up their minds about the marriage before continuing with treatment to help them implement their choice (Rice & Rice, 1986a). If they drop out, they have, nonverbally, made a choice to stay together for the present, and may return for more help when they are ready.

Stalemate situations of domestic violence may call for more intervention than merely saying, in essence, "Make up your mind already." If spousal abuse persists despite months of exploration, education, and presentation of options, the therapist, feeling that there is "nothing to loose," may want to abandon neutrality and tradition, and make a statement about the destructiveness of the status quo and the benefits of separation. Such a statement made to husband and wife together is likely to incite intensified male violence at home; battering men frequently cannot tolerate abandonment by women they need to control, and battered wives are at greatest risk for serious injury or murder by husbands at the point of departure (Lawson, 1992). Thus, if marital rather than individual counselling is ongoing for a couple containing a violent man, the wife should hear this nonneutral statement alone, in an individual session. She is then given something to think about. In case she becomes frightened and leaves treatment, she should be given specific information during this session about local shelters with unpublished addresses, as she may eventually leave her husband while she is not in treatment. If the couple remains together, she may return to treatment later, when ready for change.

In some cases, typically those where treatment has been ongoing for several months or less, the cause of unresolved marital ambivalence is not fear of marital separation, or inability to trust one's own decisions, but rather the client's relentless, obsessional way of forcing decisions prematurely. Here, a useful strategy is diffusion. The therapist can raise the issue of client fixation in a straightforward manner (e.g., "Who says you have to make up your mind this month?" or "You're putting so much pressure on yourself to get this settled! What would it be like to let this ride for a while?"), sometimes complementing this directness by simply pursuing other topics in sessions. As previously noted, clients contemplating marital separation are not necessarily in treatment to address this topic exclusively, and other issues can serve adaptively as avoidance mechanisms when the client simply needs a rest from exploring an extremely anxiety-producing topic.

Therapeutic Involvement with the Actual Move:
Impact of Differing Client Styles.

As far as the actual move, clients vary dramatically. Those who tend to be highly organized as a usual way of coping may carefully plan the move, the new banking account, any school transfer for children, and other practical matters. Such organized people sometimes handle anxiety with compulsive mechanisms, and agonizing departure rituals (e.g., last night together in the same bed) may be carried out. If dependent, these clients may want to discuss preparation and execution of the move extensively with their therapists. For example, one client added a second session to her weekly therapy schedule for 2 weeks before and 2 weeks after her move.

At the opposite extreme, other people may flee their marriages without a prior plan. For example, battered people who finally find courage to leave after provocation by a particularly violent episode sometimes arrive at a friend's or a relative's or a shelter with their children and little or no warning. Before labelling such people as "impulse ridden," therapists must remind themselves that not all people handle decisions via the long discussions that therapists generally describe as "working through." Although some divorcing clients benefit from these discussions, others may legitimately utilize a brief series of sessions as a springboard to action without protracted in-session dialogue. Sometimes these clients have little ambivalence, and need very little input to precipitate a move. Others are not highly verbal or therapy oriented, and find extensive discussion a pressure rather than a release. Others find treatment a burden because they are so busy with the demands of full-time employment and raising young children (Hicks & Anderson, 1989).

Even clients who have been in long-term treatment sometimes take major life steps without discussing them in detail with their therapists. Consequently, the therapist needs to guard against a "possessive parent" countertransference. That is, the overinvolved therapist who has lost objectivity may feel that the client has no right to sever the marital tie without talking it over with the therapist. However, rather than labelling the client as "withholding" or "unable to verbalize," the therapist needs to examine the possibility that she wants the client to be dependent on her—to be her child, or her friend, and meet an unfulfilled need for closeness. If the therapist can control this tendency, the client's own dynamics may become clear. For particularly independent people, once thoughts and feelings are aired, decisions such as whether or not to divorce become self-evident. For other people, major life changes make them feel so vulnerable that they withdraw from everyone, including the therapist. Still others may project one side of remaining ambivalence onto the therapist, and imagine a negative or critical response to departure from the marriage. With sophisticated clients, once the actual separation has occurred, it may be possible to raise the lack of verbalization of specifics in a neutral manner, and help the client see which set of dynamics has been manifest.

Helping Clients Tell Children

Once the decision to divorce is made, the children need to be told. As a first step, the therapist needs to determine if any clinical intervention is necessary at all. Even though they need help in other aspects of the divorce decision, some clients are perfectly capable of explaining to their children in a direct and sensitive manner that a split is imminent. Listening to what parents or children volunteer in session, or what they reveal in response to open-ended questions, may convince the therapist that clinical attention would be "overkill."

However, as previously noted, making the decision to divorce is tremendously draining for adults, and parental self-absorption, with consequent minimization of children's concerns, is likely. This is particularly so among adults who have not initiated the separation, and chronically narcissistic adults who had problems in parenting even while the family was intact. The sheer physical exhaustion of two working parents making arrangements to go their separate ways can also increase a tendency to avoid sitting down and talking to the children, as can the communication patterns in violent homes, where rational discussion of any topic is unusual.

In such cases, the therapist's first task is to help the parents understand what their children need to be told. Children need to know that their parents cannot get along any more, so they are separating. The decision, which was not caused in any way by children, is final. If both parents help tell the children, fantasies that one parent will take back what the other has said are forestalled. If possible, children need to know that both parents still love them, exactly where all concerned will be living, and what the visitation arrangements will be. If the custodial parent and children are moving (perhaps temporarily to the home of grandparents), or a change in employment (most often for the mother) will occur, even more concrete detail must be provided. In general, sensitive parents give the children as much information as they can absorb, to decrease anxiety and demonstrate caring. However, consideration of the young child's attention span and intellectual capacities may constrict the amount of information offered, cause parents to divide the news into manageable installments, or cause them to volunteer some information and wait for offspring questions. With children of preschool age or younger, advance discussion will have little or no effect; the task of telling them, while relevant, may not be as important as the task of dealing with their dismay and confusion when one parent actually leaves.

Sometimes adults can arrive at conclusions about what children need to be told themselves, once the therapist has raised (or re-raised) the theme of "I know you're here to work out your own issues, but what about the children?" If the parents are so self-absorbed that they cannot identify their children's need to know what is happening, they may require direct education around the above issues from the therapist. If they are exceedingly anxious about how children will react to the announcement, it makes sense to help the parents tell the children during a session, although the therapist should refrain from taking over for needy parents, and actually making the declaration herself.

Helping Parents Respond to Child, Adolescent, and Adult Offspring.

The therapist's second task is to help parents grapple with children's reactions after the announcement of impending separation. No matter how well the parents handle the announcement, the news that marital separation is inevitable often creates ongoing ripples of emotional havoc in offspring. Thus, at an already troubled time, parents may be subject to yet one more stress: children's reaction to the "big news."

Even when the marriage is fraught with discord, children do not generally anticipate marital rupture with optimism or relief (Caplan, 1990; Cherlin, 1992). Rather, they tend to verbalize, or act out feelings such as sadness, anger, or responsibility. Specifically, forthright screamed statements such as "I don't *want* to move and leave all my friends," slammed doors, and "forgotten" homework and household chores can abound. So can nightmares, bed wetting, conspicuously noticeable marijuana smoking, dawdling, overeating, and obsessive, time-consuming involvement with sports, computers, or music.

The therapist should help mothers and fathers nurture and guide children through these reactions, just when the mothers and fathers are already feeling overwhelmed by life tasks and depleted of emotional resources. No matter how experienced, every therapist, faced with the frustrating combination of needy children and needy parents who are not optimally responsive, must reinvent the wheel. That is, she must overcome any angry urge to "parent bash," and provide large amounts of support to beleaguered divorcing parents before zeroing in on exactly what the children need. Usually, what helps children is a combination of verbal recognition of feeling, along with limit setting around self-destructive acting out of these feelings. On the other hand, children who need to detach from feelings by throwing themselves into age-appropriate activities, or those who have limited tolerance for discussion of emotion need acceptance rather than a lot of talk about the divorce. Parents who over-discuss or intellectualize children's reactions display an unconscious desire to explain away offspring feelings that need to run their course. In these cases, parental discomfort is the core issue, and the therapist helps work through any parental guilt that engenders flight from children's feelings.

An interesting variation occurs when parents need the defense mechanism of isolation of affect to weather the separation decision. These people describe themselves with phrases like "tough it out," "go numb," or "use cruise control" as they make up their minds to divorce and begin planning for a drastically changed future. The therapist will realize that the parent who must detach from all feeling in order to "take care of business" will of necessity find it impossible to be sensitive to a youngster's feelings. One response is to respect the parent's defense, and see the sibling subgroup or the only child without the parents; such sessions need not extend beyond two or three if emotions are not overwhelming to the child, or acted out in a destructive manner. Another, sometimes complementary approach, is to encourage children's connections to responsive adults in the extended family. If indicated, the therapist can meet with such adults, supporting their contribution while affirming that it does not threaten parental authority.

Older Offspring of Divorce
Sometimes Need Professional Help for Themselves.

When the impending separation involves a midlife or late-life couple, as is often the case today, the offspring affected are older adolescents, young adults, and adults. In the past, their concerns were minimized or ignored in the literature (Cooney, Smyer, Hagestad, & Klock, 1986). Clinicians may have assumed that because they are relatively independent, the trauma is less severe for them. Now, though, we realize that these offspring are likely to experience shock and depression upon hearing about the demise of a parental marriage of long duration (Beal & Hochman, 1991; Bonkowski, 1989: Cain, 1989; Cooney, 1994; Cooney et al., 1986; Holdnack, 1992; Kaufmann, 1988). Therefore, we must explore with parents the separation announcement presented to older or grown children. Although the myriad of concrete detail needed to reassure younger children can be bypassed, older and grown children—like their younger counterparts—need a straightforward statement from their parents, and may feel furious and abandoned if they hear the news from someone else. Among parents divorcing past the age of 60, therapists sometimes must address a poignant twist; intense shame and a desire to protect sons and daughters from pain can cause parental secrecy that prevents geographically distant older and grown offspring from learning of the separation for weeks or even months (Weingarten, 1988).

Although they may eventually (and appropriately) become resources for their parents in a way that younger children cannot, older offspring may initially require clinical attention for themselves. The therapist with a family perspective will readily and routinely get involved with younger children needing treatment in response to the news of separation, but there is no clear-cut, across-the-board protocol regarding the therapist's responsibility for older offspring. Sometimes the therapist will offer conjoint sessions to facilitate parent/child communication, but in more charged situations a referral for individual therapy with a different therapist is preferable.

The reason is that although divorcing parents are clearly responsible for their younger children, the degree of parental responsibility for older, more fully individuated adolescents is ambiguous; for adult offspring, it is greatly diminished. When grown and almost grown offspring experience needy, confused, or angry feelings, they may benefit from discussion with a separate therapist about their response to parental split, and any resultant difficulties in college, career, or relationships. As well as gaining strength to handle their own problems, these late adolescents and young adults also gain understanding of their parents' current limitations, and their troubled parents are spared the unnecessary burden of their children's problems.

Part III

HELPING CLIENTS DURING THE DIVORCE TRANSITION

Chapter 5

Adults, Children, and Adolescents in the Divorce Transition Stage

I feel like I'm losing my mind. I'm in this crummy little apartment, working at a real job for the first time in my life, and I have three children—6, 8, and 9. They hate the new place; it's so much smaller than the house they were used to. They don't like me going to work either. I think my being so far away makes them nervous, especially since their father just took off. They never know when he's going to show up, and since he doesn't always come through with child support, there's never any money left to get them surprises. I try to have fun with them on the weekend, but who has time? After we do the laundry and go to the store, I sit down to watch TV with them—and then fall right to sleep.

> *Barbara—describing the first year of*
> *her life as a separated mother during a*
> *therapy session*

My kids are 11 and 14. I miss them terribly, but what am I supposed to do? I couldn't get along with their mother. I try to make my apartment homey, so the kids aren't like guests when they visit, but it never really works out. No matter how you slice it, it's still an apartment, and they're used to a house, where they can run in and out. I feel like I have to entertain them, because I only see them once a week. I want it all to be happy, the time is so short. So I overlook things, and I guess I do spoil them a bit. Then their mother gets on my case. But she doesn't understand what it's like, to see your own kids by appointment.

Joe, a noncustodial father—initial
psychotherapy session at a family agency

Barbara, a custodial mother, faces a mind-boggling daily overload of vocational, housekeeping, and parental tasks. Joe, a noncustodial father, suffers pangs of longing for his children. Both adults typify the many divorced parents struggling to create a viable lifestyle for themselves and their offspring in the aftermath of marital separation. Part III covers this second period of the divorce process, the transition after the actual physical split. The divorce transition period has been alternately estimated as lasting approximately 2 years (Amato, 1993; Chase-Lansdale & Hetherington, 1990; Krantz, 1988; Olson & Haynes, 1993), 2 to 4 years (Kaslow & Schwartz, 1987), and 3 to 5 years (Brown, 1989). From the practitioner's vantage point, the important thing is that this transition is profound, and spans not months, but years; the exact number of years obviously varies with the individual family.

Here, in chapter 5, we identify some issues adults, children, and adolescents face during the divorce transition, always mindful of individuals' psychological makeup and sociological reality. Then, in chapters 6, 7, and 8, we identify some relevant treatment techniques.

THE DIVORCE TRANSITION: ISSUES OF ADULTS

The Emotional Overlap of Phases of the Divorce Cycle

During the divorce process, unresolved personal struggles may disappear during one phase only to resurface later. Typically, this is because a struggle's reality basis waxes and wanes (e.g., legal battles are fought sporadically), or because an emotion is initially too painful to tolerate. Thus, in the period immediately following marital rupture, emotional residues from the preseparation phase may appear. For instance, in the first months on their own, separated people may continue to experience ambivalence, wondering if they made the right choice by leaving. Some-times ambivalence lasts because of what Robert Weiss (1975) labelled the persistence of attachment in the face of the erosion of love. Other times ambivalence lasts because powerful cultural mandates to stay mar-ried conflict with an individual's chosen course; this tension was acted out by a recently separated Hispanic woman who visited the home of her estranged husband to cook and clean when he was not there (N. G. Preto, personal communication, December 14, 1990)! Some newly separated people remain fearful, worrying, for example, that they will not be able to financially support offspring. Others experience sporadic guilt, feeling pain when considering abandoned spouses.

Emotions Typifying the Divorce Transition

After the actual separation, though, other emotional themes are added to ambivalence, fear, and guilt. Generally, depression, loneliness, anger, and other negative feelings are evoked by the numerous losses and changes inherent in marital separation. Sometimes these feelings appear in a straightforward manner, in verbalization to therapists, close friends, or family. These feelings may also take nonverbal, but relatively direct, forms such as depression manifested in diminished energy level and inability to attend to life tasks, or loneliness manifested in excessive demands on offspring or extended family. At other times, postdivorce unhappiness is masked by frenetic activity, or expressed indirectly in euphoria that is, in reality, a reaction formation against underlying pain.

Clearly, postdivorce emotions are not uniformly bleak. Some people, particularly those who initiate separation, experience relief, or pride in newfound independence. These positive emotions may alternate with the more negative ones, or be experienced along with them. Often, these positive feelings blossom gradually into a sense of mastery experienced most consistently during the final phase of the divorce cycle. Overall, though, the divorce transition is unpleasant, and people who seek profes-sional help, as opposed to those who do not, are particularly likely to be experiencing the negative aspects of the divorce transition.

In the ensuing description of divorce transition adult issues, the pre-sentation differs from the chapter 2 description of predivorce adult is-sues. In chapter 2, emotions themselves held center stage. Here, specific losses and changes in the lives of the newly separated or divorced are discussed, with reflection on the emotions generated by a particular loss or change interwoven. The reason for the shift in focus is that adults in the preseparation phase of the divorce cycle experience far more emotional upheaval than physical upheaval. Before divorce, stress may be acute, but until a physical move occurs, tangible developments are minimal. In contrast, during the divorce transition, real-world developments are rampant, and consequently organize the ensuing discussion.

Losses Experienced During the Divorce Transition

Loss of Status.

For those who have just separated, a fundamental loss is loss of status as a spouse. In this society, a single adult is sometimes viewed as less valuable than married peers. Although the signs of diminished status may be subtle, second-rate restaurant tables for solo diners, ignored comments at PTA meetings or extended family gatherings, wariness on the part of potential employers, and other signals can lead to feelings of vulnerability, isolation, and indignation.

Overall, the loss of married status is more detrimental to women than to men (Kitson, 1992); in contrast to divorced men, divorced women are frequently perceived by others as pitiful, bitter, or rejected (Hicks & Anderson, 1989). For women connected to ethnic groups (e.g., African American) or social movements (e.g., feminism) where ''single woman'' does not mean ''second-rate,'' the broader social trend is counteracted, and the loss of married status may not have strong impact. On the other hand, the loss of married status is particularly hurtful to middle-aged and older women who were raised in an era when marriage was a primary, if not exclusive, source of identity (Cain, 1988). Newly divorced women of any age whose ethnic group places high value on maintaining a marriage (e.g., Orthodox Jewish, Hispanic) may similarly feel that their whole raison d'etre has been destroyed.

Loss of Shared Life.

On a more personal level, the newly separated suffer the loss of a familiar way of life, where routines, responsibilities, pleasures, and even conflicts were shared. Those who did not initiate separation hurt most acutely. ''I can't take this; we did *everything* together. I even miss our fights,'' stated a 25-year-old electrician whose wife had just left him.

Those who initiate marital separation tend to have a more mixed loss experience. On the one hand, there is relief. The abusive, addictive, or simply incompatible spouse is gone. There is freedom to be a parent in one's own way, control household routines, seek new relationships, and generally build a new future, although that freedom may also cause some anxiety. On the other hand, like their rejected counterparts, men and women who initiate marital disruption may also find themselves shell-shocked by the loss of the familiar. Those who separate during midlife or later are particularly hard hit, experiencing the destruction of a way of life that, even if unhappy, may have taken decades to construct (Bogolub, 1991; Chiriboga, 1982).

As compared to women, men tend to be emotionally more dependent on marriage for a sense of belonging (Riessman, 1990; Ross et al., 1990; Williams et al., 1992). In part, this is because they do not have the social supports outside marriage that women generally do (Cohen & Lowenberg, 1994; Diedrick, 1991; Gerstel, Riessman, & Rosenfield, 1985; Hodges, 1991). Men may be particularly devastated by the loss of emotional moorings experienced during the divorce transition, and often experience an acute postdivorce loneliness (Guttmann, 1993; Riessman, 1990). As in the case of Joe, whose statement opened this chapter, this loneliness may be exacerbated by the loss of day-to-day contact with children.

Unlike newly divorced women, who tend to discuss feelings, newly divorced men are more likely to flee from these painful feelings into workaholism, drinking, and somatization (Myers, 1989; Riessman, 1990; Williams et al., 1992). Consequently, divorced men not only have lower overall levels of postdivorce behavioral adjustment than divorced women (Price & McKenry, 1988), but they also experience less conscious distress (Williams et al., 1992), and seek professional help less frequently (Cohen & Lowenberg, 1994; Myers, 1989).

Loss of a Dream.

Along with the loss of day to day life together comes the loss of a dream. The shared marriage was to provide lasting happiness and security, shared parenthood, shared retirement, and a companion and nurse in infirm old age. Among middle-aged and older people, who were raised in an era when divorce was rare and scandalous, this dream allows no substitute vision of fulfillment, so truncation of the marital role often brings a pervasive feeling of despair. This feeling of despair may also beset people of any age who are experiencing a second or third divorce.

Loss of Income.

Another blow whose emotional impact cannot be overstated is income loss. Most divorced mothers, whether assisted by child support or not, have to face this unrelenting, grinding reality just when loss of public married status and private married life render them already vulnerable to depression, loneliness, and anger. No matter what the original income level, the almost inevitable descent of women (whether working or not) and children to a lower rung on the financial ladder means a decreased ability to materially gratify self and children. In extreme cases, divorced women and their children become "nouveau poor" (Furstenberg & Cherlin, 1991; Marshall, 1991), and must apply for public assistance; 45% of females who apply for AFDC do so because of separation or divorce (DeParle, 1994; Kilborn, 1992). Unable to provide material necessities and/or pleasures for self and children, a woman may experience chronic worry and frustration. She may also become further depressed (Simons, Whitbeck, Beaman, & Conger, 1994), blaming herself rather than fathers who do not pay child support, the gender wage gap, or the constraints on her income created by an interrupted or nonexistent work history.

In contrast, some men experience an increase in standard of living after marital separation (Acock & Demo, 1994). Weitzman (1988) found major income increases for men after divorce; Teachman and Paasch (1993) suggest more modest gains. Accounting for these gains is the fact that even when noncustodial fathers (who comprise the vast majority of divorced fathers) pay child support, they spend less money on offspring than when part of an intact family. When child support is paid partially or not at all, the relative ease of these men increases further.

Nonetheless, some men do experience divorce-induced financial problems (Gerstel et al., 1985; Ross et al., 1990), although not to the extent that their ex-wives do. For example, some noncustodial fathers pay support regularly, and voluntarily maintain high-rent apartments large enough to comfortably accommodate children on weekend visits. Others finance sons' and daughters' private college educations, or become stepparents while continuing to support their own offspring.

Men who are custodial fathers often face day-to-day postdivorce financial responsibilities far exceeding those of men who simply pay support (Greif & DeMaris, 1990). Although these men are generally middle class, and much less likely than custodial mothers to be poor (Downey, 1994), they still bear the burden created when the same amount of predivorce parental income is distributed to cover two separate households and/or new expenses such as child care. Custodial fathers, although currently only a 10% minority among custodial parents (Johnson, 1993; Kristall & Greif, 1994), are increasing as a group more rapidly than custodial mothers (Downey, 1994; Guttmann, 1993); they currently number at least one million in absolute figures (Greif & DeMaris, 1990; Kristall & Greif, 1994). To a lesser extent, fathers with joint residential custody, another minority subgroup among divorced fathers, experience similar financial pressures. Awareness that some divorced fathers leave marriage with material loss, increased parental responsibilities, and an accompanying sense of burden and worry can prevent prejudiced, stereo-typed thinking among clinicians who work with this population.

Loss of Residence and Neighborhood.

Although family members sometimes remain temporarily or permanently in the predivorce residence, the family home may be another loss during the divorce transition. Whether the sale is court-ordered, to liquidate a joint investment (Weitzman, 1988), or voluntary, women and men who were homeowners while married give up one more pleasure, as well as visible status, when they move in with relatives, or relocate to a smaller home or apartment. The enjoyment of sufficient living space and the powerful feeling of being in charge, whether of the kitchen and domestic routines (more common among women) or the property (more common among men), is diminished or gone; we recall the bruised feelings of Joe, whom we met at the beginning of this chapter, as he moved from a house to an apartment. More crowded living in a lower status neighbor-hood and/or dependence on relatives or a landlord can be bitter pills to swallow, with increased depression a possibility. For noncustodial fa-thers who care deeply for their children, the transition to living alone may be rendered more stressful by longing for daily contact with chil-dren. In a kind of domino effect, the successive material losses of money, household, and neighborhood may lead to loss of old friends, as geo-graphical distance and status differential take their tolls.

Cumulative Effect of Divorce Transition Losses

Taken together, the multiple losses of married status, shared life, dreams of a stable and happy future, income, home, and neighborhood, can seriously decrease self-esteem. After separation, some people feel not just unrecognized, but unlovable and unworthy. For example, a recently divorced mother of two in a family agency treatment session stated, "Now I'm a total loser; I don't have anything and my kids don't have anything. The poorer we get, the more the neighbors stay away."

Such depressed feelings are perhaps most common among people who lack ego-validating social support after marital separation. These include immigrants whose families are not in this country (Chillman, 1993; Ho, 1987); adults estranged or living far from family; employed, young divorced mothers who have no time to reach out to others in similar situations (Hicks & Anderson, 1989; Kaslow & Schwartz, 1987); and abandoned middle-aged women whose married women friends now shun them as threats (Hicks & Anderson, 1989; Kaslow & Schwartz, 1987). "There but for the grace of God go I" or "There's always the chance she'll take out her anger by becoming a home-wrecker," may be the unarticulated but driving forces in these female rejections.

Acute postseparation depression may also characterize people who have chronic propensities toward depression, or those who never fully individuated as adolescents or young adults, and who then married to establish a sense of personal identity (Ahrons & Rodgers, 1987). Such people are very much "at sea" when newly alone. Consider Marilyn, a 35-year-old female divorced family agency client. A former homemaker who had lived through the accomplishments of husband and children, Marilyn presented her problem as "nervousness about being alone." She hastily remarried, and the day after the wedding, she left her therapist five messages in 3 hours with her new last name. It was as if the new name restored her personhood.

Divorce Transition Changes for Parents with School-Aged Children

The divorce transition is an extremely challenging time. Along with the demand to overcome many types of loss, there exists a simultaneous demand to master numerous divorce-generated life changes. Parents with children in high school or younger include women and men such as Barbara and Joe, whose laments begin this chapter. They are age 20 to 40, approximately, with children generally age 17 or below. During the divorce transition, the adults involved experience major changes in parental, vocational, and extended family realms. Among these adults, mothers form the vast majority of parents with custody, so our discussion begins with mothers.

Custodial Mother: The World's Hardest Job.

On the most basic level, at the time of the divorce transition, these younger mothers experience drastically reduced income and drastically increased child-care responsibilities (Cherlin, 1992; Peck & Manocherian, 1989). The only exceptions would lie among those few women whose ex-husbands provided no help whatsoever with child-care, income, or household maintenance; come divorce, the childrearing lot of these women is no harder (Mauldin, 1991; Morgan, 1991).

Although Barbara's ex-husband visits and gives money sporadically, his contribution is smaller and less steady than while they were married. As is the case for most young divorced mothers, the work of raising the children is basically Barbara's. For such a custodial mother, the list of child-care tasks is endless: giving affection, listening, guiding, sharing leisure time, obtaining medical care, laundry, shopping, chauffeuring, cooking, cleaning, making countless decisions about discipline, and much more. Because of the marital split, offspring may demonstrate a need for extra attention—both through their words and behavior—just when a custodial mother may be too depressed to give it.

However, for some mothers, particularly those with a history of adequate coping, the children provide a reason to keep going. Pride in one's ability to raise offspring under adverse circumstances can become a partial antidote to decreased self-esteem engendered by divorce-related losses. A client of mine stated that because of her 3-year-old son, she would not let herself "give in and fall apart." Mothers who learn to take care of household matters that they previously left to husbands (e.g., checkbook balancing, minor repairs) receive an additional boost to self-esteem.

On the other hand, young women who have chronic problems in organizing and coping, or those whose divorce-generated depression renders them temporarily depleted emotionally, deteriorate in their parental functioning; they are unable to give affection, guidance, or other basics. When a woman is poor as well as emotionally fragile, and lacks money for babysitters, restaurant meals, or new toys, nerves fray even more, and parenting is further depleted. When she experiences anger about her predicament but has difficulty channelling it, children can become a target; in extreme cases, verbal and physical abuse occur.

Employment Outside the Home:
It's Different with Young Children.

Particular stress exists for the younger divorced mother, who, to meet mounting expenses, returns to work outside the home after being a full-time homemaker or who, like Barbara, begins employment for the first time during the divorce transition. Trading poverty of money for poverty of time (Kissman & Allen, 1993), an employed, younger divorced mother adds to her already mammoth responsibilities. Although her family's income increases, she generally faces low wages in sex-segregated fields (e.g., unskilled office work, retail selling, elementary school teaching), or the gender wage gap (women earning 70 cents for every male dollar) in sex-integrated fields (Kissman & Allen, 1993). Typically, she must learn or relearn a job in a work environment with no particular sympathy for children who call Mom at work to make sure she has not taken off like Dad did, for occasional employee lateness stemming from a youngster's emergency, and other exigencies of single parenthood.

The range of response is wide. At one extreme are women who thrive on dual, contrasting responsibilities, each of which would be considered a full-time job by many. These women take pride in all they can accomplish. At the other extreme are overwhelmed women who experience a crushing role overload, and feel that they are doing justice to neither home nor job. In between are those who find the situation manageable or tolerable, and those whose reactions to their combined job and family responsibilities fluctuate.

If children are—approximately—under ten, and there is no family member to provide care, working mothers like Barbara also face the practical challenge of finding good child care. Because of the lack of national child care standards, problems such as untrained and overworked providers are rampant (Frankel, 1991), and maternal guilt may ensue when substandard day-care centers or day-care homes are used of necessity. Although horrors like infant/provider ratios of 8 to 1 (Zigler & Gilman, 1990) and sexually abusive employees occupy one end of the spectrum of possible day-care problems, the more mundane problems at the other end are not to be discounted; a divorced colleague of mine agonized because the day-care center her children attended after school was, in the winter, to use her son's words, "always cold." Quality child care with ample, trained staff and appropriate physical plant does exist, but there is not enough to go around and its cost is beyond the budget of most divorced mothers (Zigler & Gilman, 1990).

Extended Family Can Help.

To an extent, support from family can decrease the divorce-engendered stress of young mothers who work full-time or nearly full-time. Sometimes, extended family provide money and childrearing assistance to divorced mothers while mother and children maintain a separate domicile. Other times, custodial divorced mothers move in with their own parents. In these cases, overcrowding may ensue, and, as previously noted, feelings of loss of one's own "turf" may occur. However, living costs are controlled, and grandparents, particularly if not employed outside the home, become involved in both the concrete and emotional aspects of raising grandchildren (Bogolub, 1989).

Among Black families, the lack of stigma associated with the three-generational household and the flexibility with which people change roles (Del Carmen & Virgo, 1993; Slonim, 1991) can promote a smooth adaptation to the new arrangement, which often involves a divorced or single grandmother. However, employed Black grandmothers in their forties may themselves experience an overload that interferes with the less conflicted involvement characterizing their older counterparts (Timberlake & Chipungu, 1992). To compensate, the geographically accessible extended family members often help (Hatchett & Jackson, 1993). These may include adult siblings of custodial mothers, and parents of noncustodial fathers, even when the noncustodial fathers themselves are uninvolved (Boyd-Franklin, 1989). Although extended family, when available, appear to be generally beneficial to Black divorced women, the drawback is the potential for disagreement about childrearing between a mother and other family members, particularly maternal grandmothers (Boyd-Franklin, 1989).

Female-headed Hispanic families consolidating with grandparents after a divorce have the similar advantages of nonstigmatized, cheaper living arrangements and built-in child care. Particularly relevant to the young divorced Hispanic mother is the loyalty of adult sisters and other female relatives, who may feel obligated to assist her with tasks considered off limits to Hispanic men because of the generally strictly delimited masculine/feminine sex roles (McGoldrick et al., 1991). When available, such assistance eases her burden considerably, as she returns to the labor force. Complications may occur, however, if relatives, because of adherence to traditional roles, are critical of a young divorced mother's employment. Likewise, complications may also occur if relatives, because of their adherence to Catholicism, are critical of divorce (Del Carmen & Virgo, 1993).

When divorce gives rise to extended family households among recently emigrated Soviet Jews, the people involved, like their Black and Hispanic counterparts, are generally accustomed to three-generational households. These are common in the former Soviet Union due to both longstanding cultural norms (Belozersky, 1990), and a major housing shortage (P. Berger, personal communication, January 4, 1991).

However, for other American Jews, three-generational households are unusual, and may prove a mixed blessing for divorced women and their children. In contrast to Black culture (Slonim, 1991), Jewish culture does not particularly emphasize flexibility with regard to role change. In contrast to both Black and Hispanic culture (Fulmer, 1989), Jewish culture does not maintain a value of children as "belonging" to a whole family. Thus, when a divorced Jewish woman goes to work because of financial necessity, and grandparents assume a larger responsibility in child care, the amount of time and energy lost from the maternal role can be upsetting to her (Schlesinger, 1991), as can grandparents' inevitable control over some aspects of grandchildren's day-to-day life. For example, I recall a divorced, employed Jewish mother in treatment at a family agency who was extremely upset because her daughter's grandmother (i.e., the client's mother) had cut the little girl's hair while the mother was at work without checking with the mother first. From a broader perspective, conflict between parents and grandparents in divorced Jewish families over childrearing may be viewed as one example of the greater prevalence of parent–grandparent conflict in nonminority families, as compared with minority families (Del Carmen & Virgo, 1993).

Joint Custody and Paternal Custody.

Although mother-headed homes are most common after divorce occurs, there are other, less common arrangements. With joint residential custody, children alternate between maternal and paternal households. Two reasons for the infrequency of this arrangement are:

1. Joint custody parents are generally a self-selected group characterized by high income, ability to sustain two domiciles of adequate size, and father willingness to pay child support (Arditti, 1992; Pearson & Thoennes, 1990).
2. Not all children respond well to constant moves between two residences (Wallerstein, 1993).

With joint residential custody, young women are spared both time poverty, and isolation from adults who can help them. These women generally feel less overwhelmed than do their sole custody counterparts, particularly the sole custody mothers who lack extended family support. Interestingly, though, joint custody mothers experience only slightly less discord with their former spouses than sole custody mothers do (Maccoby, Depner, & Mnookin, 1990).

Also infrequently, the father is the custodial parent. Most often, this is because of a) the mother's emotional problems, b) the children's desire for paternal custody, or c) the father's superior financial position (Greif & DeMaris, 1990; West & Kissman, 1991). Most custodial fathers of young children adapt well to their role, in part because the financial strain on them is generally not as great as on their female counterparts (Downey, 1994); fathers who have chosen rather than assented to custodial parenting do even better (Greif & DeMaris, 1990). When custodial fathers do encounter problems in raising their children, the source of difficulty is often a) a lack of generally agreed-upon norms for role performance (Germain, 1991; Greif & DeMaris, 1990), or b) gender-based difficulty in deep interpersonal engagement with offspring (Cooney, 1994; Downey, 1994). These obstacles, which also beset fathers with joint residential custody, contrast with the financial strain and role overload that plague young divorced mothers.

Most commonly, though, the father in young divorced families has neither joint nor sole custody. Rather, he is noncustodial, and gradually becomes a shadow figure, first intermittently available for visits and financial support, then generally fading to financial and parental noninvolvement (Hetherington & Clingempeel, 1992; Furstenberg & Cherlin, 1991). Interestingly, although men are generally more involved raising their sons than their daughters (Katzev et al., 1994; Seltzer & Brandreth, 1994), there is no consistent evidence for greater postdivorce paternal involvement with sons (Seltzer & Brandreth, 1994).

Divorce Transition Changes for Families with Late Adolescent, Young Adult, and Adult Children

Like their younger counterparts, recently divorced women and men who are middle-aged (age 40 to 60, approximately) or older (age 60 and over) experience major life changes. These changes occur in the areas of family relationships and employment.

The Changing Relationship of the Generations.

Middle-aged and older divorced women cannot usually depend on parents, who may be ill, aged, or dead (Peck & Manocherian, 1989), so emotional support from grown and almost grown sons and daughters becomes critical. Although exceptions occur among older offspring who are governed by memories of unhappy childhoods, and do not want to help, most older sons and daughters feel protective of their divorced mothers (Bonkowski, 1989; Cain, 1989; Cooney, 1994; Kaufmann, 1988). This is particularly true if their mothers have been rejected for younger women (Bonkowski, 1989; Cain, 1989). Another reason for loyalty to divorced mothers is that divorced mothers, as opposed to divorced fathers, have generally been deeply involved in raising their families (Kaufmann, 1988).

Usually, when older offspring listen, encourage, or assist with concrete tasks, feelings of loss and depression are reduced for their recently divorced mothers. However, psychological factors sometimes interfere with the helping process. For example, a divorced woman whose predivorce self-esteem depended on always being in charge finds it difficult to accept her own divorce-generated needs and her changing, increasingly dependent relationship with her children. She feels diminished rather than enriched when children offer help, and accepts only with difficulty or not at all. Newly divorced women who are excessively concerned with being a burden also turn away childrens' concern. Such disruptions of the helping process are somewhat less likely among Black and Hispanic families, where three- and even four-generation households, and extensive cross-generational give-and-take are common (Del Carmen & Virgo, 1993).

On the other hand, when middle-aged and older divorced women become excessively dependent on offspring, their capacity to function as parents is diluted. Although spared the numerous parental demands facing younger divorced mothers, mothers of older offspring are still responsible for facilitating separation, both physical and psychological. For example, when a mother's income is inadequate, she may depend partially on earnings of a working daughter or son residing at home. This dependence may create guilt in a daughter or son who wants to move out, or to pay college tuition (Bogolub, 1991). Likewise, a lonely divorced woman's frequent and wistful inquiries about a daughter's social plans may send a covert message that a 20 year old's life task is not to grow up, but to take care of her mother. Overall, although grown or almost grown children can often ease life for divorced mothers, and simultaneously get maternal encouragement to move ahead with their own lives, many complications occur.

Compared with their ex-wives, middle-aged and older divorced fathers are more likely to be ignored by their grown children (Cooney, 1994; Cooney et al., 1986), or to be the targets of anger (Kaufmann, 1988). In general, such hostility is directed at fathers who left wives for younger women (Bonkowski, 1989), fathers who were not deeply involved in childrearing (Kaufmann, 1988), and/or fathers who attempt to bribe offspring into desired behavior with money (Kaufmann, 1988). Alternately, the whereabouts of the divorced father are simply unknown. As with younger divorced families, then, there is generally more deterioration in the postdivorce father/child relationship than in the mother/child relationship (Cooney, 1994). As with younger divorced families, this trend should not blind us to the many middle-aged and older divorced fathers who love and help their children.

Universal and Age-Related Employment Issues for Divorced Women.

In some ways, vocational issues for middle-aged divorced adults parallel those of younger divorced adults. In both age brackets, the man is far more likely to have an uninterrupted work history and a higher salary, while the woman, as previously noted, faces low pay in sex-segregated fields and the gender wage gap in sex-integrated fields. In both age brackets, the woman often encounters sex discrimination when she attempts to advance, and Black women, because of their extensive work experience and the Black cultural emphasis on women's employment, may be better prepared for postdivorce economic survival divorce than other women (Fine et al., 1992).

In other ways, employment issues for divorced adults differ according to age bracket. The newly divorced middle-aged woman does not usually face the role overload or child-care dilemmas that exhaust her younger counterpart. However, unless she is among the few who have steady full-time work histories in well-paying fields, the newly divorced middle-aged woman sees a particularly painful contrast in earnings compared to her ex-husband, who is often at his earning peak (Wallerstein, 1986). If the woman was raised to experience identity through her husband's achievements rather than her own, she may bitterly resent the divorce-engendered need to work for a living (Wallerstein, 1986). If she has been a homemaker, or even if she has intermittent or part-time job experience, the newly divorced middle-aged woman may become quite discouraged, as she is generally eligible only for low-paying jobs (Weitzman, 1988), and, in an ageist job market (Rayman, 1987), may face stiff competition from younger women for available positions.

Even the blue-collar middle-aged divorced woman, who has often worked all her life, may never have attained economic self-sufficiency, because her income while married was supplemental to her husband's (Rubin, 1979). Such a woman faces age discrimination as she seeks to maximize income after her divorce, but she is not generally burdened by resentment or embarrassment at having to work full-time.

The Older Divorced Woman, Employment, and Money.

Some recently divorced older women (60 and up) do not have financial problems, but in general the financial situation for this group is bleak. True, women whose socioeconomic status while married was blue-collar or better may have their own pensions, and additionally receive funds from ex-husbands' Social Security pensions if they were married for 10 or more years. But, such fixed income almost always means a reduction in the marital standard of living (Germain, 1991), sometimes to the poverty level. Additionally, these older divorced women may also be cut off from husbands' medical insurance just when they need it most (Germain, 1991).

Of course, not all older divorced women had a socioeconomic status of blue-collar or better while married, and not all have pensions. Likewise, not all ex-husbands have worked long enough for Social Security to generate retirement checks, and many couples do not have health insurance that can be shared upon divorce. In these cases, an older woman's poverty is deepened by divorce, and she must apply for public assistance and Medicaid if she does not already receive these.

What distinguishes the older poor divorced woman from the poor divorced woman who is young or middle-aged is that the older woman is truly trapped in poverty. As a result, depression is extremely common among this group. It is unlikely for employers to hire a woman older than 60, particularly if she has a sparse or nonexistent job history (as is common), except for "unskilled" caretaking positions, such as live-in companion or sorority housemother. These jobs may improve diminished self-esteem, providing company, a place to live, and a sense of purpose to women who may otherwise find good reasons to see life as lonely and futile. However, such jobs do not significantly improve income or insurance coverage, and some older divorcees lack the prerequisite physical and emotional stamina.

Children, grandchildren, and other relatives can make a difference in the finances of the older divorced woman, by offering either money or a place to live. The former would be more likely in Jewish families, who tend to be middle- and upper-middle class (DeFrain et al., 1991; Soifer, 1991), and the latter in Hispanic and Black families, where three-generational living is common (Chillman, 1993; Fulmer, 1989; Minkler, Roe, & Robertson-Beckley, 1994).

THE DIVORCE TRANSITION: ISSUES OF CHILDREN AND ADOLESCENTS

Three Major Losses for Children and Adolescents

What do the family shifts described above mean for youngsters experiencing the divorce transition? Like parents, a child caught up in a new divorce is bombarded with unsettling losses.

Loss of the Noncustodial Parent.

Perhaps the major loss for children is the daily presence of the noncustodial parent, usually the father. Among children of preschool age or younger, the response to this loss is generally confusion. Because of limited cognitive capacity, a 2- or 3-year-old simply cannot understand that Daddy does not live here anymore, or why he is gone; the child is likely to be utterly bewildered (Kalter, 1990). Among older children, no matter how carefully parents prepare them, hurt and anger about the father's departure are almost universal (Gardner, 1990; Kalter, 1990). Even an older adolescent attending college or living independently can be devastated when visiting a mother in a house or apartment where both parents formerly resided. For children of all ages, if the relationship with the father was warm and loving, the loss is particularly painful, though it may be counteracted, to an extent, by regular support payments, visits, and phone contact (Kalter, 1990).

If the relationship was more distant or troubled, the decline in contact with the father is still upsetting for offspring. Surely, exceptions occur in instances of severe paternal brutality, when a father's departure evokes relief. But in general, daughters and sons need routine and stability. The loss of contact with a parent clearly thwarts this. Also, children and adolescents are forming their identities, in part through interaction with significant adults, so they are dependent on fathers for contact and nurturance, albeit sometimes less than optimal. When contact with the father becomes diluted during the divorce transition, the void is keenly felt. In other words, poor fathering while married generally does *not* lead to offspring indifference following a divorce.

After departing, the father sometimes reveals himself as inconsistent in his phone and in-person contacts. I recall, for example, the dejection of a 10-year-old Hispanic boy whose father usually visited in accordance with the visitation agreement, but failed to arrive for a scheduled outing on the first Christmas after separation. In these situations, the child is placed on an emotional yo-yo. A youngster may be very angry one day and may miss his father terribly on the next. Also common is a yearning for parental reconciliation.

Mother-only homes and divorce are very common among Black Americans, but it would be a serious clinical error to hypothesize that a Black child or adolescent whose parents have recently separated is less likely than a White counterpart to miss a father (P. M. Hines, personal communication, November 19, 1990). The tendency of Black youth to be somewhat circumspect in their verbal expressions of feeling should not distract therapists from the pain that may exist below a "cool" facade (A. J. Franklin, 1992; Gibbs, 1989).

Loss of the Custodial Parent Through Decreased Quantity and Quality of Involvement.

If a mother begins work or returns to work after a stint as a married homemaker, the daily presence of the residential parent as well as the nonresidential parent is diminished. This may leave offspring very uneasy; they fear they will lose their mother, just as they lost their father. Younger children governed by egocentric thinking may feel that their behavior is causing the mother to distance herself. Consequently, they may present a "too-good" facade, to retain her.

More important, if a woman does not thrive on multiple roles, or if she is unsupported by extended family, she may be so overwhelmed, physically and emotionally, that the quality (not just the time amount) of her relationship with her children is diminished. Barbara, quoted earlier, is a full-time working mother who falls asleep during the few hours a week theoretically reserved for family fun. Even if a newly divorced mother is a homemaker (either because she receives AFDC, cannot obtain a job, or—almost never—because she can afford it), her children often find her preoccupied with her own problems (Kalter, 1990; Soldano, 1990), and excessively permissive (Acock & Demo, 1994; Demo, 1992; Thomson, McLanahan, & Curtin, 1992).

Children and adolescents may also find that their mother wants them to reverse roles by becoming her supporters. As previously noted, help from offspring to parents is appropriate for older children of divorce, and a circumscribed amount of extra responsibility for younger children in single-parent families may actually benefit their self-esteem (Kissman & Allen, 1993). But, a pervasive sense that "mom is out of it, so we have to take over," can be extremely anxiety producing.

Also anxiety producing is a custodial mother's reliance on offspring as an antidote to loneliness. On occasion, an unwanted, excessive attentiveness to the concerns of sons and daughters barely conceals the parental need to live through children, and to skip the hard work of filling adult voids in an adult life. Until they are fully grown, sons and daughters need to feel that parents are interested when offspring need them, not when parents are lonely.

Loss of the Predivorce Standard of Living.

The third major loss children incur is the predivorce standard of living. Newly middle-class or newly working-class children are suddenly without vacations, movies, sleepaway camp, and new school clothes. Newly poor or newly poorer children must go without birthday presents, McDonald's, and the sneakers that other kids have. When poor custodial mothers await late child support or AFDC checks, they delay trips to the doctor or laundromat, and forego needed toilet items for self and children. For children who do not have the resignation and apathy born of years of poverty, the cumulative effect is one of constant frustration

(Simons et al., 1994). Feelings of anger and deprivation are prominent, and frequently compounded by reactions to the diminution of paternal and maternal functioning described above.

More subtly, financial loss can produce the constant gnawing feeling of having a worried parent who is always thinking about money even though she tries not to talk about it. When their capacity for empathy develops, somewhere between the ages of 9 and 12 (Kalter, 1990), awareness of a mother's struggles may induce guilt over anger at deprivation.

As cognitive capacity matures, children may feel betrayed by fathers who do not pay child support. Even if mothers do not overtly criticize nonpaying fathers, children sense the numerous gaps in day-to-day life nonpayment brings. Although a father may dispense toys and charm during visits to cover over his omission, children are not easily fooled. In a family seen at a social agency, a 12-year-old boy who had frequent stomachaches in the year following his parents' separation finally shouted in session, "My father *makes me sick*. He says he loves me but he's a liar. If he really loved me, he'd give money to Mom to buy me new clothes."

If there is a household move, children lose friends and switch schools. Even under the best of circumstances, a household move requires energy for mastery; when other divorce-engendered losses absorb so much of a youngster's energy, starting in a new school, and making new friends become even harder. Children may also have to get used to a new neighborhood (Hodges, 1991) (perhaps less affluent and more dangerous than the previous one), a new place to live (perhaps more crowded and plainer than the previous one), and the residential presence of any extended family who now share quarters.

The comments of a 9-year-old boy seen in agency practice in New York City describe typical feelings. He and his recently divorced mother had just moved out of a suburban home, and into his maternal grandmother's apartment. "There's no place to put my stuff, and no place to ride my bike. My old friends aren't allowed to visit me here. The new kids think I'm a spoiled brat because I'm from the suburbs. I *hate* it here," the youngster screamed. He was inconsolable.

Offspring Reactions to Divorce Transition Losses

In short, the losses of the divorce transition are usually highly anxiety provoking, and represent a diminution of the security, stability, and routine that all children need. Generally, children of preschool age and younger react to the losses of the divorce transition with a general sense of confusion and bewilderment, while older youngsters demonstrate a progressively wider, more differentiated range of feeling. Thus, older children and adolescents, at different times, experience anger, sadness, anxiety, fear of further abandonment, and yearning for the parents' reconciliation.

Depending on the child's age, reactions to the divorce transition are expressed differently. Very young children tend to regress, losing recent developmental accomplishments such as toilet training, speech, or ability to drink from a cup rather than a bottle (Bray & Berger, 1993; Kalter, 1990; Soldano, 1990). Children who are school age or older are not only better able to express their reactions to divorce in words, they are also better able to distance themselves emotionally from their upset (Bray & Berger, 1993). For example, they may visit frequently with friends whose parents provide nurturance and interest. Hispanic children may develop stronger connections with *compadrazgo*, or nonblood kin created during life-cycle events such as baptism or marriage (Chillman, 1993; Germain, 1991). Alternately, children may utilize defense mechanisms such as avoidance and sublimation, and escape from the concerns of the divorce transition into activities. Although driven, compulsive behavior should not govern a child, and must sometimes be examined in sessions, avoidance and sublimation are frequently adaptive.

Thus, therapists must be sensitive to the sometimes hostile environments of low-income children, where opportunities for avoidance and sublimation are few or nonexistent. For example, sometimes the neighborhood school is a place of fear, where interest groups and academic challenges are nonexistent, and serious study is ridiculed by other students (Gibbs, 1989). For poor Spanish-speaking children, even if they are bilingual, feelings of alienation in school are intensified by the absence of the mother tongue in daily proceedings (Carrasquillo, 1991).

When older children and adolescents lack opportunities to distance themselves from their parents' divorces, or to express their feelings about the divorce in a healthy manner, they may act out their reactions self-destructively (Bray & Berger, 1993). These actions run the gamut from blatant, dangerous, attention-seeking behavior (e.g., shoplifting, substance abuse) to more subtle phenomena, such as constriction of creativity, somatization, or slight decrease in academic performance. Overall, therapists need to keep in mind that for children and adolescents, acting out reactions to the divorce transition (as to most situations) are far more usual than straightforward verbal expression.

Forces Modulating the Divorce Transition
for Children and Adolescents

In chapter 2, temperament, siblings, and extended family were identified as forces that might heighten or diffuse the impact of marital discord on sons and daughters. These forces are similarly influential during the divorce transition. The only difference, one of degree, occurs when custodial parents become increasingly dependent on extended family during the divorce transition. This is quite common, as noted. In these cases, the impact of extended family on sons and daughters is intensified, either as a support, a source of conflict, or both.

Community involvement modulates divorce impact, too. The church in the African American community has a long history of maintaining hope in times of adversity, providing substitute family, and supporting prosocial behavior (Germain, 1991; Ho, 1992; McGoldrick et al., 1991). African American children and adolescents whose support network has been disrupted may benefit from church-sponsored activities, both formal (e.g., recreational opportunities) and informal (e.g., contact with concerned adults; Boyd-Franklin, 1989). For Hispanics, the church is less of a resource; even though most Hispanics are Catholic, many are distrustful of the church and organized religion (McGoldrick et al., 1991). However, Hispanic children and adolescents, particularly those of Puerto Rican origin, may benefit from peer group involvement stemming from ethnically based neighborhood social clubs (Germain, 1991).

Likewise, synagogues are not always a major resource for Jewish children and adolescents during the divorce transition. Compared to intact Jewish families, single-parent Jewish families are much less likely to be synagogue members. Although some synagogues do have reduced membership rates for needy families, single-parent families' failure to obtain or maintain synagogue membership frequently stems from the cost (Keysar, 1994). Additionally, a bias favoring two-parent families prevalent among some Jewish leaders (e.g., Bayme, 1990; Bayme, 1994; Reisman, 1994) may discourage single-parent Jewish families from synagogue affiliations that could identify them as "second class." On the other hand, as a group, Jews readily avail themselves of mental health services (Hines et al., 1992); parents and youth benefit from Jewish social service agencies which frequently offer divorce-specific counselling (e.g., Hulewat & Levine, 1994; Shapira & Tiell, 1994).

Chapter 6

The Mental Health Professional's Role: Individual Adult Divorce Transition Concerns

FOCUSSED TREATMENT GUIDED BY MULTIPLE GOALS

The divorce transition presents a challenge to the therapist that is very different from the challenge of the preseparation phase. During the preseparation phase, clients may be unready to fully face their marital dilemmas, and therapists must respect client need to intersperse marital issues with other issues as clients' approach-avoidance conflicts are manifested. If preseparation counselling addresses a treatment topic (marital dissatisfaction) that needs to be handled as a "big fish," divorce transition counselling addresses a treatment topic (coping with multiple, fundamental losses and changes) that needs to be handled as an emotional Hiroshima. Of course, avoidance and denial may still operate, and the pace of treatment will be affected by the client's characteristic ways of handling stress. But generally, treatment during this phase of the divorce

109

process is more focussed and concentrated than during the preseparation phase, as major emotional and tangible challenges that cannot be stopped have been set in motion.

While the goal of treatment during the preseparation phase can be conceptualized in a unitary manner (i.e., precipitate a decision about the marriage), treatment during the divorce transition must be conceptualized as having four goals. Based on a broad range of empirical research about what improves life for adults, children, and adolescents after divorce (Furstenberg & Cherlin, 1991), these treatment goals are:

1. Improve the emotional status of individuals within the family, in part by helping them understand, control, and resolve their feelings about the divorce.
2. Improve financial and social support for the custodial parent, usually the mother.
3. Improve the relationship between offspring and the custodial parent.
4. Decrease conflict and increase cooperation between parents, when it is possible to involve them both.

Not every goal figures prominently in the work with each client, and their importance relative to each other will vary from case to case. And, sometimes the goals must be modified. For example, a father disappears after divorce, the mother becomes so dependent on alcohol that she is unfit to raise her children, and the therapist helps a child develop strong ties with a foster parent or grandmother rather than a parent. Likewise, sometimes only limited achievement of goals is possible. For example, total decrease in conflict between divorced parents who could not get along while married is usually not possible. But overall, therapists can use these four goals to guide the choice of treatment foci and techniques during a phase of the divorce cycle when so much is happening that it is sometimes difficult to know where to start.

This chapter, and the two that follow describe some techniques therapists use as they pursue these goals, while assisting individuals and families as they pass through the divorce transition. Although the concerns of individuals and families overlap, this chapter emphasizes treatment of individual adults, addressing their psychological, vocational, and social struggles. Chapter 7 emphasizes treatment of individual adults, addressing their functioning in the role of custodial parent. To a lesser extent, chapter 7 emphasizes treatment of individual children and adolescents. Chapter 8 emphasizes treatment of the newly divorced family in a broad social context.

The proviso given in chapter 3, which covered techniques for dealing with predivorce emotional issues, remains in effect here: The separation of treatment techniques in the ensuing chapters is for discussion purposes only. In actual practice, the therapist combines or shuttles flexibly between them according to the needs of the clients in a given session.

DIVORCE TRANSITION TECHNIQUES
FOR INDIVIDUAL ADULTS

Facilitating Mourning

Because of the many behavioral challenges that arise during the divorce transition (e.g, job hunting, increased parenting responsibility, household move), therapists may rely particularly heavily on task-oriented and cognitive-behavioral clinical skills to help clients during this period. However, the first goal for the divorce transition (improvement of emotional status) suggests that a period of mourning-related individual treatment is sometimes a necessary preliminary or accompaniment to a challenge to move ahead. Without the opportunity to express feelings about the many losses experienced during the divorce transition, client movement to improved levels of coping may be impeded by disguised expressions of hurt, anger, and disappointment (Sprenkle, 1989).

Helping Adults Mourn is Usually, but not Always, a Good Idea.

Why is attention to mourning the losses adults experience during divorce only sometimes a good idea? First, ethnicity may discourage expression of divorce transition pain. As previously noted, Black and Hispanic women may place far greater importance on their children's lives than their own (Hines, 1990; Neff & Schluter, 1993), and may feel reluctant to talk about themselves. Also, African American women tend to be stoic about pain (McGoldrick et al., 1991), and sometimes underrate the complexity of their own lives (P. M. Hines, personal communication, November 19, 1990). For Black and Hispanic women, then, the urging of a therapist to focus on adult loss may stimulate discomfort rather than release. This is particularly true if the client has not been involved with the therapist during the preseparation phase, and is now involved in a relatively new treatment relationship. Second, adults of any ethnicity may mask pain with euphoria. As a defense (viz., reaction formation) that allows people to "do what they have to do," euphoria should be left intact during the first part of the divorce transition, if preliminary exploration reveals it is entrenched; it should be more actively challenged only in later phases of the divorce cycle, when it has persisted for an unduly long period.

Helping Adults Mourn the Universal and the Particular, the Present and the Past.

But for many divorcing adults, the opportunity to describe the loss of a marriage to someone who is not afraid to really listen is of immeasurable importance. In most cases, the pain, anxiety, anger, and loneliness at the beginning of the divorce transition are profound and omnipresent, and therapists can help clients express, control, and, ultimately, slowly let go of these emotions. In session, clients typically alternate between catharsis and discussion of "getting on with life." Over time, they often feel a shift from "just existing" to "living again."

As well as addressing grief universals, therapists must also address individual grief variations. For example, although noncustodial fathers are frequently perceived as the villains in divorce, these men often need desperately to share with another person their longing for daily contact with their children, and their feelings of being "out in the cold" after exiting the family home (Mitchell-Flynn & Hutchinson, 1993; Umberson & Williams, 1993). Likewise, other divorced clients must learn not to act out in an impulsive, haphazard fashion that works against them (e.g., angry outbursts at work), and to realize that they cannot realistically ask others to give them special consideration for divorce-engendered pain.

As well as balancing the universal and the particular in treatment, therapists may, with more sophisticated individuals, help their clients understand how the divorce is magnified or otherwise reshaped by prior experiences. For example, Mary's sudden childhood loss of her father causes her adult abandonment by her husband to be experienced not just as pain and shock, but as a sign that all relationships with men end precipitously; her mother's remarriage subsequent to Mary's father's death injects an element of optimism into Mary's psyche which can be explored in treatment after her initial grief outpourings have run their course.

Emotional Recovery is a Matter of Degree.

During the approximately 2 years or more of the divorce transition, many younger clients (both initiators and assenters) involved in such mourning processes gradually gain or regain autonomy, self-esteem, hope, and coping skills to build their futures. These clients are aided not just by their therapists, but by the social and vocational opportunities bestowed upon them by a youth-oriented society. In fact, such progress is common among divorce initiators in all age brackets. As mourning proceeds, some of these clients may even benefit from the therapist's suggestion that they "reframe" (Kissman & Allen, 1993) the divorce experience as an opportunity to develop emotional strength.

In contrast, many middle-aged and older divorced women whose husbands have departed for new partners achieve emotional recovery only partially, and after many years—or not at all (Farnsworth, Pett, & Lund, 1989; Kitson, 1992; Wallerstein, 1986). In most cases, what sets these women apart is their near-permanent sadness and anger, as well as their experience of ageism; the social and vocational prejudices they face will only grow worse with the passage of time. With such clients, therapists need to give up standard notions of mourning as a process that ends (Leon, 1992). The goal with regard to emotional status is more limited than for other divorced adults: Help clients live with, or encapsulate, their emotions. Although client feelings of self-esteem, hope, and satisfaction with postdivorce life may be minimal and precarious, at least bitterness and self-destructive acting-out can be avoided.

The Relevance of Individual and Group Treatment.

In general, adult mourning is best addressed in individual sessions, or in treatment groups (Byrne, 1990; Grych & Fincham, 1992; Sprenkle, 1989). Individual treatment nurtures adults whose divorce transition experience is so shattering that they are literally incapable of paying attention to the troubles of others, including fellow group members. Group treatment is better suited to those whose ability to relate is more intact. Like individual treatment, group treatment promotes expression and handling of emotion (Byrne, 1990). It also counteracts loneliness (Sprenkle, 1989), normalizes emotion, and provides models of coping behavior (Kissman & Allen, 1993).

Therapists Must Beware of Countertransference during Adult Mourning.

When working with the grieving, newly divorced client a common countertransferential problem is to be "too soft." Clearly, therapists grappling with the problems of newly single clients should accept an extra measure of client dependence, even digging for it when it appears buried. On the other hand, the pain and anxiety of the newly divorced adult sometimes evoke pity in the therapist, or guilt over what one has if the therapist is happily married (Wallerstein, 1990). If the therapist is not aware of these depotentiating emotions, she may mistakenly act as a friend to her client

(Brown, 1989). If the therapist is White, and the client is not, this tendency to be overly solicitous may increase (Berg & Miller, 1992; Boyd-Franklin, 1989; Devore & London, 1993); respect for the client's experiences of racist oppression may prevent the therapist from pointing out behavior such as self-destructive wallowing or inappropriate reliance on children.

A particular variation of intervention that is too soft arises when working with the severely disturbed. Unless the therapist is very careful, intensely angry clients who unconsciously and primitively seek restitution from their therapists for the pain of divorce sometimes elicit the therapist's unconscious tendency to mollify them (Wallerstein, 1990).

For example, Cara, a 28-year-old White divorced mother sought help at a family agency because her 5-year-old son Eric ''has been wild since his father Steve took off five months ago.'' Of blue-collar status while married, Cara and Eric had recently begun receiving public assistance.

In treatment, Cara mourned the loss of her marriage, and developed parenting skills which had been depleted by her experience of marital disruption. To ease her burden and enrich Eric's experience, the agency provided Eric with a male college student volunteer, John, age 21, as a ''big brother.'' John appeared regularly at the family apartment, politely said hello to Cara, and took Eric on outings. Three weeks after these visits began, Cara lashed out during her session, ''How do you think I feel when that nice guy shows up to take *Eric* out? How about a new boyfriend for me?'' As she spoke, neither humor, nor perspective on the unrealistic nature of her remarks was evident. She clearly wanted her therapist to give her a new relationship, and compensate her for the loss of divorce.

The therapist, with the help of her supervisor, was able to do more than offer sympathy. She helped Cara see that ''I have a chip on my shoulder,'' and that ''I think everyone should be supernice to me just because Steve took off.'' The therapist respected the raw feelings of the divorce transition, realizing that mourning cannot be quickly explained away, but she also helped Cara to modify the alienating way she presented herself.

Addressing Employment Concerns

Compared with the preseparation period, the divorce transition more often requires a clear focus on the issue of employment. As noted, prior to divorce, a woman under the same roof as her husband may not want to reveal her interest in a job search or job training. Or, consumed by indecision about her marriage, she may have no energy to even consider employment outside the home. But once she is separated, secrecy and indecision about marital separation do not remain barriers to earning a living.

In addition, of course, financial urgency increases. Earlier, this chapter established that a goal for treatment during the divorce transition is to improve the financial position of the custodial parent, usually the mother. As we have seen, child support payments, when available, provide a custodial mother with "gravy"; her most important source of income improvement is generally her own employment. Clearly, therapists should be sensitive to clients' working conditions and satisfactions. However, if they approach women's postdivorce employment from the vantage point of income as well as fulfillment, they are generally best able to connect with clients seeking help during the divorce transition, particularly those choosing social agencies because they are unable to afford private practitioners. For both younger and middle-aged women clients, relevant session topics include realistic goals for responsibilities and salary, exploratory job search phone calls, and job interviews. For dependent clients with little employment experience, actual in-session role-play of calls and interviews may be helpful. When clients efforts are not fruitful, and no self-defeating behaviors can be discovered, it may be necessary to remind clients of sometimes discouraging job-market realities, in order to forestall depression.

Also of interest to both younger and middle-aged women facing the job market are issue-oriented groups where a leader and guest speakers present on employment opportunities, vocational training, and job-hunting skills (Bogolub, 1991; Kissman & Allen, 1993). In addition to education, these groups provide mutual support. Such support is particularly relevant to middle-aged women who approach the job market with trepidation, sometimes because they came of age before the birth of feminism and were raised to live through husbands; through the group experience, these women may be galvanized by younger women's ideas about an independent, proactive view of life (Bogolub, 1991).

Younger Women: Clinical Skills for Age-Specific Vocational Issues.

During the divorce transition, a young working custodial mother must do more than find and keep a job, sometimes her first. As noted in chapter 5, unless she thrives on multiple responsibilities, she may also need to learn to juggle raising a family and working full-time. In this vein, a common clinical theme is the need for an overwhelmed young divorced mother to decrease standards for herself. For example, in session, young divorced women sometimes decide that at this point in their lives, their children require so much energy that geographical closeness is more important than job stimulation, although they recognize that the balance may shift later, as child-care demands wane (Shapira & Tiell, 1994). In such situations, feminist therapists for whom career is very important must be careful not to impose their values on clients.

Young divorced working mothers must also face the guilt about the effect of maternal employment and/or substitute child care on young children, as indicated in chapter 5. Linda, a client I saw in a family agency, was a secretary with two "latchkey" children aged 8 and 10. In session, Linda reproached herself: "They always find some excuse to call me up at work as soon as they come home from school. I think they're afraid I'll take off the way their father did. I worry that my boss won't like the calls, but I just can't tell the kids to stop. I suppose I should feel good about the money I'm earning to keep us going, but mostly I'm worried that I'm making my children into nervous wrecks. Are they afraid they'll become orphans?''

In addition to expressing themselves, women like Linda also sometimes need help in gaining perspective on the brief duration of the period during which the custodial mother's new employment situation affects children most painfully and intensely. They also may need help in reassuring their children of continued interest and affection. Finally, just as presentation of facts about the job market may lift spirits of an unsuccessful job hunter, facts about the lack of consistent evidence for any negative impact of maternal employment on child well-being (Greenstein, 1993; Silverstein, 1991) may ease the emotional burden of Linda and others like her.

Likewise, young divorced mothers with children who attend after-school or all-day day-care centers may benefit from learning about the lack of consistent evidence for any negative impact of substitute child care on child well-being (Greenstein, 1993; Silverstein, 1991). At the same time, these mothers (generally low- and middle-income) may benefit from encouragement for their efforts to obtain the best available care for their children, and their efforts to advocate for improvements in care facilities.

Middle-Aged Women: Clinical Skills for Age-Specific Vocational Issues.

Among middle-aged divorced women, former full-time homemakers and women who have worked part time or intermittently may need assistance in seeing how emotions such as resentment of having to work for a living (Wallerstein, 1986) or a fear of competition with younger women (albeit realistic), could inadvertently affect behavior in a job interview, and sabotage a job search. Sometimes, they also must learn to accept unskilled work temporarily, simply to survive. In this circumstance, the humiliation of the middle-aged homemaker-turned-salesclerk is generally far greater than that of a younger counterpart. The middle-aged woman who feels degradation needs empathy with her humiliation, and a good deal of encouragement 'from the therapist.

On the other hand, therapists should not relate to middle-aged divorced women seeking to improve their vocational situation as unfortunate victims. For example, therapists can present the possibility of training for positions (e.g., paralegal, computer programmer) that require vocational education but not extensive college background. Initially, these women may need assistance in overcoming intimidation about training, due to prolonged absence from educational settings. If they master their fears, they can be encouraged to pursue training while maintaining themselves through the nonpreferred positions initially obtained. At this time, therapists can highlight the middle-aged women's job-search advantages: personal maturity, and lack of intensive childcare responsibilities.

Middle-aged divorced women can also be encouraged to obtain or utilize rehabilitative alimony (Fine & Fine, 1994; Zastrow & Kirst-Ashman, 1990) as they pursue job training, and will sometimes benefit from discussing what it means to fight for what is due them. Finally, therapists can encourage the middle-aged divorced women with a bent toward political activism to take note of any ageist discrimination she experiences in her job search, training, and employment experiences, and to work through organizations and politics to counteract it.

Addressing Employment Issues Among Women of Varied Ethnicity.

With Hispanic clients, therapists sometimes have to reckon with particular employment complications. First, because of the traditional homemaking role expectations and lack of enthusiasm for women's economic self-sufficiency in Hispanic culture, it is rare for Hispanic women to approach a job search without emotional conflict (Del Carmen & Virgo, 1993). Non-Hispanic therapists need to be both direct and respectful here; a simple question like "Can you tell me what going to work means for you as a Hispanic woman?" goes a long way. Clients can also be asked to reflect on their mothers, grandmothers, sisters, and aunts; some may live nontraditional lives. Then, without directly or subtly criticizing cultural mandates, therapists can help clients decide how they, as individuals, feel about the mandates of their ethnicity. In some cases, zest for a job search develops.

Second, because of the stigma associated with divorce in a largely Catholic culture, the Hispanic client may be rejected by family during the divorce transition (Del Carmen & Virgo, 1993). When this happens, the therapist must sometimes help the client obtain the child-care assistance that nonrejecting Hispanic families readily offer (Chira, 1994); this practice would be in line with the treatment goal of improving social as well as financial support for the custodial parent. Later, family sessions on the topics of forgiveness and help for the working divorced mother may take place.

Finally, therapists sometimes need to help non-English speaking Hispanic women decide if they want to learn English, thereby broadening their job options. If clients are interested, therapists must help them decide if it is realistic to learn English during the divorce transition, when so many other challenges arise, or if it is better to defer this endeavor until a less stressful period.

It has been noted (e.g., Fine et al., 1992; Del Carmen & Virgo, 1993; Ho, 1987), that as compared with Hispanic and Jewish women, Black women are better prepared for employment demands post-divorce, even though they must face racial discrimination. Preceding divorce, Black women were usually involved in marriages in which their employment counted heavily, and they have, in general, had a long history of employment outside the home. For therapists, it is important not to impose an unwanted spotlight on the employment area with Black divorced women if no conflict is hinted at or manifest. This is particularly so as Black clients tend to be quite sensitive to communications that might be perceived as condescending (Boyd-Franklin, 1989).

With regard to employment, Jewish women benefit from a variety of treatment skills during the divorce transition. For Soviet emigrant Jewish women, the cultural mandate for employment is similar to that experienced by Black women. Although conflicts around employment per se are unlikely, the therapist must sometimes help these women adjust to the relatively low status of jobs they can initially obtain in the United States. Education and experience that made Soviet women (as well as their male counterparts) well respected before emigration generally do not provide a competitive edge in the new country (Handelman & Miller, 1990). Once survival needs are met, such women can pursue retraining if so inclined (Handelman & Miller, 1990). Additionally, Soviet women may need English classes, as well as facts and tips about practical matters (e.g., want ads, employment agencies, phone calls) that are second nature to those who have lived here since birth.

The Orthodox Jewish woman is similar to the Hispanic woman in that she may need considerable attention to psychological conflicts around the relative importance of employment and motherhood, before she is ready to seek employment. Sometimes, the therapist's reference to the long tradition of Jewish women in the business world (Hines et al., 1992) helps. Since business employment was perhaps more common among the grandmothers of today's Jewish clients than among their mothers (Hines et al., 1992), the therapist evokes memories and role models that may be literally buried by the numerous emotional and physical demands of the divorce transition.

For mainstream Jewish as well as Orthodox Jewish women, therapists sometimes need to help clients work through embarrassment attached to the divorce-engendered necessity of working for a living (Schlesinger, 1991). This embarrassment is sometimes manifested in the masking of financial problems with new clothing and other material trappings, in session and elsewhere. Such secrecy, when combined with a therapist's unthinking tendency to assume Jewish wealth and ignore Jewish poverty (Kaye/Kantrowitz, 1991), can generate a collusion to avoid a central fact of the client's life. When a recently divorced Jewish woman seeks treatment, clinicians need to probe directly but gently about money if the client does not raise the issue herself. Although the role models of the past may provide the client with some inspiration, attention to feelings of shame, caused by current comparisons to other women who have not experienced divorce, may also be warranted.

Helping Men with Employment Concerns.

What of men and employment during the divorce transition? Relative to their female counterparts, most men are in an easier position postdivorce. True, if they are responsible about paying child support, and voluntarily take on expenses such as high-rent apartments or college tuition, some fathers experience increased financial demand postdivorce. As previously noted, these fathers face a financially constricted lifestyle as a result. Stress increases when such men remarry, and is only rarely balanced by "moonlighting" income, because visitation takes the time that might be filled by a second job. However, in contrast to women, men are far more likely to have income improvement postdivorce, and continuous employment histories. They are also far less likely to have young children living with them. Some time poverty and child-care dilemmas do occur among custodial fathers and those with joint physical custody, but they are buffered by these fathers' mainly middle- and upper middle-class status, by their exercise of choice in the custody arrangement, and by the likelihood of their holding jobs with flexible schedules (Downey, 1994; Greif & DeMaris, 1990).

Although employment is thus much less likely to be a theme for male clients during the divorce transition, certain therapeutic skills are relevant. For instance, like their female counterparts, some responsible noncustodial fathers, as well as fathers with sole custody or joint physical custody, may need help in facing the anger and frustration stemming from a financially constricted lifestyle following divorce (Ross et al., 1990). They may also need help with developing acceptance of their changed reality, and with specific money management skills. Responsible fathers may also need help in negotiating in a workplace that does not have much sympathy for a father (custodial or not) who takes time off from work for a child's orthodontist's appointment, or a school play (Chira, 1993). Another workplace issue pertains to the garnishing of paychecks for child support payments. Noncustodial fathers who react angrily to what they see as an invasion of privacy may need assistance in negotiating confidentiality (e.g., limitations on number of people aware) regarding these deductions.

Assisting Clients with Concerns about Dating and Social Life

Two broad goals of treatment during the divorce transition are improvement of the emotional status of adults, and increase in social support for the custodial parent (usually the mother). Clearly, stable and caring personal relationships help move newly divorced adults toward these goals. Such relationships may be sexual or nonsexual, and may occur with or without cohabitation, with partners, or with friends. Most therapists who have worked with the newly divorced can give many examples of adults who, quite understandably, seek companionship, affection, and sexual pleasure as natural parts of life, and as counterbalances to the trauma recently experienced.

Not All Clients Want New Relationships:
The Relevance of Therapist Neutrality.

General goals may or may not apply to the case at hand. During the divorce transition, many clients, for various psychological reasons, lack interest in new relationships. For instance, drained by the process of detaching themselves from unhappy marriages, some adults have absolutely no emotional energy to develop closeness with anyone else. Others, rejected by former spouses, may stay aloof from new contacts because they yearn for reconciliation. The newly divorced may distrust their own ability to pick suitable associates, or they may feel, in despair, that human relationships bring trouble, and should be avoided. Finally, children's reconciliation wishes may inhibit dating. A single parent feeling guilty about children's disrupted lives may be reluctant to further upset offspring who have not yet accepted the separation, or too weary to face their acting-out.

Ethnicity may also mute the desire for socializing among the newly divorced. Some divorced Hispanic woman, particularly those who move in with extended family, may find themselves infantilized and emotionally desexualized by relatives (G. Serrano, personal communication, December 7, 1990). Thrust back into the role of daughter, the Hispanic woman may be pressured not to date. The influence of Roman Catholicism, which has a strong stand against divorce, may reinforce this pressure. Likewise, Black women (who, as previously noted, are less likely than other women to remarry) may eschew dating, often because they are unable to find mates of equal education and social class (McGoldrick et al., 1989).

In contrast, among Jews, there are no cultural forces that inhibit post-divorce dating. If anything, with regard to dating, the cultural emphases on marriage as preferred (Bayme, 1990; Bayme, 1994; Reisman, 1994) and on single parenthood as lower-status (Fishman, 1989) may create encouragement or even pressure to date. However, therapists must be aware of a group of Orthodox women who are ineligible for remarriage because they are separated from husbands who refuse to provide a Jewish bill of divorcement, which can be granted only by a man (Breitowitz, 1994; Heschel, 1991). In these cases, therapists must respect that the religious convictions of the *agunah* (literally, stranded woman) may prevail over her human needs, and cause her to avoid socializing with men; of course, the similarly religious men who form her pool of eligible partners would likewise probably see her as off limits, too.

Because of such emotional and ethnic mandates, therapists working with the newly divorced must carefully assess each adult client, to see if she or he in fact wants to pursue new relationships. After the divorce transition has passed, if a client remains aloof from people, the therapist may want to assertively raise the topic of relationships, and initiate analysis of impediments to new human connections; at that time, client hesitance engendered by ethnicity must be examined with the greatest respect, by the technique of inquiring how the client feels about the cultural directive, rather than questioning the directive itself. During the divorce transition, however, the therapist's more neutral stance conveys to clients that "it is okay to be single." This stance can bolster self-esteem, particularly among women who were raised to believe that being single is simply a transitional state leading to the more desirable state of being married (Hicks & Anderson, 1989; Kissman & Allen, 1993).

Helping Clients Who Want New Social Connections: Identifying Age-Specific and Gender-Specific Experiences.

To help clients who are not ready for new social connections, the therapist uses a low-key stance that affirms "singlehood" as a viable lifestyle. To help clients who express some readiness for new social connections, the therapist must begin with awareness of the social experiences of the newly divorced of various age and gender groups.

Since the social world emphasizes physical beauty (Peck & Manocherian, 1989), younger clients generally have an asset. For women, this asset may be short-lived; midlife body changes such as facial wrinkles and grey hair diminish both the perceived attractiveness (Sands & Richardson, 1986) and the remarriage rates (Rubin, 1992; Uhlenberg, Cooney, & Boyd, 1990) of women but not men. Overall, in both younger women and younger men, therapists find that clients' awareness of their own desirability sometimes contributes to the confidence required for new social ventures, although newly divorced young people are certainly not without anxiety about new social situations.

On the other hand, a liability younger custodial parents (both women and men) face is that after a week spent both at the office and caring for children, they often feel too physically exhausted to socialize with strangers. They may also prefer not to spend precious time away from young children, even if free child care in the form of extended family exists. Since the mother is most often the custodial parent, younger women, as a group, experience greater stress about new social ventures postdivorce than do younger men.

As age increases, the social experiences of women and men during the divorce transition diverge further. For women, development of new contacts becomes increasingly difficult, due to the erosion of confidence that frequently accompanies midlife body changes (Sands & Richardson, 1986). Additionally, the middle-aged woman experiences a social world that has probably changed considerably since the last time she dated. She may become anxious because of changed mores in sexual behavior, payment for restaurant meals, and other areas (Bogolub, 1991).

With regard to a changed social world, her male counterpart may be uneasy, too. Although his greying appearance may be perceived as distinguished, and numbers are on his side with regard to remarriage, therapists must be careful not to stereotype him as problem-free. Not all middle-aged men who divorce do so because of involvements with younger women, and some are quite nervous about beginning to date again—nervous not just about changing sexual mores, but also about their own changing sexual performance.

Helping Clients Who Want New Social Connections:
The Relevance of Issue-Oriented Groups.

Like clients grappling with postdivorce employment issues, those grappling with the formation of postdivorce social connections may benefit from issue-oriented groups featuring both guest speakers and professionally led discussions (Bogolub, 1991; Kissman & Allen, 1993). Topics applying to a broad range of clients include loneliness toleration, fear of rejection in social situations, and handling oneself during the initial phases of a new relationship during the age of AIDS. Age- and gender-specific topics include explaining dating to young children, maintaining social confidence during midlife, and the initiation of social plans by women and men in a newly egalitarian world. Because reaching out for new relationships generally occurs without clear guidelines and with much anxiety, the support of a group, as well as the shared humor and reports of others' experiences, can be invaluable. Overall, the aim is to help the client feel as comfortable—and as adventurous—as possible about extending herself socially.

Generally, new friendships as well as new sexual relationships are discussed in these groups. New friendships are particularly relevant for middle-aged women, as these women tend to be lonelier than their younger counterparts, who are often busy with children (Bogolub, 1991). If they are lonely, divorced middle-aged women may benefit from encouragement to extend themselves to begin new friendships, and if necessary, to overcome ideas inculcated during childhood about female friendship being a relatively unimportant type of relationship.

Helping Clients Who Want New Social Connections:
The Relevance of Individual Treatment.

For many clients, the ideas and encouragement stemming from a group experience are sufficient to help them through the age- and gender-specific dilemmas—and the almost universal anxiety and ''stagefright''—that accompany the social endeavors of the newly divorced. However, some clients have concerns requiring the depth and privacy of individual treatment.

For example, when a client's anxiety and stagefright are unusually strong, the individual therapist may draw upon the technique of visualization, so as to pinpoint the anxiety-producing elements of social situations. If necessary, the therapist will also explore impediments that prevent clients from really extending themselves in social situations. Such impediments include low self-esteem, messages presented during childhood about sexuality outside of marriage, and divorce residues that leave people psychologically unavailable. For example, clients sometimes feel that their divorces make them unattractive, and that other people will shun them once they know them.

Individual treatment also makes sense when clients have left marriages because of realizations, at varying degrees of consciousness, that they are homosexuals. Here, therapists may face a client's ambivalence about the nature of her or his own sexuality that can go on for months or years. In such cases, the clinical techniques required closely parallel those used to explore ambivalence around ending a marriage (see chapter 3). Alternately, if a client has left a marriage because of a homosexual awareness, the focus in sessions is likely to be on self-acceptance, and "breaking the news" to others. With homosexual clients, therapists must carefully monitor themselves for hostile countertransference, particularly where minor children are involved.

In other cases, the therapist may, in individual sessions, provide assistance to a client who has become involved since the divorce in a new sexual relationship. Here, the therapist must walk a fine line, inquiring about the relationship without sounding like a controlling, overprotective parent. One potential countertransference to check is viewing with rose-colored glasses the client and the people she chooses as companions. In our eagerness to accept divorce as a normal process, we sometimes hesitate to acknowledge that during the divorce transition, people are particularly vulnerable (Myers, 1989). Newly divorced people sometimes choose partners who they imagine will save them from loneliness or single parenting. A woman may want to be rescued from financial decline, while a man may be desperate for someone who can keep house. People of both sexes may relive adolescence, or claim an adolescence they never had (Textor, 1989). They may also be drawn to people who resemble the prior spouse.

Should a client in fact make a self-destructive choice, the therapist must ask questions and make statements that will draw the client's attention to it. The aim is to support the client's desire for human contact, while generating client anxiety about the particular choice of partner at hand. If denial operates, the therapist will have to back off, monitor the situation by listening carefully, and attempt to raise the issue again at a later date. In these cases, raising client self-awareness about social choices becomes a long-range project. With more sophisticated clients, the therapist may tie such awareness to longstanding client patterns in human relationships that predate the divorce.

A Contrasting Approach Will Help Newly Divorced
Older Women Address Issues of Social Connection.

In some ways, older divorced women (60 and up) suffer the most in the area of social relationships. Although adult children and grandchildren can provide comfort, the friends and siblings (particularly sisters) who mean so much to younger and middle-aged women have often died, or relocated because of retirement (Cain, 1988). Older women friends still alive and nearby may be "old-fashioned"; in a social scenario not experienced by younger or middle-aged women, they sometimes reject "the gray divorcee" as a violator of morality (Cain, 1988).

Additionally, the tendency to extend one's self to meet new people decreases with age. This is because (a) physical decline saps energy, and (b) the older divorcee, who is often bound by a strict morality, may feel so disgraced that she hides socially. Despite the paucity of peers, the sometime presence of moral opprobrium, a decreased tendency to socialize, and an almost infinitesimal chance of remarriage, social hunger among older divorced women may not be as pronounced as among the middle-aged. The reason is that older people, in general, tend to be oriented to the past (Weingarten, 1988); although they are concerned with future illness and death, meaning and solace are often found in memories rather than anticipated new experiences (Bee, 1994).

Thus, with socially isolated newly divorced older women, skills geared to increasing the client's social connections may have limited utility. The technique of "life review" (e.g., Wallace, 1992) may be more helpful. When the client reflects on previous human connections (e.g., friendships, children, and sibling and collegial relationships), her emotional status may improve, at least to an extent. Although she may remain somewhat depressed because of multiple losses, she benefits from thinking about accomplishments that cannot be taken from her like her husband or her health, even if these accomplishments were attained during the now-defunct marriage.

Chapter 7

The Mental Health Professional's Role: Strengthening the Custodial Parent during the Divorce Transition

In chapter 6, we saw that an adult seeking help during the divorce transition is generally struggling to resolve concerns in at least one of three areas: mourning the prior marriage, improvement of vocational situation, and development of personal relationships. At the same time, such an adult must cope with new family tasks, as parents, sons, and daughters experience a home life affected on every level by marital rupture.

When handling the family concerns of adults during the divorce transition, therapists face parents with problems that include inconsistent discipline, excessive reliance on offspring, and resentment of adult responsibilities. In light of these problems, the present chapter emphasizes the strengthening of the custodial parent. Although much more has been written about helping children of divorce than about helping divorced parents (Grych & Fincham, 1992), my own clinical experience,

127

supported by the thinking of other authors (e.g., Brown, 1989; Simons et al., 1994), suggests that strengthening the custodial parent (most frequently the custodial mother) is perhaps the most fundamental aspect of divorce transition family treatment. Chapter 7 also covers those occasional instances where individual or group therapy is necessary for a child or adolescent.

Therapists must maintain awareness that parents who have recently experienced the upheaval of marital separation often manifest a psychological openness—or even desperation—borne of crisis and need (Parad & Parad, 1990). For this reason, intervention during the divorce transition is particularly likely to matter, and can set the tone for patterns in living for the entire postdivorce experience (Ahrons & Miller, 1993). Mirroring the multilayered life of the divorced parent, individual and family sessions focussing on issues of the custodial parent can be flexibly combined with the individual sessions that are generally used to address mourning, employment, and socializing.

THE THERAPIST RESPONSE TO THE CUSTODIAL MOTHER

We begin with recently divorced mothers. This is not because recently divorced mothers have more problems as parents than do recently divorced fathers. Rather, it is because divorced mothers are most frequently the custodial parent, and generally have more lasting and formative relationships with children than do divorced fathers, whose ties with offspring often erode over time (e.g., Ahlburg & De Vita, 1992; Booth & Amato, 1994). In fact, most clinicians who work with divorced mothers would probably agree that in many cases, the most striking feature about these women is not the help they need, but their strength.

Consider Lynn, a recently divorced 36-year-old mother who sought help at a family service agency. She commuted an hour each way on a train to her nine-to-five secretarial job. One night a week, Lynn brought her two latchkey sons, ages 10 and 11, to the agency during its evening hours. This entailed a separate round-trip train ride, undertaken after giving the boys a quick supper. Although she needed guidance in approaching her two boys with increasing firmness as they neared adolescence, her sheer physical stamina and calm demeanor were remarkable. Lynn typifies the many mothers who need professional help during the divorce transition, and who also cope in a way that merits the greatest respect.

Work with custodial mothers like Lynn is generally based on the divorce transition treatment goal of promoting a strong relationship between children and at least one parent. Research indicates that most children of divorce do well in the long run if their custodial parents (generally mothers) are involved and caring (Furstenberg & Cherlin, 1991). Even though the loss of contact with the father can hurt deeply, and should be minimized or reversed if possible, permanent scars can generally be avoided if the mother/daughter or mother/son relationship is strong (Furstenberg & Cherlin, 1991). As explained in chapter 1, this knowledge makes it possible for the clinician to approach mother-headed divorce transition families optimistically, without worry that the children are bound for long-run damage no matter what intervention the therapist tries.

Strengthening the Custodial Mother

During the divorce transition, a custodial mother like Lynn is frequently less consistent in discipline than parents in intact families (Acock & Demo, 1994; Grych & Fincham, 1992). Specifically, compared with a mother who has the support of another adult residing with her, the solo custodial mother imposes less supervision, fewer demands, and fewer restrictions on behavior (Simons et al., 1994; Thomson et al., 1992). Explanations include maternal guilt over having subjected offspring to a divorce (Hodges, 1991), desire to have children meet the need for peer companionship (Asmussen & Larson, 1991), and physical exhaustion. When a custodial mother is governed by such conditions, and overly permissive as a result, her children may be left feeling that she does not care very much. This is true even when intermittent strictness or spoiling interrupt the overall pattern of nonattention to the parental role.

Exceptions to this trend of divorce transition maternal laxness are perhaps most common among recently divorced African American families, where the broader cultural mandates of strict discipline (Hines et al., 1992; Ho, 1992) and extended family input (Hines, 1990; Ho, 1992) may buffer the unsettling effects of marital rupture. Pseudoexceptions occur among possessive, dominating, or overly protective custodial mothers of any ethnicity. In these cases, although there is an appearance of maternal involvement, it is generated by adult need for companionship and control at a time when the divorce transition upheaval has eliminated both. Again, the underlying dynamic is divorce-generated inattention to offspring needs.

Given the stress of custodial mothers during the divorce transition, the last thing in the world a clinician should do is pass judgment on her client—or hold her to an impossible parenting standard. However, in the context of a supportive relationship, the therapist must frequently help custodial mothers to delineate their parental roles (Brown, 1989; Peck & Manocherian, 1989), and carry them out with greater zest. If a therapist has paid careful attention to a woman's personal, nonparental concerns (mourning, vocation, and/or socializing), the therapist then has leverage to additionally focus on encapsulating adult troubles and increasing attention to daughters and sons.

Promoting Ventilation of Guilt, Fatigue, Loneliness, and Anger.

To promote encapsulation of adult problems, and increased attention to the parental role, a number of techniques can be used. For women like Lynn, who are stressed by the divorce transition, but not seriously impaired psychologically, the therapist must promote ventilation about the divorce transition, and then promote reflection about how it affects parenting.

In individual sessions, therapists can help custodial mothers ventilate (a) guilt about damage they imagine they have done to their children, (b) fatigue stemming from the simultaneous demands of employment and parenting, (c) loneliness generated by carrying out parenting without the live-in support of another adult, and (d) anger or resentment about parental responsibilities. Although not all custodial mothers experience each, these four emotions are among the most common that custodial mothers express at this time. Individual rather than family sessions are critical. Negative feelings about parenthood should not be shared directly with offspring of any age; their sense of security has already been severely shaken by the divorce transition, and would be further damaged by hearing that their custodial mothers think they are hurting them, or do not want them.

Although it is relatively simple for most clients to express guilt, fatigue, and loneliness, it is harder for them to express anger about parental responsibility, because this anger is socially unacceptable. To unearth such anger, the therapist must go beyond simply exploring clients' dropped hints, and beyond open-ended questions like "When you think about Jimmy, is there anything else that goes through your mind?" If the therapist senses the client is holding back "bad thoughts," she may have to add something like "At times, most parents resent their kids even when they know they shouldn't. Have you ever had that kind of feeling?" In response, clients may say things like

Client A: If it weren't for Susie, I could afford to go out to a club on Saturday. I can't always ask my mother to watch her, and sitters are just too expensive. If I didn't have Susie, it would be a lot easier to meet new men.

Client B: Sometimes I wish they weren't there. It's just so much work. I mean, checking the homework, and listening to all their stories. I know it sounds awful, but sometimes I ignore them.

Client C: My teenagers have so much fun. Sometimes I get jealous.

Clients are often relieved to say such things in a nonjudgmental atmosphere; their feelings are not so shameful that they cannot be shared, understood, or discussed rationally. To promote these "angry parent" disclosures, the therapist must sometimes identify and put aside countertransferential feelings of contempt for women who have temporarily and understandably lost sight of the "bottom line" of parenthood, which is putting the needs of another ahead of one's own.

Ethnic Variation and Ventilation of Anger.

On the other hand, for some custodial mothers, particularly those with strong ethnic identities, resentment about the pressures of the mother role during the divorce transition may be diluted. For African American (Hines, 1990), Hispanic (Hines et al., 1992), and Orthodox Jewish women, motherhood is considered a sacred responsibility, essential to one's identity, rather than an optional role that one plans or rationally chooses. To be fundamentally angry about a cultural directive accepted as natural throughout one's life simply because one has recently divorced, while not impossible, is quite unlikely. In addition, when extended family assists, loneliness is minimized, and anger is further prevented.

Thus, from African American, Hispanic, and Orthodox Jewish women, the therapist is more likely to hear about occasional resentment over specific chores, than about the overall burden of motherhood. In these cases, it is important not to push clients, or imply that they must work through their resistance to anger, and get past complaints to a deeper resentment. In fact, such women may need extra support in order to integrate any irritation at all. As will be seen below, expression of any negative feeling about parenting (ranging from irritation to full-blown rage) is beneficial in that it frees clients to nurture themselves, and function more effectively as parents.

Promoting Reflection.

Inexperienced therapists sometimes stop at ventilation of guilt, fatigue, loneliness, and resentment, but ventilation is not an end in itself. To facilitate effective parenting, such ventilation must be followed by the promotion of client reflection about the impact of these emotions on parental behavior.

For instance, when working with a guilty, permissive custodial mother who wants to compensate offspring for hurt she has inflicted, the therapist can clarify the difference between the temporary short-term pain divorce usually causes offspring, and the client's fantasies about long-range harm. The therapist can also present factual information about the general long-range well-being of children of divorce (e.g., Barber & Eccles, 1992; Walsh, 1991). When the short-term nature of hurt to offspring is established, and the mother realizes there is probably no permanent damage to make up for, the therapist can help the mother formulate her own ideas of what true parent-to-child giving is. For example, she might ask, "Does being giving mean only being nice?" Usually, the realization that discipline is in fact not an additional blow, but a way of expressing love, follows readily.

Likewise, when assisting fatigued mothers who have trouble being energetic, the therapist helps them get in touch with temporarily buried feelings of parental pride. This is accomplished by saying, "I wonder what your life would be without the kids," or something similar. I have found that almost inevitably, such a comment elicits a response like "I can't imagine life without them. All the work sometimes gets me down, but raising them makes me proud. They're my kids." Occasionally, I have found such a comment elicits a client's tears too. Overall, the recently divorced mother becomes more conscious of the satisfaction of being a parent, and gains pleasure from reinvesting herself in the parental role. One result is increased sensitivity to feelings of offspring; those in less obvious need, such as the "too-good" child or the "mature" adolescent or young adult, are particularly likely to be emotionally neglected when custodial mothers become overwhelmed.

Loneliness can affect parental discipline adversely. A lonely, recently divorced mother who wants desperately to be liked by her children (Asmussen & Larson, 1991) must learn that while her insecure feelings are natural, acting upon them by granting a knee-jerk "yes" to offspring requests is destructive. When adolescents test to see if a parent cares enough to say "no," the consequences of overpermissiveness can be particularly severe, due to the potential for dangerous acting-out behavior. Likewise, a mother who is excessively dependent on adolescent or young adult children must learn that she is not attending to her job of facilitating emotional separation; if she and her offspring are not influenced by ethnic norms promoting multigenerational living, she may be inhibiting age-appropriate physical separation as well.

If a custodial mother is frequently angry, it is sometimes useful to help her identify the feeling on the spot. Then, she can nurture and soothe herself, so that she does not take out her anger on her family, or simply allow the feeling to spill out unchecked.

Sometimes, though, reflection does not enable clients to grasp the link between divorce-generated emotions and substandard parenting. With such clients, the therapist may use confrontation to cut through avoidance or denial. For example, Pam, a client of mine, reported doing parental tasks in a dogged manner, but avoided discussion of the resentment which accompanied them. Pam brushed off questions designed to heighten awareness of the way her simmering anger quietly poisoned her relationship with her daughter Laura. Finally, I said, "You know, when Laura grows up, she may say, 'I always felt like a burden to my mother. She always did what she had to, but she would have been much happier if she didn't have to take care of me.' " Pam flinched and began to cry. In a true breakthrough, she began her next session with reference to my statement. Her new understanding made it possible for her to begin working on expression and containment of resentment, and on self-nurturance and reoriented parenting.

Translating the Idea of Strengthened Parenthood
into Action in Family Sessions.

Ventilation and reflection do not work in isolation, but must be combined with other techniques that strengthen parental functioning. Via questions like "How would you like to translate that good idea into action?" renewed interest in parenting must be broken down into specific tasks (Kissman, 1991; Kissman & Allen, 1993), such as sticking to bedtimes, planning one meal on the weekend that everyone cooks together, or asking a neighbor rather than a teenager for household help when the teenager is studying.

Additionally, in family sessions, youth can be asked to describe parents' different moods (frequently expressed in jargon such as "out of it" or "into it"). Complementing the type of direct feedback offered to Pam, the family session is an alternate route for parents to see their impact on children, adolescents, and young adults. After such discussion, parents can be encouraged, in front of their daughters and sons, to formulate more youth-oriented, involved stances. Since many custodial mothers are so overwhelmed that they minimize or ignore offspring responses to the divorce (Kalter, 1990; Kitson, 1992; Walsh, 1991), this type of intervention is common.

Black and Hispanic youth often need a lot of encouragement before coming forth with criticisms of their mothers. First, they may be reluctant to speak out because of peer warnings that mental health professionals do not really help much (Ho, 1992). Second, in contrast to Jewish families, who place a high value on discussing problems with experts (Hines et al., 1992), Black and Hispanic parents may feel pressure to conceal problems, and may initially encourage children, adolescents, and young adults to "put their best foot forward" with mental health professionals. Children (and older offspring, to a lesser extent) may worry that they will "get in trouble" at home for speaking out in session about what they do not like in family life, and may need mothers' reassurance that it is acceptable, in fact desirable, to express themselves.

For example, a working-class mother-headed Hispanic family was seen at a family agency when Juan, age 7, was referred for behavioral problems in school. For the initial appointment, Juan appeared in a suit and tie, with hair carefully combed. His mother had obviously made him don his best clothes, and seemed more concerned with the impression her son made on the therapist than with helping him express himself. In such cases, explicit acknowledgment of maternal care, and clear statements about the relevance of disclosure to accomplishment in treatment can help mothers to open up, and to encourage their children to do the same.

In addition to helping parents become more consistently involved with their daughters and sons, parents and offspring also can be asked in family sessions to describe what they like to do together, or what the "funnest" part of the week is. Recently divorced mothers struggling with major losses and changes are sometimes so overworked and upset that they need reminders about the existence of enjoyment. The therapist's conscious effort to avoid emotionally joining custodial mothers in their "blues," while maintaining empathy, is very helpful.

Assistance in Developing a Social Life.

During the divorce transition, youth often react to the custodial mother's dating by "giving her a hard time." Young children may whine, pout, or refuse to speak in the presence of new boyfriend, while teenagers and young adults may forget to relay phone messages from him.

Typically, offspring make themselves obstacles to romance because a new man is both a dramatic sign that their father is no longer a member of the household, and competition for their mother's attention. Sometimes mothers submit to offspring pressure to stop dating, because they are too weary to stand up to it, or guilty about upsetting sons and daughters with romantic involvement. This capitulation can occur subtly, as when a mother who is ready for dating holds herself back. It is always a mistake, because it gives children too much power in running the household.

In individual sessions, the therapist can help a mother realize that daughters and sons with too much power are emotionally abandoned. Then, by planning her own social life, the mother can make it clear that she—not her kids—is in charge. Sometimes, the knowledge that offspring may eventually benefit from a mother's dating helps her develop necessary firmness; although casual dating may not improve a woman's emotional status or her youngsters' social network, a meaningful relationship will lift a woman's spirits as a mother as well as a sexual being, and may introduce a valuable new source of attention to her youngsters as well.

Simultaneously, the therapist helps the custodial mother provide reassurance of her love. Sometimes, a mother needs the protection and structure of a family session to begin this process; annoying, provocative reactions to dating may make it hard to focus at home on a son's or daughter's poignant, masked fear of more divorce-generated loss.

The Importance of Limited Treatment Goals.

Throughout the therapeutic work with the divorce transition custodial mother and her children, the therapist must remember that no matter how skilled the intervention, parenting during the divorce transition is generally somewhat diminished (Hetherington & Clingempeel, 1992; Wallerstein, 1994). Thus, the therapist must strike a balance between challenging parents to be parents, and accepting their temporarily constricted capacity for growth. In fact, if a family presents an overly rosy picture of progress, the therapist should say something like, "I see things are going pretty well. But there must be some moments when it's hard to have the kind of family life you want." In this way, the family is divested of any internal pressure they may feel to please the therapist.

When clients are freed of this pressure, the therapist may then hear beleaguered custodial mothers say things like, "Since I've had these sessions, I know I should be doing more with the kids. But sometimes I just can't." Then, the therapist can respond with acceptance, and queries about the shifting overall balance of maternal involvement and noninvolvement, even if "this was a bad week." The therapist can also inquire about whether the client thinks she will remain this physically and emotionally depleted on a permanent basis. If the client is not able to see that her energy level and spirits will probably lift eventually, the therapist may even share with clients information on the generally recognized time limits of the divorce transition, i.e., several years (see chapter 5). Overall, limited gains, and a two-steps-forward, one-step-backward process are typical for custodial mothers during the divorce transition.

Helping the Seriously Disturbed Custodial Mother

Sometimes, a recently divorced custodial mother is more disturbed than Lynn. Custody does not necessarily indicate adequate parenting potential; often, a woman has custody by default. That is, she is the only parent whose whereabouts are known, or the only one who will assent to the job. In extreme cases, the divorce transition can push a fragile custodial mother with minimal parenting capacity into neglectful or abusive behavior, particularly if poverty and/or lack of social support add further stress.

When faced with serious pathology, a therapist's nonjudgmental attitude about divorce should not blind her to the client's limited growth capacity (Myers, 1989). For such a client, ventilation is not catharsis, but pointless outpouring. There is little or no capacity to understand one's impact on a child, and little or no spark of parental pride to be fanned by the therapist into new behavior. In these instances, an approach that involves ventilation of emotion, reflection on the effect of emotion on behavior, and translation of newly developed ideas on parenting into concrete action, while not entirely pointless, may accomplish only very limited gains.

Depending on the level of disturbance, other techniques must supplement or replace those used with women like Lynn. For example, in individual sessions, a therapist can carefully supply a self-absorbed custodial mother with specific information or education on offspring needs for affection, guidance, and discipline; if these needs are presented in a straightforward but caring manner, some increase in parental skills may occur. Likewise, in family sessions, a therapist can literally model appropriate behavior with youngsters, and then ask the mother to describe or try out what she has observed. While a higher functioning custodial mother would probably find this insulting, her lower functioning counterpart may find it useful, particularly if she has received inadequate parenting herself.

Preventing Abuse and Neglect: The Case of Fran.

In a particularly vivid form of education, the therapist may have to define abusive and/or neglectful behavior for the client, and either make a report to child protection officials, or inform the client of the possibility of such a report, should the client be unable to stop a downward behavioral spiral. Again, our empathy for the highly stressed recently divorced custodial mother cannot blind us to children's ongoing needs.

For example, Fran, a 28-year-old recently divorced White custodial mother, was seen at a family agency. Fran was home on public assistance with three children under 8 years old. Fran's parents and siblings saw her divorce as shameful, and offered no support—emotional, practical, or financial. They hoped that if Fran's life alone was very difficult, she would pursue reconciliation, and reduce their shame. Fran confided in her therapist that she was "going crazy because she was always alone with the kids," and that she was considering leaving them alone for an hour or so from time to time, to get a break. "Andy, my oldest is very mature for a 7-year-old; he can watch the little ones," she stated.

The therapist told Fran that even though she understood how trapped she felt, a call to the local child protective agency would be necessary if Fran carried out her plan. Related therapist comments centered on children's developmental needs, and the possibility of developing a babysitting exchange with neighbors. The following week, Fran said, "I stayed up the whole night after our last session worrying about what you told me about calling the government." Aware that it is sometimes a clinical responsibility to heighten rather than assuage anxiety, the therapist was pleased. She deliberately refrained from any supportive comments about the irritation of sleepless nights, and responded, "It sounds like you were really thinking hard. What went through your mind?" Then followed a discussion of Fran's realization that "I guess I can't walk out on them just because I feel like it."

Although Fran never became a particularly sensitive parent, she was able to stop treatment after several months. In addition to absorbing some ideas about children's basic needs, Fran also experienced a decrease in the intensity of the divorce transition. Initially, the shock of the rejection by her ex-husband, who had literally disappeared, seriously compromised her already limited parenting. Fran's gradual acceptance of the end of the marriage complemented the therapist's intervention, and contributed to the achievement of circumscribed but genuine gains.

WORK WITH INDIVIDUAL CHILDREN AND ADOLESCENTS: EXCEPTIONAL CASES ONLY

Mental reference to the divorce transition treatment goal of strengthening the bond between the child and the custodial parent suggests that individual sessions for younger children are generally unnecessary. Whenever possible, energy should be directed to connecting children to parents, not to therapists. In fact, a countertransference to guard against when working with depleted divorce transition custodial mothers is the desire to rescue their children (Springer, 1991), and emotionally foster or adopt them by unnecessarily scheduling individual sessions for them.

Sometimes, though, separate treatment for youngsters is needed, either because of (a) a youngster's serious emotional disturbance (preexistent or divorce-generated), or (b) a youngster's social/emotional isolation. Such isolation typically stems from the psychological disturbance of a parent or parents, coupled with a lack of grandparents, godparents, or significant others who might partially fill the parenting gap. In such cases, individual and/or group treatment can certainly help a disturbed or isolated youngster through the divorce transition.

The Case of Andy: Combined Individual and Group Therapy for a Socially Isolated Child

Seven-year-old Andy was the child whom Fran, his 28-year-old custodial mother, wanted to put in charge of his two younger siblings. During the divorce transition, Andy experienced increased material poverty, as the family status changed from working poor to public assistance recipients. He also experienced the deterioration of his mother's parenting skills, inattention from extended family, and the loss of his father. Because his brother and sister were ages 3 and 1, he also lacked sibling support. Despite multiple losses and intense social isolation, he was a capable and seemingly cheerful child. Andy's appealing nature appeared partly due to temperament, and partly due to a need to endear himself to any adults in his life (e.g., teachers, mental health professionals) capable of offering him attention.

The therapist working with Fran, Andy, and his siblings concluded that behind Andy's "little man" facade, there probably lay considerable sadness and anger, as well as anxiety around being so alone. The therapist knew that helping Andy express these emotions to his mother in a family session would be fruitless, due to her inability to respond, or even see Andy as a little boy. So, the therapist combined two other approaches.

First, she saw Andy for a limited number of individual sessions, utilizing a "divorce monologue" (Kelly & Wallerstein, 1977) during each. In this format, the therapist talks to a child about divorce transition emotions and experiences he is likely to have, without any demand (overt

or covert) that the child respond verbally. Although the divorce monologue technique was developed many years ago, it retains its relevance
today. Since Andy was not a child who readily discussed his problems,
this technique seemed appropriate for him.

During the divorce monologues, the therapist spoke very softly about
how tough divorce is for an 7-year-old (e.g., short-tempered mother,
decreased standard of living) and some of the things that other kids feel
that he might be feeling too (e.g., resentment, sadness). Andy did not
say a word, but he listened carefully. The therapist's talks helped Andy
identify and organize his carefully hidden feelings. They also helped
Andy learn that he could find nurturance in the world. Yet, the therapist
did not become a substitute mother; she contracted for a series of six
sessions with Andy, and adhered to the contract.

Second, the therapist referred Andy to an ongoing school-based support group for children who had recently experienced parental divorce;
such groups are common for this population of children (Farmer &
Galaris, 1993; Grych & Fincham, 1992). Pleased with any adjunct that
would ease her burden, Andy's mother readily permitted his participation. During the group, Andy listened as the leader and the other youngsters discussed anger, loss, and yearnings for parental reconciliation.
Gradually, drawing on the divorce monologues, and his therapist's nurturance, Andy was able to make sense of these discussions, and participate in them. As a result, his pain and anxiety diminished. He also
became more open about his feelings, which enabled him to develop
some meaningful friendships with other children in the group.

Other Approaches to Children and
Adolescents Needing Individual Treatment

For Andy, whose problem was social isolation rather than individual
disturbance, the combination of short-term individual sessions and longer
term group therapy worked well. As noted in the discussion of the preseparation phase, more disturbed youngsters (e.g., those manifesting
dangerous behavior) may need a long-range relationship with an individual therapist, to work toward goals such as mastery of impulses, and
verbalization—rather than acting-out—of feelings.

In such cases, parents and other involved adults must also be seen, to
heighten their awareness of their youngsters, and to focus on parenting
skills. Even with the best therapy in the world, someone like Andy's
mother probably would not make great gains in the subtleties of listening
to children's feelings, but less disturbed parents more clearly justify the

investment of therapist effort in developing responsiveness. However, because of the almost inevitable decrease in level of parenting during the divorce transition (Hetherington & Clingempeel, 1992; Wallerstein, 1994), individual therapy for the dangerously acting-out child or adolescent remains critical during the divorce transition.

THE THERAPIST RESPONSE TO
THE CUSTODIAL FATHER

For several reasons, therapists are far less likely to encounter custodial fathers than custodial mothers either during the divorce transition or afterwards. First, although the proportion of custodial fathers is increasing (Downey, 1994; Guttmann, 1993), custodial fathers are a minority population, currently comprising only approximately 10% of divorced households (Johnson, 1993; Kristall & Greif, 1994). Second, custodial fathers are overwhelmingly middle and upper income, highly educated, and White (Guttmann, 1993). This means that compared with his female counterpart, a custodial father is much more likely to be able to afford household help, and to bypass problems such as "role overload" and time poverty which cause custodial mothers to feel overwhelmed, and to seek treatment. Third, custodial fathers have generally sought custody actively (Kissman & Allen, 1993); default custody, which can set off serious parenting problems among the resentful or emotionally disturbed, rarely comes into play. Finally, men in general (Meth & Passick, 1990)—and divorced men in particular (Myers, 1989; Cohen & Lowenberg, 1994)—seek mental health help less often than women.

Custodial Fathers: Heroes or Humans?

Nonetheless, the therapist must be prepared to assist custodial fathers who do seek assistance during the divorce transition. To limit detrimental countertransference, she must consciously avoid the widespread public view of these men as heroes (Johnson, 1993). If the therapist sees her client as a hero, she may be supportive to the point of being saccharine, and gloss over rather than explore problems. If a male client feels pressured by his therapist's hero mind-set to be "father of the year," and already has trouble acknowledging the guilt, fatigue, and resentment which women more readily express, the combination of therapist and client avoidance can create a superficial pseudotherapy. If anything, it behooves the therapist to dig a little harder with male clients, who frequently mask emotion (Kissman & Allen, 1993).

Specialized Techniques for Assisting Custodial Fathers

Depending on the client's particulars, the therapist may utilize some of the techniques described as pertinent to custodial mothers (ventilation, reflection, translation of ideas into action via family sessions, reliance on limited goals). However, these techniques hinge on access to feelings, and it may be difficult or impossible for a custodial father to get in touch with feelings that impede parenting, even with therapeutic encouragement.

Psychoeducational and Cognitive Techniques.

If it is not possible for a man to identify emotions, the therapist uses alternate approaches. For example, psychoeducational or other cognitively based, directive techniques are sometimes employed (Greif & DeMaris, 1990; Kissman & Allen, 1993); because of their socialization, men are more likely than women to resonate to approaches stressing logic and task implementation. For example, when presented with a custodial father and an acting-out school-aged son, a therapist began by suggesting that the father reserve one afternoon and one evening per week for father-son activities. In the therapist's judgment, this was initially more helpful than exploring the father's feelings; such exploration occurred only after the structured father-son task had solidified the man's rapport with the therapist.

Expanding the Role of Father.

Just as custodial mothers sometimes must learn to be the disciplinarian and tolerate offspring anger, custodial fathers sometimes must learn to nurture, empathize, and relate to offspring feeling (Downey, 1994). But because of the way men are raised in this society, they may find feelings embarrassing. For instance, fathers who respond to offspring pain or sadness with concrete gestures (e.g., gifts, outings) that youngsters sometimes find distancing need help in giving verbal recognition to emotion, so that children feel understood.

Additionally, the previously noted lack of norms for custodial fathers (Germain, 1991) frequently leaves them uncertain as to what to do in a variety of situations. A useful technique is to help a custodial father develop his own norms. Typically, the therapist's first set of questions revolves around what kind of father the client wants to be; the second set of questions promotes consideration of the model presented by the client's own father. Specifically, the client is helped to consider how he wants to emulate his father, and how he wants to be different.

THE THERAPIST RESPONSE TO
JOINT RESIDENTIAL CUSTODY PARENTS

When parents share joint legal custody (but not joint residential custody), youngsters live full time with one parent, whose experience, as previously noted, is for all practical purposes that of a sole custody parent (Arditti, 1992; Johnson, 1993); relevant issues have generally been covered in the material pertaining to custodial mothers and custodial fathers. However, the small minority of divorced parents with joint residential custody (Pearson & Thoennes, 1990; Maccoby & Mnookin, 1992) have contrasting experiences. In some ways, their emotional stress is less than that of sole custody parents. They may experience some of the problems affecting sole custody mothers (e.g., resentment, fatigue, loneliness) and sole custody fathers (e.g., lack of norms), but the stress is less intense because of the recurring respites built into joint residential custody. In addition, the generally middle- and upper middle-class socioeconomic status of joint custody parents (Pearson & Thoennes, 1990) protects them from severe financial hardship. Thus, with this population, the therapist will probably call upon the techniques described for sole custody parents, but to a lesser extent.

In addition, the therapist will have to handle a dilemma unique to joint residential custody parents, namely, parents' reaction to the constant separations from their children. Some parents may find these separations stressful. These parents have a hard time letting go of their kids when the switch to the other parent takes place, and may unwittingly induce guilt over leaving ("I'll miss you *so* much, sweetheart!") Other parents may welcome the separations, and unwittingly induce offspring guilt over staying. Such a parent might, for example, spend an inordinate amount of audible telephone time planning a weekend trip, leaving her children with the idea that Mom (or Dad) is happier when they are elsewhere. Alternately, parents may have varied reactions to offspring coming and going, depending on their own emotional state and social life.

When working with joint residential custody parents, the therapist must explore for client reaction to the regular separations from sons and daughters. Sometimes, the therapist must help parents understand and modify the detrimental effect of these reactions on their children.

The Mental Health Professional's Role: Realigning Relationships in Divorce Transition Families

In chapter 7, we considered ways to strengthen the custodial parent during the divorce transition. Here, in chapter 8, we add a broader perspective on treatment conducted during this period, by looking at mental health interventions with (a) the single-parent household, (b) the separated spouses, and (c) divorced parents and their children as they interact with extended family and the broader community. These interventions are related, respectively, to the divorce transition treatment goals of (a) improvement in the relationship between offspring and the custodial parent, (b) decrease in conflict and increase in cooperation between the separated parents, insofar as possible, and (c) increase in social support for the custodial parent.

THE SINGLE-PARENT HOUSEHOLD: HELPING THE CUSTODIAL PARENT PROMOTE OFFSPRING MOURNING

During the divorce transition, it is sometimes necessary to help custodial parents put aside their own feelings of loss, and respond to their youngsters' specific reactions to the divorce (Kalter, 1990). Chapter 5 reported that preschool children are likely to be confused by the separation, while older children, adolescents, and young adults generally experience anger, sadness, anxiety, and fear of future abandonment. Although their needs are sometimes masked, these young people are generally very much in need of understanding and attention during the divorce transition.

In some ways, the work of the therapist with the custodial parent during the divorce transition is similar to the work the therapist did with parents who have just announced an impending separation, described in chapter 4. That is, the therapist should help the custodial parent give extra nurturance, discuss feelings, curtail self-destructive acting-out, and avoid intellectualization. Also, offspring can be encouraged to connect with significant others. However, during the divorce transition, the degree of parental self-absorption the therapist must cut through may be even greater than before the divorce, given the concrete problems as well as emotional stressors that arise at this time.

New Expressions of Offspring Mourning

Additionally, during the divorce transition, the therapist must help custodial parents address new expressions of offspring mourning stemming directly from the actual physical separation. For example, the cognitive confusion of very young children does not really begin until the father literally moves out (Kalter, 1990); I recall a recently divorced mother who sadly related how her 3-year-old daughter, Candy, shouted "Daddy" whenever she saw a red car (like her father's), only to burst into tears when the car did not stop. In such cases, custodial mothers must be helped to see that even though patient, repeated explanations are in order, very young children will not readily appreciate them, and confusion must run its course.

Similarly, newly divorced custodial parents must sometimes learn to "read" puzzling behavior in light of recent marital rupture (Kalter, 1990). For example, 14-year-old John tinkers obsessively with his bicycle. His mother, initially annoyed, realizes in session that the tinkering helps John feel close to his father, whom he now sees only on alternate weekends in which father-son bicycle outings figure prominently. Rather than discouraging John's tinkering, the mother decides to say, "I think it's nice the way you like to take care of your bike so much lately. I know you miss Dad, and it kind of reminds you of him." For both Candy and John, a therapist helped a custodial mother respond verbally to an acted-out reaction to the loss of the father, thus helping a youngster feel understood.

Sometimes, youngsters' displays of mourning during the divorce transition are maladaptive. For example, a 10-year-old angry about his parents' divorce takes to embarrassing his custodial mother in public. A 22-year-old young woman who had always been attractive feels that her world has come apart when her parents divorce. She becomes highly anxious about almost everything, and gains twenty pounds in a year. Again, in both cases, the therapist helps the custodial mother read behavior. She also helps her bypass criticism, and talk to the youngster about divorce-generated anger or anxiety. Additionally, limits on maladaptive behavior are encouraged for the school-aged boy, but not for the young woman. Because of her developmental level, it is no longer appropriate for a parent to direct her behavior, although individual treatment may be encouraged if increased parental understanding does not lead to self-correction of maladaptive, attention-seeking behavior (in this case, over-eating).

As offspring mourn the loss of their former life, custodial parents (overwhelmingly female) may also have to learn to address questions such as: "Are you and Dad gonna get back together?" The therapist must help the custodial mother to get past feeling interrogated or attacked, and to validate the underlying feelings of youngsters testing to see if the two-parent family is really gone. While children miss the noncustodial parent, and long for the two-parent household (Caplan, 1990), they simultaneously experience a need for stability in the new living situation. The best responses sidestep a youngster's prickly, challenging demeanor, honor her longings for the past, and acknowledge that it may take a while for the new household and new rules to feel like home.

Unrealistic Parents Can Short-Circuit Offspring Mourning

An adult who is not happy about the separation, and wishes for reconciliation (Guttmann, 1993) finds it particularly difficult to take either the single-parent home or offspring mourning seriously; the wish is that both will vanish. In these cases, the therapist's job is to help the divorced parent realize that desire for reunion with the former spouse, while legitimate, should not prevent acceptance of the fact of the separation. The therapist must also help the client resist dangling reconciliation before the children, either directly or indirectly.

INTERVENING IN THE PARENT–CHILD DYNAMICS
OF SINGLE-PARENT HOUSEHOLDS

Like all families, families headed by custodial mothers (or fathers) present various patterns, some dysfunctional. If the therapist wants to address such patterns, she usually takes the initiative; parents during the divorce transition are often so overwhelmed that they minimize family problems (Kitson, 1992). The divorce transition patterns that follow do not comprise an exhaustive list. However, they are some of the more common patterns facing today's therapists, both in agency and private practice. In each case, adult needs have unconsciously and negatively influenced the parent-child relationship. In each case, the therapist must help recently divorced adults modify their parenting, and base it on the needs of children rather than adults. The therapist must also be able to involve children and adolescents in sessions as indicated.

Scapegoating

Scapegoating occurs in all family types (e.g., intact two-parent family, family headed by a never-married woman), but it acquires a particular flavor in the household of a custodial parent. Specifically, the therapist frequently observes a mother "picking on" a child or adolescent (usually a boy) who unconsciously symbolizes to her the estranged husband, toward whom she retains much anger (Kalter, 1990). In addition to the usual line of inquiry employed when any scapegoating occurs (e.g, finding out if the "bad" child is praised for anything at all), the therapist asks questions such as: "Who does he look like?" and "Who is he named after?" A disclosure that "He's the spittin' image of Tom," can lead to realizations such as "I'm always in knots with the poor kid; I get so busy thinking about his creepy father, I never see him just for himself." More nurturing, less hostile maternal behavior often follows.

These realizations, which may occur in individual or family sessions, can be buttressed by use of the sibling group in family session. For example, the therapist may share observations about how other siblings react to the scapegoating; they may participate in the process, or protect the scapegoat. Such observations heighten the custodial mother's awareness of the far-reaching ripples of her displaced anger. Likewise, the therapist may ask the scapegoat to tell his mother what it feels like to be picked on, which may put the mother in touch with buried loving feelings.

Skin Tone and Scapegoating.

In Black and Hispanic families, resemblance based on skin tone may also be a factor in scapegoating. In both ethnic groups, the topic of skin tone is so emotionally charged that people often avoid it (Boyd-Franklin, 1989; Montalvo, 1991). Therefore, the therapist must bring it up, if she senses a youngster (male or female) whose skin tone is similar to the father's is receiving negative attention. The therapist must also bear in mind that in both groups, there is some tendency to prefer lighter skin tones (Hall, 1992; Montalvo, 1991). This tendency may or may not apply to the family at hand, but the worker must explore issues of jealousy or contempt, as well as those of resemblance. As with other charged topics (such as sex or money), the therapist must proceed with a balance of confidence and gentleness, and be prepared for some edgy responses masking deep feeling. If the therapist is White, the exploration is particularly challenging, but the tendency to be overly solicitous and let clients of an oppressed group "off the hook" with regard to charged topics (Boyd-Franklin, 1989; Berg & Miller, 1992; Devore & London, 1993) does not promote in-depth clinical work.

Parentification

Like scapegoating, parentification is a type of parental focus on one child (Guttmann, 1993). Generally, in scapegoating, the custodial mother's anger towards her ex-husband (or toward men in general) affects the mother-child tie. In parentification, the custodial mother's dependency (discussed earlier with regard to lenient discipline and the need to be liked) takes effect. She relies on one youngster, usually the oldest. The parentified child carries out household tasks, and may also may provide care to younger siblings.

Functional and Dysfunctional Parentification.

Unlike scapegoating, parentification is not always destructive. If the mother is employed, the parentified child's household contribution is usually virtually essential, and can build a sense of self-esteem and responsibility (Boyd-Franklin, 1989; Del Carmen & Virgo, 1993; Kissman & Allen, 1993). If the parentified child is praised for her contribution, and also allowed time for homework, peer involvement, and other age-appropriate activities, damage is not done. In other cases, reliance on the parentified child is excessive; the mother demands much work, and has no awareness of the need of a younger child for approval, or the need of an adolescent or young adult for support in developing emotional separation and an independent life.

When functional parentification occurs, the therapist must be supportive, reflecting, for example, that "It's tough in a family with only one parent at home, and you have really figured out a way to get everything done. This is a family where everybody pitches in." Such supportiveness can only stem from a true conviction that the single-parent family is a valid family form (Kissman & Allen, 1993). For a middle-class therapist with a bias toward the two-parent intact family as the best family type, supervision or introspection may be necessary for genuine articulation of support.

When parentification is dysfunctional, the therapist is probably faced with a narcissistic parent who sees her child as existing simply to gratify her. In such cases, the therapist must work within the woman's limitations. Since the mother is obviously extremely needy, she needs much recognition about how hard her life is. Then, in a nonjudgmental fashion, the therapist presents information about the negative consequences of the parentification. The appeal is made to the mother's self-interest, not to her sensitivity to her child. For example, a divorced mother who kept her 11-year-old son home from school to attend to child care and household tasks while she worked learned from her therapist that her son would eventually be taken from her, and be forced to live someplace else, if she did not permit him to attend school. Then, the therapist initiates problem solving and/or provides information about help sources (e.g., government-financed homemaker, extended family, or neighbors) that could replace the labor of the parental child, at least partially. Problem solving around the mother's ability to handle a somewhat greater number of tasks is also useful.

When the dysfunctionally parentified child is late adolescent or young adult, the therapist generally sees both parent and offspring in conjoint and individual sessions. In the work with the very limited parent, the emphasis is again on help sources that could partially replace the contribution of the parental daughter or son. The work with the parentified daughter or son focuses on the conflicts that impel the child to acquiesce to the mother's verbal or nonverbal cues that she or he give up her or his own life; because of age and developmental level, issues of parent-child complementarity and responsibility in creating a "two-way street" must be brought to the surface and resolved.

Parentification in Emigrant Families.

When Hispanic families emigrate, their divorce rates rise. Wives' success in obtaining jobs and salaries superior to those of their husbands strains marriages based on traditional female and male roles (Drachman & Shen-Ryan, 1991). Despite occupational success, loss of parental authority for the divorced Hispanic woman is inevitable, because she and her children remain part of a culture where household authority lies traditionally with men (Del Carmen & Virgo, 1993). When children learn English and parents do not, children become their parents' teachers of mainstream customs and mores, and maternal authority is further diminished. If migration has isolated a divorced Hispanic mother from blood kin and *compadrazgo* members, her marginalization intensifies.

Parentification of offspring can further weaken the authority of the divorced, recently emigrated Hispanic mother. Such parentification becomes dysfunctional when offspring feel that because of a mother's multifaceted status loss, they are free to disregard her. However, treatment can sometimes reverse this process. For example, divorced, recently emigrated Hispanic mothers may gain self-respect and parenting skills through mothers' groups comprised of members with similar backgrounds (Chillman, 1993; Kissman & Allen, 1993). Concrete results might include curfews, insistence on homework completion, and the confidence to intervene in emotionally charged areas such as suspected substance abuse. These mothers are generally disadvantaged by circumstances rather than psychopathology, so the ability to see offspring needs as separate from one's own can be utilized in both group and individual treatment.

In recently emigrated Soviet Jewish families, the parentification of sons and daughters because of newcomer status is less intense. Soviet Jewish divorce rates do rise with emigration (Belozersky, 1990), and offspring do generally absorb mainstream language and culture more quickly than parents (Castex, 1992). However, in contrast with her Hispanic counterpart, the Soviet Jewish mother's culture stresses male/female equality (Belozersky, 1990; Castex, 1992). This egalitarian tradition supports authoritative functioning in the custodial mother role, although some difficulty maintaining leadership due to emigration stress can still occur (Belozersky, 1990: Castex, 1992). Thus, when working with Soviet Jewish custodial mothers, the need for therapists to bolster parental confidence and assertive behavior, while not eliminated, is diminished.

Sexualization

In parentification, adults' lack of time, psychopathology, or cultural dislocation contributes to a role reversal between custodial parent and offspring, and children and adolescents become household managers. In another postdivorce transformation of the parent-child tie, lonely, newly single adults may, without awareness, enlist their adolescent and young adult sons and daughters as social peers (Brown, 1989; Guttmann, 1993). With the recent explosion of knowledge about actual incest, we must not lose sight of subtly sexualized parent-child bonds, which are less dramatic, but also destructive. The damage to offspring during the divorce transition caused by sexualized mother-son or father-daughter relationships may explain the finding that overall, boys with divorced parents fare better when they live with their fathers, while girls with divorced parents fare better when they live with their mothers (Aquilino, 1994; Guttmann, 1993).

Assessment and Treatment of Sexually Toned Relationships.

While sexualization is usually more subtle than scapegoating or parentification, a skilled therapist learns to sense it. In family sessions, clues arise from seating arrangements, as when mother and son (not sibling and sibling) sit next to each other on the only available sofa. Similarly, mother–son or father–daughter dyads may answer the therapist's questions like a married couple, that is, looking at each other for verification, correcting each other in a loving way, and so forth.

Therapists should also be alert as to what is omitted. For example, if a custodial mother, when asked to describe a typical day, stops at dinnertime, her therapist should help her fill in the missing hours. Typically, the therapist uses inquiry that is behavior oriented rather than feeling oriented, asking, ''Tell me what happens after dinner,'' not ''Tell me what it feels like after dinner.''

Although identification of a subtly sexualized parent–child bond can evolve from either family or individual sessions, its treatment is best handled in separate individual sessions for the parent and the youngster. For example, a therapist learns that a custodial mother insists that her teenaged son eat dinner out with her (''just the two of us'') every weekend. If the matter is discussed in a family session, the son will probably feel smothered and confused by his mother's sexual and social longings. Awareness of these longings may cause him to withdraw in a panic from all social situations, or, alternately, to act out sexually, to counteract the pull of the mother.

A better approach is for an adult who sexualizes the parent–child bond to discuss the matter in individual sessions. Then, the parent can be asked to consider the impact of this sexualization on a youngster, as well as on the parent's own pursuit of new social relationships. Likewise, a youngster needs to discuss the development of her or his own interests individually. An introspective and expressive youngster may also share feelings about the parent with the therapist, with catharsis and insight preceding the focus on an increasingly independent life. Overall, the strategy for treatment of sexualized parent–child relationships is enhancement of boundaries, and containment rather than sharing of sexual overtones. After these goals are accomplished, parent–child sessions regarding other matters can be beneficial.

Using Children

During the divorce transition, adult mourning over the loss of the marriage is generally not complete, and separated spouses often remain quite angry with each other (Peck & Manocherian, 1989). Sometimes, this anger is a smokescreen for lingering feelings of attachment (Wallerstein, 1990). Adult feelings of both anger and attachment can negatively affect the parent–offspring relationship, when newly divorced adults rely on youngsters as tools to express these feelings.

Offspring as Spies and Weapons.

Often, an angry or inappropriately attached parent pumps the children with questions about the other parent (Isaacs, Montalvo, & Abelsohn, 1986). They may be asked if a parent is dating, how much food is in the pantry, and whether the home is clean or dirty. Alternately, a parent may relate to a child or adolescent as a weapon. For example, to hurt her ex-husband, a mother will cancel a visit, even if the youngster wants it (Brown, 1989). In extreme cases, a child becomes a pawn in a custody battle, but these are very rare (Guttmann, 1993), occurring in only approximately 5% of divorces in the United States (Johnson, 1993).

Generally, parents who use children as spies or weapons are so consumed with raw feelings toward the former spouse that they do not realize they are upsetting their youngsters. But, if a daughter or son is overtly or tacitly asked to spy, or take sides in a battle, the child feels constantly guilty or disloyal for loving the "enemy" partner. Additionally, when youngsters sense that they matter only as information sources or weapons rather than as persons, self-esteem suffers, compounding the feelings of disloyalty or guilt. Although adolescents may feel free to disregard parental directives (either overtly or covertly), younger children are more likely to feel they must do as they are told. Consequently, the possibilities for psychological damage are greater in this age group.

Interestingly, divorced parents with joint residential custody have only slightly less conflict than other divorced parents (Maccoby et al., 1990), so the dual residence situation, with its frequent comings and goings, magnifies the opportunities for use of offspring as spies or weapons. Likewise, the possibility for psychological damage to exploited youngsters is magnified too.

Identifying and Correcting the Pattern.

Use of children and adolescents as tools in adult conflict can be blatant or subtle. For example, although a custodial mother may not volunteer that she withholds visits, the information is not hard to elicit. On the other hand, reminders to notice what kind of car Mommy's boyfriend has are more elusive; embarrassment will cause many parents to omit reference to instructions to spy even when the therapist asks specific questions. To further obfuscate matters, instructions to spy, unlike the sexualized parent-child bond, cannot be readily sensed via therapist observations of nonverbal in-session cues. Although specific questions to individual adults sometimes elicit information about this kind of exploitation of children and adolescents, questions asked in family sessions are generally more fruitful, as children and adolescents are more likely than adults to ''spill the beans.''

Consider Elena, a 30-year-old Hispanic woman, who began treatment because of the withdrawal and depression of her 6-year-old daughter, Maria. About 18 months before, Elena had left her ex-husband, Jorge, because of his possessiveness and jealousy. Although Jorge refused contact with the social worker, he did provide child support, and adhered religiously to a court-ordered visitation schedule.

In Elena's presence, the therapist talked to Maria about her visits to her father. As is frequently necessary when treating children, both Elena and the therapist explained that Maria would not get in trouble for what she said in session. Finally, the therapist asked Maria what Mommy talked about when she got Maria ready for her visits to Jorge. Maria revealed that Elena wanted her to find out about Jorge's relationship with a woman he had begun dating. ''Mommy asks me if Daddy smooches her, and Mommy asks me if she sleeps over,'' Maria said, with visible constriction and discomfort. Elena hung her head.

Verbalizing the feelings evoked by Elena's directions was clearly beyond the capacity of a 6-year-old. So, relying on Wallerstein's divorce monologue (Kelly & Wallerstein, 1977), the therapist told Maria that kids usually feel ''yukky'' when grownups ask questions like that. She also said that it was not fair that the visits were not fun for Maria. So as not to interfere with the stability of Maria's world, the therapist was careful to also say that Mommy loved Maria, and had brought her to therapy to make things better.

Equally important, in individual sessions, the therapist helped Elena bring out her remaining feelings of attachment to Jorge. Although Elena had left Jorge because he was so possessive, she missed his attention, and was unready for his new romantic relationship. Once Elena was aware of her lingering ties, she could contain them, and focus more on giving Maria an enjoyable visitation experience.

Throughout, the therapist worked hard to control occasional angry impulses toward Elena, and to remain warmly related to her. The therapist's recognition of instances where she herself had been blinded to the needs of loved ones by strong emotions was instrumental in this process. In this case, as with all of the identified single-parent household dysfunctional interactional patterns, a major emphasis was restructuring of the family system via individual and family sessions, so that the capacity for a warm, loving parent-child relationship could be maximized.

INTERVENING WITH SEPARATED SPOUSES

The level of conflict between separated spouses is a powerful determinant of offspring response to the divorce experience (Simons et al., 1994); the less conflict, the easier it is for children, adolescents, and young adults (Amato, 1993; Donnelly & Finkelhor, 1992; Peck & Manocherian, 1989). In other words, it is the ongoing give-and-take between separated spouses, rather than the technical form of custody (e.g., sole maternal, sole paternal, joint, residential), that matters most (Maccoby & Mnookin, 1992). So, the therapist during the divorce transition often helps the ex-spouses develop a new coparental relationship (Maccoby & Mnookin, 1992). Sometimes this happens through conjoint sessions. Other times, the therapist reaches out through an ex-spouse in treatment to an originally untreated ex-spouse, so that person can receive separate treatment around parenting issues. Other times, both conjoint and individual treatment are used. Whatever the form of treatment, ex-spouses learn, ideally, to separate their adult and parental roles; they learn to prevent emotions such as grief, anger, and attachment from influencing a relationship between ex-spouses that, at best, is cooperative and businesslike (Ahrons & Rodgers, 1987; Greif & DeMaris, 1990; Maccoby & Mnookin, 1992; Peck & Manocherian, 1989).

The benefits of increased coparental cooperation may be most far-reaching for young children. This is because the contacts of young children with nonresidential parents are completely orchestrated by parents, while adolescents and young adults can exercise some independence in planning and carrying out phone calls, visits, and other contacts.

Limited Goals: An Ongoing Issue

Just as therapists who work with solo custodial parents have limited goals regarding improved strength and energy for their overburdened clients, therapists who work with recently separated spouses have limited goals too. Although a cooperative, businesslike relationship is the best possible outcome (Maccoby & Mnookin, 1992), there are two reasons it is rarely achieved totally. First, during the divorce transition, the therapist meeting with a recently separated couple sometimes encounters a minefield of emotion, with ex-spouses vacillating wildly in their feelings toward each other (Tschann et al., 1989). Some of these feelings can be resolved or controlled only gradually, and they often influence the coparental relationship during the first postdivorce years. In some cases, for example, pain is so close to the surface that people have trouble with telephone communication, and/or are literally unable to sit in the same room with each other. In these cases, parallel, rather than cooperative parenting (Furstenberg & Cherlin, 1991; Maccoby & Mnookin, 1992) is the best possible outcome. In parallel parenting, as noted in chapter 1, each parent does what he or she thinks is best for offspring, but communication is minimal and the child's experience is necessarily disjointed.

Second, many divorced fathers, over time, become less available with regard to visitation, financial support, and other forms of support, such as health insurance and school event attendance (Bray & Depner, 1993; Teachman & Paasch, 1993). During the divorce transition, therapists generally aim to prevent this decline in paternal involvement. But sometimes they cannot, and the options of cooperative and parallel coparenting wane. In such situations, therapists who operate on the premise that paternal involvement is desirable but not necessary will be flexible, and convey therapeutic optimism about the possibilities for children's growth in a mother-only home.

Introducing the Topic of Dual Treatment Involvement

As we have seen, spouses who have recently separated physically are generally not yet separated emotionally. Consequently, the therapist often encounters reluctance when attempting coordinated clinical work around parenting during the divorce transition.

Introducing Custodial Mothers to Treatment Involvement for Nonresidential Fathers.

As the vast majority of children live exclusively with their mothers in the postdivorce period (Guttmann, 1993), the therapist most often suggests treatment involvement for both separated spouses to a custodial mother. Typically, the custodial mother expresses the wish to keep her ex-husband away from sessions, often by telling the therapist, "He won't come," or "It won't do any good." Fearing their clients will leave treatment if the issue is pursued, new therapists sometimes back down when confronted with such comments. However, experienced therapists realize that usually, the client's dependence on the therapist underlies the resistance to involving the ex-husband. The client does not want to share the therapist with another adult, particularly her ex-husband; she may experience the primitive desire to be favorite, and wonder whom the therapist will like better. Additionally, she wonders what her ex-husband will say about her, and whom the therapist will believe.

Only the most sophisticated clients will tolerate a thorough discussion of these dependence issues. With less sophisticated clients, the therapist reassures the client that introduction of the ex-husband into the treatment does not curtail her opportunity for confidential sessions, and explains that maximum benefit to children flows from maximum involvement of both parents. In essence, the therapist presents herself as a firm, caring parent who refuses to have a favorite child. To counter fears of the ex-husband's criticism, the therapist clarifies that she knows how recently separated ex-spouses can exaggerate or distort, and also that she is here to help, not judge.

Other resistances to the ex-husband's treatment involvement are less primitive, and pertain to the marriage itself. Sometimes, a woman is repulsed by the thought that she was ever involved with "someone like that," and wants to eliminate her ex-husband from her life and that of her children (Bogolub, 1984). This is particularly likely if an ex-husband had problems such as substance abuse or criminal justice involvement. In these cases, a custodial mother needs help in thinking about what is best for her children; if the husband expresses interest in the children, it is not fair to deprive them, either of his presence, or of the benefit that may accrue from sessions involving separated spouses. The mother also needs to discuss how it will become easier to relate to her ex-husband as a coparent over time, as feelings of emotional separation from him strengthen (Bogolub, 1984).

On the other hand, it is not necessary to work through the resistance of custodial mothers formerly married to violent or sexually abusive men. If these women do not want to see their ex-husbands in treatment or elsewhere, their wishes should be respected. Assuming legal recognition of the man's pathology, his visits with children will be either prohibited or court-supervised. If there are no visits, there would be no need for coparental contact. Even if visits are court-supervised, the need for coparental contact is eliminated, because the parents do not make their own arrangements for contact with youngsters. All in all, there would be no need for such a woman to encounter her ex-husband in a treatment session (Garber, 1994).

In fact, in these situations, the therapist may have to help the woman keep the ex-husband out of her life. When domestic violence precedes marital rupture, it often follows it as well; the tendency of abusive men to react wildly to abandonment is well-known (Johnston & Campbell, 1993). In these cases, if unwanted intrusions occur, women must be helped to seek orders of protection (see chapter 4). They must also be helped to make phone calls requesting that police arrest violent ex-husbands who violate court orders, or threaten ex-wives' safety or welfare.

How to Involve Nonresidential Fathers in Treatment.

My clinical experience suggests that once the custodial mother understands the merit of paternal treatment involvement, she should be given the option of contacting the ex-husband herself, and inviting him to a session. This enables her to exert control over the process, if this matters to her. The therapist must go over what the client might say ("The therapist thinks fathers are very important," rather than "The therapist thinks you don't do enough for Johnny"). If necessary, the therapist also goes over how the client might make the initial disclosure of treatment involvement. Ideally, the fee for the initial contact with the father should be waived, in that he has not sought help.

Alternately, the therapist contacts the father directly; the phone call must be made at a time when the father can speak privately, even if this is inconvenient for the therapist. A therapist will make the call if the mother does not want to broach the subject, or if the mother tries and "fails" to get the father in. Sometimes the mother will go through the motions of asking, and triumphantly present the therapist with "He won't come in. I *told* you, it's hopeless." In this case, the therapist should tell the client something like, "You know, it really is better for the kids if I meet with him. Perhaps I'd better get in touch with him." If the mother balks, the therapist can either accept the mother's stance, or she can continue to address resistance. Eventually, if necessary, she can rely on professional authority, and refuse to continue treatment without an attempt to involve the father. However, a gentle but firm insistence stressing the benefit to youngsters often cuts through the client's refusal.

When the therapist reaches out to the nonresidential father, she must be careful not to collude with the mother's view of "father as villain" (Kruk, 1994). Many reasons underlie the seemingly callous behavior of fathers who do not visit, call, or make support payments. For instance, to handle the pain of separation from offspring, with all its strangeness and loneliness (Mitchell-Flynn & Hutchinson, 1993), some divorced fathers plunge themselves into work, and distance themselves from human beings (Kaslow & Schwartz, 1987; Riessman, 1990). Because of gender role stereotyping, others underestimate their importance to children (Myers, 1989; Peck & Manocherian, 1989), or do not know how to relate to children if they do not share parenting with wives (Furstenberg & Cherlin, 1991). Still others may be afraid of their potential for violence (Isaacs et al., 1986). Some are pressured by new partners who resent financial and emotional claims of children from a prior relationship (Kaslow & Schwartz, 1987). Black fathers sometimes absent themselves if extensive extended family input gives them the erroneous idea that their involvement is superfluous (Del Carmen & Virgo, 1993).

Awareness of the many reasons underlying "deadbeat" behavior makes it easier for therapists to demonstrate empathy and patience, both of which are required when seemingly uninterested men test the therapist's concern with hostility, monosyllabic communication, and other forms of resistance. During telephone contact, these fathers may require sustained outreach as well as diffusion of issues around support arrears, which should be addressed only in person. With Hispanic men (or others who have a background stressing the traditional male role), it is sometimes helpful to inject an appeal to *machismo* via comments like "You were the head of the family, and your views would really help me understand your children."

Much less frequently, the therapist encounters a father who "plays Santa Claus," showering his children with gifts and costly outings during visits. In this case, he may be competing with his wife to be the children's favorite (Myers, 1989), compensating for his guilt over leaving, or seeking peer companionship from a son or daughter (Asmussen & Larson, 1991). It is considerably easier to enlist these men as clients, as they often welcome one more opportunity to show how much they love their children.

Between obtaining mothers' cooperation and reaching out to fathers, involving noncustodial fathers in treatment during the divorce transition is very hard work. Given the amount of work, and the abundance of material generally presented by the custodial household, it is sometimes tempting to simply skip the whole process. Another inhibiting variable is therapist pessimism about growth potential for fathers who were not very involved with their children before the divorce. This pessimism, however, is not warranted; empirical research has repeatedly demonstrated that there is no correlation between paternal behavior predivorce, and paternal behavior postdivorce (Bray & Berger, 1993; Kruk, 1994). Overall, significant opportunities for intervention are lost if the effort to involve divorced fathers in treatment is not made.

Custodial Fathers and Noncustodial Mothers.

Much less frequently, the therapist will attempt to arrange treatment for custodial fathers and noncustodial mothers. Custodial fathers generally do not want communication with their ex-wives (Maccoby et al., 1990). However, contrary to popular stereotypes, noncustodial mothers are as a rule neither unfit nor self-centered (Depner, 1993). Often, they are simply the less affluent spouse (West & Kissman, 1991). Since custodial father/noncustodial mother couples are almost as likely to experience conflict as other separated spouses (Maccoby et al., 1990), the therapist must find ways to engage them.

Custodial fathers, who are generally successful in their new roles and comfortable financially (Greif & DeMaris, 1990), must be helped to see that they cannot "do it all alone." While their accomplishments must be supported, their veneer of independence must be challenged (Kruk, 1994). These men need to see that the noncustodial mother is important, too, and that the child benefits from a coordinated effort by both parents.

In contrast to the noncustodial father, it appears that the noncustodial mother may not be hard to involve, once the ex-spouse is willing to proceed. Compared to their male counterparts, noncustodial mothers are less likely to be under child support orders (Depner, 1993), and thus less likely to be in arrears, so they have less to be defensive about. In addition, noncustodial mothers are frequently objects of prejudice as "unnatural" mothers (Greif, 1987). The burden of this stigma, combined with the relative ease with which women seek therapy after divorce (Cohen & Lowenberg, 1994), may cause noncustodial mothers to respond readily to therapist outreach. In fact, the therapist must guard against any unacknowledged prejudice of her own (Greif, 1987) that might create a subtly critical, nontherapeutic response to a "mother who walks out on her own children."

WORKING WITH SEPARATED SPOUSES ON ADULT ISSUES

Once both parents are available as clients, the therapist helps them prevent the adult issues of the divorce transition from interfering with effective parenting, insofar as possible. Among these adult issues, some of the most common are (a) emotional ties between former spouses (b) one parent's self-absorption, and (c) one parent's disengagement from the parental role.

Working with Emotional Ties

Attachment.

Sometimes, separated spouses remain emotionally attached, as when a mother lingers while delivering her daughter to her ex-husband's for a visit, and then accepts his invitation to stay for lunch. Such behavior confuses children regarding the finality of marital separation, and makes them anxious. The therapist's task is to help the clients examine their attachment, which is sometimes based on a true ambivalence about ending the marriage, and other times simply on a fear about moving on socially as a newly independent adult. The therapist also highlights the effect of the parents' attachment behavior on their children.

The case of a separated couple seen in a family agency illustrates the therapeutic handling of attachment. The first few sessions were held with the custodial mother, or the custodial mother and the children. Then, because the therapist detected hints of extended contact between the separated spouses, she requested a conjoint session for them. Because she wanted to avoid the stimulation of reconciliation fantasies, the children were not invited. Although the mother had attended prior sessions in casual attire, at the meeting with her ex-husband, she arrived fashionably dressed and carefully made up, while he wore a suit! The ex-husband was relatively open and verbal, so it was possible to proceed quickly to interpretation of their nonverbal (viz., clothing) cues.

Rather poignantly, both adults acknowledged that the unexplored wish for a new partner, rather than a personal bond to each other, was motivating their sexualized presentation in session. Both adults revealed their fears about reaching out socially. With some help from the therapist, they were also able to see how they confused their children by sometimes "acting married." Since prolonged conjoint treatment would have only encouraged counterproductive relating as a couple, this portion of the treatment was kept purposefully brief. Because both parties wanted continued help, the man was given his own therapist. Conjoint sessions coordinated by both therapists were held only occasionally, for child-focussed issues (e.g., planning an approach to a graduation both former spouses had to attend)—not to provide the adults with a social outlet.

Anger.

At the other extreme, anger links former spouses. For example, the fury of those who have been rejected, or the exasperation of initiators who feel pursued may be acted out. Thus, an ex-wife may withhold visits with children from an ex-husband who delays support checks. He, in turn, delays checks because he is convinced his ex-wife would spend the money on herself, not the children. The psychological cost to children who are used in parental battles (feelings of disloyalty and guilt, and diminished self-esteem) has been identified earlier in this chapter.

In such cases, conjoint sessions can be used to help former spouses replace blaming with introspection. Ideally, each adult takes some responsibility for nursing a desire to punish the other. Ongoing tit-for-tat punishment may then give way, at least partially, to a decrease or encapsulation of anger, and an increase in mature behavior oriented to child well-being.

In other cases, only one adult is carrying on protracted hostile behavior. For example, an ex-husband refuses to provide his 18-year-old son with the college tuition he had always promised. Although the ex-wife does not interfere with visits, the son is anxious because of the tension he senses between his parents—as well as anger about the broken promise. In such cases, conjoint (or family) sessions may penetrate the denial of the hostile ex-spouse; when that person's behavior diminishes or ceases, tension is reduced and a less warlike environment for children or adolescents is created.

If necessary, complementary individual sessions are used, too. For example, with regard to withheld college tuition, the therapist can certainly present the impact on offspring of withholding behavior in a more rational manner than an outraged woman or young adult. In such cases, the man's experience and point of view must be considered; he should be treated as a client, not a criminal. Nonetheless, the need to form a relationship with a client should not be used as an excuse to avoid the issue of responsibility (Myers, 1989).

Sometimes, hostile behavior between separated spouses during the divorce transition takes place around relatively minor issues, and includes activity such as arriving late for visits, or undermining the other parent's discipline (Maccoby et al., 1990). In these cases, the issue is often not real anger, but rather hanging onto the relationship by bothering a former spouse. In conjoint sessions, a skilled therapist can work her way through the nuisance behavior to previously described attachment issues: the need for human contact, and the fear of starting anew.

Working with Self-Absorption and Lack of Cooperation

Sometimes, a parent is very caught up in creating a "new life" during the divorce transition. For example, an adult seeks postdivorce fulfillment through a new career, or a personal interest requiring a major time commitment. In such cases, a legitimate desire for a changed life is not the problem. Rather, the problems are (a) parental self-absorption and (b) an accompanying lack of cooperation between former spouses that is very destructive for children. Generally, the therapist respects the new commitment, while simultaneously drawing attention to coparental responsibilities. A related treatment topic (which affects separated couples struggling with a variety of divorce transition adult issues) is the need to establish norms for the separated couple's ongoing interaction (Germain, 1991); unless such norms are explicitly developed, even the most well-meaning parents may have trouble creating a unified, relatively non-contradictory environment for their children.

The Impact of Ethnicity.

An interesting variation of this pattern occurs when a parent who desires a change of lifestyle rejects or partially rejects her or his ethnic heritage. For example, a divorced Hispanic woman begins a career in computer programming. She incurs the wrath of her ex-husband, who accepts the need for her employment, but views her new-found professional orientation negatively; rather than subject herself to his overt and covert criticism, she curtails contact with him. As a result, the coparental relationship becomes strained.

Or, consider Arthur, an Orthodox Jewish man who left his wife, Nadine, and, within a year, married a woman who was not Jewish. In a pattern common in stepfamilies involving one Jewish member (Friedman, 1994), Arthur gave up compliance with Jewish laws for daily living. For example, in his new home, he served food that was not *kosher* (i.e., not acceptable according to Jewish law), and stopped complying with Sabbath proscriptions.

Arthur and Nadine had joint residential custody of their 10-year-old son Joey. When Joey was at his father's, he was served food that was not *kosher*, and asked to perform tasks forbidden on the Sabbath, such as writing. Arthur genuinely loved Joey, and paid support regularly. However, Arthur ignored Joey's conflicts related to religious practice. Returning to his mother's, Joey told her he felt like a criminal for breaking the law at his father's.

When Nadine sought professional help, Mark, the therapist worked hard to engage Arthur. After two individual sessions, during which Mark listened nonjudgmentally to Arthur describe his transition to a new, less religiously observant lifestyle, Mark arranged a series of conjoint meetings for Arthur and Nadine, to penetrate Arthur's self-absorption, and help Arthur and Nadine consider the totality of Joey's experience in two different households. In this case as in others, joint residential custody proved to be no guarantee against dysfunctional parallel parenting.

Mark realized it would be a serious clinical error to characterize Nadine as the sensitive parent and a model for her insensitive coparent, Arthur. Mark also realized it was important not to be swayed by prevailing ideas of political correctness, and not to establish a value-laden dichotomy between culturally aware and assimilationist identities. Rather, because his task was to promote cooperation, Mark supported the strengths of both parents. Arthur's strengths included his genuine interest in joint residential custody, and his responsible child support payment behavior. Then, Mark had Nadine explain what Joey told her about the time he spent at Arthur's. Once Arthur grasped his son's pain, Mark had Nadine and Arthur problem-solve around how to diminish it. Without much resistance, Arthur decided to provide Joey with *kosher* food, and to stop asking him to perform forbidden activities on the Sabbath.

With Nadine and Arthur, as well as with other divorced couples, Mark also worked to help the couple establish *norms* in the coparental relationship, for example, alternate adult attendance at events such as open school week, and phone conversations about Joey on Sunday night. Such norms would encourage the separated couple to solve any subsequent conflicts without a therapist. Mark knew that, like other couples, Nadine and Arthur would need such norms for an extended period, as events such as medical emergencies and graduations would require their combined efforts for years to come.

Working with Disengagement from the Parental Role

We have seen that during the divorce transition, some noncustodial parents, most typically fathers, become less and less involved with their offspring, both financially and emotionally (Ahlburg & DeVita, 1992; Booth & Amato, 1994; Furstenberg & Cherlin, 1991). Debates in the empirical literature center on how extensive the postdivorce decline in father-child contact is (Bray & Depner, 1993) and how long it takes to occur (Bray & Berger, 1993), not on whether or not it exists. We have also seen that although the "deadbeat Dad" looks culpable from a non-clinical point of view, care and concern sometimes exist beneath his seemingly callous veneer.

How can a therapist help in such a situation? As a first step, she must introspect about her own possible hostility towards absent or irresponsible fathers. Unless a therapist believes there may be a viable parent hidden beneath a man's display of irresponsibility or apathy, any further clinical contact with him is wasted. Remembering the male tendency to act out rather than talk out emotions can aid the therapist in bypassing personal anger, as can concentrating on the previously noted dynamics that constrict paternal involvement (e.g., avoidance of emotional upset over separation from sons and daughters, ignorance of parenting skills, minimization of one's own importance to offspring).

Generally, a seemingly uncaring father expects the therapist to chastise him. Therefore, in the early sessions with disengaged fathers, the therapist should avoid examining the effect of the father's behavior on others. Rather, the therapist initially concentrates on eliciting the father's own divorce transition parenting experience, which generally encompasses loss of control (Umberson & Williams, 1993), pain, and diminished status; the issue of diminished status during the divorce transition is particularly salient for Hispanic men, who generally assume an authoritative or *macho* role in their families of procreation (Del Carmen & Virgo, 1993). Comments such as these are typical:

"The whole idea of seeing someone I love according to a schedule the court is in charge of makes me sick. It's like I'm being bossed around with my own kids."

"How can you *visit* with someone you should be living with? Aunts and uncles are supposed to visit, not fathers."

Once the father feels understood rather than chastised, the therapist helps the father see that while he may feel like a cipher, he still matters greatly to his children. Building the client's self-esteem, the therapist conveys that a disengaged father can move beyond depressed, erratic behavior, and think assertively about his effect on his offspring. Typical inquiries would include "What do you think it's like for Johnny when you skip a visit?" and "What do you want Johnny to remember about your visits?"

A vivid example of the difficulty disengaged fathers sometimes have in noticing their impact on offspring concerns money; these fathers sometimes think children and adolescents are not aware when they do not provide financially. However, youngsters as young as 6 or 7 are acutely aware of a difference between the two households in standard of living, and of a mother's anger toward a father who has less financial strain than she, and yet does not fulfill his obligations.

As previously noted, the therapist should not be afraid to raise the issue of missed child support payments, or re-raise it if the father proves evasive (Myers, 1989). If the father fears the therapist will discuss his payment behavior with government authorities, the therapist may have to reassure the father about confidentiality. Clearly, the therapist should also provide empathy about any difficulties the father has in maintaining payments, and help him budget when necessary. All this emotional support, though, is a means to an end: helping the man understand his obligations, and that children do notice when he doesn't pay.

Sometimes a therapist feels that she will lose her client if she talks about support arrears. In this case, she might. But an experienced therapist will realize that it is better to lose a client who is not ready to face facts, than to placate him, and collude with his denial. Sometimes, though, a client respects the therapist for not letting him evade her, and appreciates her belief in him as a person who can do better.

After he has ventilated about his parenting experience during the divorce transition, bolstered his self-esteem as a parent, and raised awareness of his impact on his children, a disengaged father may be ready to move to a more related stance with ex-wife and children, both inside and outside of treatment. At this time, conjoint sessions with the ex-wife may address issues of avoidance of grudge holding, and elimination of the alignments an angry ex-wife sometimes forms with her offspring against their father (Johnston, 1993). Also important in conjoint work are the development of norms for future parental participation, discussed above.

When sons or daughters have been reluctant to have anything to do with the father, either because of his ex-wife's brainwashing or because of his own behavior, conjoint sessions for father and youngsters may help. Other times, a particularly angry youngster may refuse such a session, or more frequent contact with a previously disengaged father. Such refusal is most likely among adolescents and young adults, whose pull to independence sometimes engenders a denial of the need for parents. When rejected in this way, the father must learn that although he may be very hurt that his desire to ''change things'' has been ignored, he cannot force a son or daughter to draw closer. Rather, patience and gentle offers of contact are in order (Johnston, 1993).

INTERVENING WITH EXTENDED FAMILY
AND THE BROADER COMMUNITY

As noted, members of the extended family (including but not limited to grandparents) can provide much-needed support to adults and children who have recently experienced marital disruption. So can resources in the broader community (e.g., churches, synagogues, schools, lawyers, and the courts). During the divorce transition, work with extended family and community resources often complements the work conducted with the single parent, the children, and the separated couple.

The Complexities of Intergenerational Helping

Although early (and male) writers in the field of divorce (e.g., Dell & Applebaum, 1977; Gardner, 1976) often portrayed three-generational living as destructive to a divorced mother's independence, recent thinking is less critical of this arrangement. Respect is given to longstanding Black and Hispanic traditions of three- and even four-generational cooperation (Chillman, 1993; Fulmer, 1989; Minkler et al., 1994); currently, 12% of Black children and 5.8% of Hispanic children, as compared to 3.6% of White children, reside with their grandparents (Minkler et al., 1994). Respect is also given to 1990s financial realities that often pose extended family households as the only postdivorce alternative to public assistance.

Postdivorce intergenerational helping is complex. Awareness of what grandparents and other kin provide (emotional support to adults and offspring, financial support, child care, and household assistance) must be accompanied by awareness of the emotional fallout of multigenerational living. First, grandparents who help often experience stress. Helping offspring and grandchildren is emotionally satisfying, but it also may tire a grandparent, make it hard for her to carry out employment responsibilities, or restrict her freedom (Jendrek, 1993; Timberlake & Chipungu, 1992). Second, longstanding child-parent conflicts between the adult generations may persist during intergenerational helping (Spitze et al., 1994), sometimes sending children of divorce overtly or covertly into the fray (Whitbeck, Hoyt, & Huck, 1993). Third, the original criticism that increased dependence results in regression or frustration for the custodial parent, while not the sine qua non of intergenerational helping postdivorce, is relevant in some cases.

Ethnicity and Intergenerational Helping

Ethnicity also influences intergenerational helping. Del Carmen and Virgo (1993) present research indicating that compared with Black and Hispanic families, non-minority (i.e., White) families in which grandparents assist postdivorce experience more conflict and more harmful psychological effects for grandchildren. In fact, the studies by Spitze et al. (1994) and Whitbeck et al. (1993) describing postdivorce intergenerational conflict and its negative effects for children are based on samples composed largely of White people that are not influenced by longstanding norms of three-generational living. Although Del Carmen and Virgo do not specifically refer to Soviet Jewish families, it is reasonable to expect that the experience of these families resembles the less conflictual experience of Black and Hispanic families, due to the norm of three-generational living and cooperation (Belozersky, 1990) shared with these groups.

Still, three-generational Black, Hispanic, and Soviet Jewish families are susceptible to the grandparental overload mentioned earlier. And, although they may have comparatively few longstanding intergenerational problems, they are susceptible to particular forms of intergenerational conflict, some of which are divorce specific. For example, in Black families, after a young divorced mother has occupied a sibling role vis-à-vis her own child, and has relied on her mother (the child's grandmother) to parent two generations, the young mother eventually matures, and wants to reclaim her children. At that time, competition may exist between mother and grandmother over who the real parent is (Boyd-Franklin, 1989). In such cases, role flexibility, a strength of Black families, is overshadowed by conflict (Boyd-Franklin, 1989).

In Hispanic families, as previously mentioned, tensions sometimes arise when grandmothers and sisters provide culturally mandated practical help to custodial mothers, at the same time criticizing the divorce from a Roman Catholic perspective. Because of the traditional Hispanic male/female role structure (McGoldrick et al., 1991), family members may also criticize the custodial mother's employment.

In Soviet Jewish families, recently emigrated grandparents frequently become depressed. In contrast to Hispanic families, where divorced women often migrate alone, even enduring separations from children (Chillman, 1993), Soviet Jewish families may be forced by the government to emigrate together (Castex, 1992). Sometimes, grandparents who did not wish to move experience the loss of a whole way of life, and anticipate little future happiness after relocation (Castex, 1992). Their depression can intensify upon a divorce in the middle generation, and reverberate throughout an entire three-generational family. Generally, although grandparents and other relatives in many ethnic groups provide much-needed assistance to divorce transition parents and children, the three-generational family experiences various complications, which sometimes respond to professional intervention.

Working with Extended Family

Beginnings.

During the divorce transition, it is custodial parents who usually apply for mental health help. Sometimes, particularly when the family is of an ethnicity where three-generational involvement is accepted, the custodial parent is open about the involvement of grandparents or other relatives in family life. However, we should not assume openness about all extended family involvement in Black, Hispanic, or Soviet Jewish families. Secrecy may mask the participation of a particular person or group—for example, an absent father involved in a Black family (Boyd-Franklin, 1989; McGoldrick et al., 1991). In White families guided by norms of independence rather than interdependence for adults (Bogolub, 1989), the original client sometimes downplays the role of extended family, even in cases of coresidence.

With clients of any ethnicity, three-generational data may pertain not just to the topic of help extended, but alternately to the topic of help denied. For example, shame about an adult child's divorce sometimes engenders grandparental avoidance, and a temporary inability to give expression to the desire to help grandchildren. With clients of any ethnicity, as soon as possible after a trusting relationship has been established, the therapist must elicit information about extended family whose divorce transition involvement or rejection is suspected.

Although specific skills such as use of genograms, and asking of open-ended questions like "Who else lives in the house?" and "Who else helps you out?" (Boyd-Franklin, 1989) are important, the therapist's attitude is a more important variable in eliciting extended family data. To develop relevant hunches and ask the right questions, the therapist must be free of a two-parent nuclear family bias, and operate from a three- or even four-generational perspective (Bogolub, 1989).

Once the relevance of extended family in a particular case is established, the therapist works to involve them just as she works to involve the nonresidential parent. In both situations, in order to convey a serious message, the therapist must believe that the presence of additional clients is necessary, not optional. To obtain the participation of grandparents or other relatives, the therapist uses techniques described with reference to noncustodial fathers. That is, when necessary, she explores resistance of the original client to treatment participation of another adult. Here, when the new client is a grandparent (in most cases, the mother of a custodial mother) rather than an ex-spouse, resistance tends to center on fear of exposure of the bond between adult child and grandparent. The therapist also collaborates with the original patient on outreach to extended family, and, if necessary, makes personal phone contact to invite the participation of grandparent or other relative.

Three-Generational Involvement.

Once the cast is assembled, the emphasis parallels that used in work with single parents and work with separated spouses. That is, the therapist helps to delineate responsibilities, strengthen boundaries, clarify the lines of family authority, and improve communication. As with separated spouses, the therapist may also work to reduce adult conflicts, and prevent them from contaminating the experience of children and adolescents. If necessary, to fill gaps in the support network, the therapist reaches out to additional family members as treatment progresses. Although some individual sessions (e.g., for beleaguered grandmothers who need to ventilate about their burdens) may be in order, the major emphasis is on structural family sessions that are focussed in the here-and-now and goal oriented (McGoldrick et al., 1991). Discussion frequently centers on the concrete realignment of dysfunctional relationships. Throughout, the therapist must tune in to issues that cross ethnic lines (e.g., overloaded grandparents), as well as those that tend to appear in particular ethnic groups (e.g., availability of godparents and other *compadrazgo* members as resources for Hispanic families).

Working with Community Resources

To further decrease gaps in the support network, the therapist may help the family reach out to or improve connections with community resources (e.g., churches, synagogues, schools, day-care centers, lawyers, and the courts). These connections range from reasonably straightforward (e.g., resuming lapsed attendance at a church) to complex (e.g., working with an attorney to alter a visitation or child support agreement). The more complex the situation, the more detailed the therapist's discussion with the client. If clients do not speak English, or lack skills for negotiating the environment, the therapist may have to share the actual work of accessing these resources, as discussed in detail in chapter 4.

Additionally, the therapist's professional views are sometimes needed by other professionals involved in her clients' lives. Although the work of an expert witness in a child custody case is the most vivid example here, such testimony is relatively rare. A more common, and no less important (though less dramatic) example is the sharing of a professional assessment with a teacher at a loss as to how to handle a troubled child during the divorce transition.

Whether the therapist is helping clients connect with community resources, or collaborating with other professionals, a crucial variable is her attitude about assistance provided outside of the therapy session, such as travelling to meetings and making phone calls. If the client senses the therapist views these tasks as ancillary—or worse, as a nuisance— the client may conclude that her practical concerns are not significant. When a client's self-esteem is fragile, the feeling of insignificance may extend to herself as a total person; weakened treatment involvement or even premature termination ("I'm not important. What's the point of all this anyway?") may result.

Case Example: Reluctance About Extended Family Counselling

Helen C., a 37-year-old White custodial mother with two children, Paul, age 8, and Lisa, age 3, sought family agency help a year after Helen's ex-husband Art moved out. When the separation occurred, Helen began working full-time as a bookkeeper. Helen's mother, age 67, and father, age 70, both retired, moved in to assist her with the children. At that time, Paul began to exhibit classroom problems of "babyish" behavior and inability to concentrate on in-class assignments. The persistence of these problems caused his school to refer the mother-headed family for professional help.

Regarding Art's involvement, Helen cooperated readily. Couple and father-children sessions revealed no contradiction of the initial presentation of Art as a responsible noncustodial father. However, Helen balked at the idea of involving her parents. She wondered what they had to do with Paul's behavior, and was vague when describing their ways with him.

Aware of the importance of the three-generational perspective, the therapist, named Barbara, persisted. Barbara was able to obtain Helen's acknowledgement that "My mother has always been dominating." This acknowledgement freed Helen to envision and eventually try three-generational sessions. And, Helen trusted Barbara enough to accept her comment that "We've looked at Paul's situation from all angles except that of your parents' involvement, and we haven't gotten to the bottom of his school troubles yet.''

During the first family session involving Helen, her parents, Paul, and Lisa, each child sat on a grandparent's lap, with Helen some distance away. The nonverbal message that Paul was babied while his mother was becoming a marginal person in the family was substantiated by grandparental disclosures. Paul and Lisa were both treated as 3-year-olds after school; Helen's requests that her parents get Paul started on his homework were ignored. Barbara concluded that while the grandparents provided valuable household assistance, they were also infantilizing Paul, and involving him in the power struggle over ''Who is the boss?'' that was occurring between Helen and her parents.

The treatment flowing from this three-generational assessment was straightforward. In a brief series of couple sessions, Helen's parents gained perspective on their resentment of the divorce which they felt ''cheated us out of our retirement''; they decided that ''We didn't have to move in, but we really wanted to.'' Most sessions focused on Helen and her parents. While supportive of all three adults, Barbara identified a pattern of constant grandparent-parent power struggles, which was acknowledged. Then, Barbara helped Helen and her parents get past this pattern to the underlying question of authority. Her parents were able to say that they had gotten carried away with their new responsibilities, and that ''Helen really should make the rules.'' Barbara did not emphasize longstanding conflict between Helen and her parents or Paul's reaction to this. Rather, she emphasized the divorce transition as a time of change, and encouraged concrete planning for the care of Paul and Lisa, with a stress on household hierarchy and division of childrearing labor.

Contacting the School.

When Paul experienced more age-appropriate demands from his grandparents, and less confusion over who was in charge of the house, his report card indicated some decrease in immature behavior, and some improvement in ability to concentrate. However, it also stated there was still room for improvement in both areas. Barbara felt that Paul's teacher, Ms. Jones, should be sensitized to the recent changes in Paul's life. So, in an individual session, Barbara obtained permission for school contact from Helen—not the grandparents! Helen chose to tell Paul about this contact herself. Barbara helped Helen anticipate both Paul's probable appreciation of the school contact as a sign of caring, and his probable questions (e.g., ''Will Ms. Jones tell the other kids I have a counselor?'').

In a conference at the school, Barbara mentioned the divorce, Paul's grandparents, and Paul's infantilization at home, sharing as few details as possible. Although Ms. Jones knew about the divorce, she had not known about changes in family structure. Subsequently, Ms. Jones found it easier to be patient with Paul, and easier to keep asking for and praising age-appropriate behavior. Explicit discussion with Ms. Jones confirmed the confidentiality of Paul's treatment. While Paul's symptoms did not totally disappear, Ms. Jones' increased sensitivity facilitated further improvement in classroom behavior and ability to concentrate.

Case Example: Involving Black Extended Family and Community

Maxine J., the 32-year-old Black, divorced mother of George, age 12, and Becky, age 8, had resided with Maxine's 58-year-old widowed mother, Alice, since marital disruption occurred 3 years ago. Maxine and Alice were both registered nurses. When Maxine, George, and Becky came to live with Alice, Maxine was a mature woman, and she did not assume a sibling position vis-à-vis her own children. Although George and Becky were nurtured by both mother and grandmother, Maxine always maintained parental authority.

Maxine's ex-husband, Ed, had left town about a year after the separation, and soon lost contact with his family. For several months after his father disappeared, George lost interest in school, but soon resumed his usual high level of achievement. Overall, the divorce transition proceeded unusually smoothly. Then, George began to cut classes, and resist his mother's authority. At this point, Maxine sought family agency help.

"Three females and one male, and George is starting to grow up. No wonder he's acting out; he misses Ed" was the first thought of Sam, the therapist assigned to the case. Sam had worked in a clinic serving an ethnically varied population for some time, so he never assumed that the frequency of divorce among African Americans (Cherlin, 1992) made family disruption or father absence easier for any particular African American child.

Because the family was Black, and oriented toward doing, as opposed to feeling or talking (McGoldrick et al., 1991), Sam was careful to be straightforward about the purpose of sessions ("to figure out how to get George back on track"). Additionally, he was warm but not condescending (Boyd-Franklin, 1989; Gibbs, 1989). Since George initially hid emotions behind a "cool," nonverbal facade typical of Black males (A. J. Franklin, 1992), Sam proceeded slowly with George, without pressuring him to talk about his feelings (Gibbs, 1989). While Sam considered other possible trigger factors for George's behavior (e.g., peer models), Sam's initial hunch proved correct; George finally told Maxine in a family session that "you never even looked for Dad after he took off. You just let him go." Although Maxine froze briefly, she then said, "I never realized Dad was so important to you."

Again respectful of the African American orientation toward action (McGoldrick et al., 1991), Sam involved the family in a discussion of what could be done to find Ed. Alice suggested that Maxine contact Ed's parents, which she did. Although surprised to hear from her, they did not blame her for the marital demise, and did not receive her in a hostile manner. In fact, they expressed interest in renewed contact with George and Becky, although they did not know Ed's whereabouts. George maintained a tough facade, but he agreed to every get-together his paternal grandparents suggested. Sometimes, the paternal grandparents, George, and Becky spoke about missing Ed, and their hopes that he would reappear.

Sam sensed that this indirect connection to Ed helped, but he also sensed that George wanted a male adult with whom he could share experiences, and emulate. Sam was aware of the research indicating that the overall development of children such as George is not generally impaired by father absence (e.g., Furstenberg & Cherlin, 1991; Ihinger-Tallman et al., 1993; King, 1994; Maccoby & Mnookin, 1992), but, as a therapist, Sam was also interested in the alleviation of the pain at hand.

In a family session, he wondered if George might like to "hang out with guys and men more, since where you live, it's all females." George nodded. Maxine felt that if the whole family increased attendance at the church, George would have a chance to associate with more adult males. Sam was aware that the church in most Black communities is more than a house of worship, but also a source of organized activities and informal relationships (Boyd-Franklin, 1989; Ho, 1992), so Maxine's suggestion made sense to him. Informal associations with fathers of other boys developed in church; these did not replace Ed, but they helped. Equally important was Maxine's effort to give George the church experience; George's complaint to her in the early family session was not just about Ed's absence, but about his mother's inaction.

Overall, the introduction of the paternal grandparents and the church into George's support network made a difference. Sam did not feel it was necessary to obtain George's explicit verbal confirmation of the value of the increased warmth and nurturance in his life. Rather, Sam felt that the decline in behavior that he had read as a cry for attention was sufficient. Although George did not become a model youngster, his truancy decreased, and his cooperation at home increased, as a result of the interventions.

Part IV

HELPING CLIENTS POSTDIVORCE

Chapter 9

Adults, Children, and Adolescents in the Postdivorce Stage

It's been 5 years now since Tom and I split up. I'm 35. I must say, I'm quite proud of myself, the way I've come through all this. I'm working fulltime, and the kids go to a day-care home after school. They're 8 and 10 now, and I think they've finally settled down. Maybe it's because I have! Their father doesn't pay that much attention to them, but we're all pretty used to that by now. I couldn't have done it without my mom, though. She'll take the kids for a weekend once in a while, when I need "time out." And if they get really sick—stuff like that—I just call her up, and she helps me figure out what to do. And something else—I used to get so depressed I had to pull the covers over my head every so often. The last year or two, I just don't feel like that anymore. And I'm not afraid that I'll forget my kids are kids, either. The only thing is money is so tight. And I get so lonely. I've been seeing this guy lately. In a way it's serious, but I just don't know if he's right for me.

Janet—a custodial mother, initial
session at a family agency

When Joe left me I was 45. Now I'm 50. It's been 5 years, and I still
feel like I'm just existing, not living. Actually, I'm getting worse. I guess
you could say I have nothing to look forward to. I never believed I'd have
to keep working, so I never fought for rehabilitative alimony. I always
thought Joe would come back, but here I am selling clothes in a boutique
to make ends meet. When he remarried 2 1/2 ago, it was a disaster for
me.
    My kids were still teenagers at home—13 and 15—when Joe left, but
they're 18 and 20 now. I put on a good front about encouraging them to
move on with their own lives, but deep down I'm terrified to let them go.
I'm afraid they see that, even if no one else can. And my mom has gone
downhill so fast. I can't cry on her shoulder any more. She's too old for
that. Now I have to help her, and it's very, very hard to do it all alone.

*Victoria—a custodial mother, initial
session at a community mental health clinic*

    Janet and Victoria are both custodial mothers who have been divorced
for 5 years. Janet, age 35, seeks help because she is considering remarriage. Victoria, age 50, seeks help because of ongoing depression. Both
women are facing issues that sometimes occur during the postdivorce
phase of the divorce cycle, the long period subsequent to the 2–5 year
divorce transition.
    In contrast to the wide-ranging concrete and emotional upheaval of
the divorce transition, the postdivorce phase is a time for deepening
one's accommodation to a now-altered reality, and settling into a new
life. While the postdivorce phase does present characteristic life changes,
such as the remarriage Janet is considering, these life changes are generally less sweeping and upsetting than those of the divorce transition.
    Perhaps because of this relative quiescence, people are much less
likely to need professional help during the postdivorce phase than during
the earlier preseparation and divorce transition phases of the divorce
cycle. In major recent studies, Kitson (1992) and Maccoby and Mnookin
(1992) found that most people are coping well with their economic and
parental responsibilities by 3–3 1/2 years after the actual separation.
They are also feeling much better than they did when recently separated,
although a minority of women (such as Janet and Victoria) continue to
report being troubled by divorce (Kitson, 1992; see Note 1). In all
likelihood, this is because of women's financial and child-care burdens,
as well as the decline in their remarriage possibilities as they age.
    Researchers cite occasional women (though not men) who blossom
beyond the postdivorce norm of consolidated coping skills and emotional

equilibrium. These "super-women" have exciting, new careers and increased zest for life in general (Hetherington & Tryon, 1989; Wallerstein, 1986). During the postdivorce phase, children and adolescents also generally demonstrate higher functioning abilities and less distress than during the divorce transition (Furstenberg & Cherlin, 1991), although they are not entirely unscathed. This chapter explores issues that people confront during the postdivorce phase. The next chapter will present ideas for assisting these people when necessary.

THE POSTDIVORCE PHASE: ISSUES OF ADULTS

As noted previously, phases of the divorce cycle overlap. Thus, during the postdivorce phase, divorced adults sometimes experience depression, loneliness, anger, and other negative emotions that characterize the divorce transition. These negative emotions can be evoked by major events, both happy and challenging, that one would prefer to share with another adult—for example, holidays, special occasions, illnesses, or difficult decisions. Negative emotions can also be evoked by a reminder of the now-defunct marriage, such as an anniversary or a location.

By and large, though, during the postdivorce phase, negative emotions are joined or supplanted by feelings of competence, pride, and mastery. People experience these feelings for good reason. Having weathered the divorce transition, they are less preoccupied with ex-spouses, and have fine-tuned their skills as custodial or noncustodial parents. They have ironed out some coparental difficulties with their ex-spouses, or they have grown apart. If they wish, they may have found new social relationships. They have faced new vocational demands, handled increased financial pressure, and drawn on extended family and community in new ways. Since many single parents have low incomes, their overall well-being reminds us that neither single parenthood (Boyd-Franklin, 1989) nor poverty (Hines, 1989) is a condition that defeats all or even most people.

However, during the postdivorce phase, predictable life changes sometimes create new challenges for those who are generally doing well. And, certain subgroups among the divorced who have not successfully negotiated the divorce transition actually deteriorate during the postdivorce phase.

Predictable Life Changes During the Postdivorce Phase

The Changing Relationship with the Ex-Spouse.

By the end of the postdivorce transition, only a small minority of former spouses remain locked in chronic disputes (Johnston, 1993). By this time, most divorced parents have either developed a reasonably coopera-tive relationship, or (more often) drifted into a parallel parenting situa-tion (Furstenberg & Cherlin, 1991). In the latter case, custodial mothers do most of the work, and fathers either do nothing or help out when they are so inclined (Furstenberg & Cherlin, 1991).

Regardless of the nature of the coparental relationship, children's maturation often forces new encounters between former spouses during the postdivorce phase. For example, when adolescents want to spend more time with their friends, divorced parents need to make new visita-tion arrangements. These arrangements may decrease the amount of time spent with the nonresidential parent, or, in cases of joint residential custody, allow for increased offspring input regarding time spent in each location. Likewise, parents may have to consider the wishes of a teen-aged boy who has been living with his mother and now wants to move to his father's. Other times, changes in parental employment may neces-sitate review of child support arrangements (Koel, Clark, Straus, Whit-ney, & Hauser, 1994).

If parents have developed cooperation skills during the divorce transi-tion, the actual negotiations and court appearances necessary to finalize new visitation and support arrangements generally go smoothly (Koel et al., 1994). If parents have drifted after marital rupture, as most do, their personal maturity will determine if negotiations and court appearances can be businesslike and child-oriented. Otherwise, both can become fo-rums for expressing—or heightening—unresolved adult conflict.

Even when children of divorce become adults, the need for coparental contact does not stop. Weddings, graduations, and medical emergencies all cause ex-spouses to interact, although without the pressure of court involvement. If norms for interaction on such occasions have been devel-oped during the divorce transition, they can proceed smoothly. Other-wise, feelings such as loss and longing can interfere with an adult's composure. Additionally, as when divorce agreement modifications con-cerning younger offspring are necessary, unresolved adult conflicts can impede optimal handling of delicate situations.

The Possibility of Remarriage. (See Note 2)

About two thirds of divorced women and three quarters of divorced men remarry (Cherlin, 1992). On average, divorced women remarry within

3 to 5 years of marital rupture, and men remarry even sooner (Cherlin, 1992). Yet, the redivorce rate is higher than the divorce rate (Fursten-berg & Cherlin, 1991; Ganong & Coleman, 1994), and the average remarriage lasts only 5 years (Bray & Berger, 1993). The high redivorce rate has been attributed, in part, to the complexities of stepfamily life (Cherlin, 1992). These include lack of adult privacy in the remarriage (Visher & Visher, 1988), difficulties in becoming a stepmother or stepfa-ther (Pasley, Dollahite, & Ihinger-Tallman, 1993), and a feeling of being left out of the relationship between one's new spouse and her or his biological child (Whitsett & Land, 1992). The high redivorce rate has also been attributed to personal predispositions (Cherlin, 1992; Ganong & Coleman, 1994). That is, people who are inclined to leave an unhappy marriage once will be inclined to do the same thing again (Cherlin, 1992; Ganong & Coleman, 1994).

Although remarriage is common, it is far less common among Blacks and Hispanics (Del Carmen & Virgo, 1993). For these groups, the sup-port provided by extended family may make remarriage less important as a potential support network (Del Carmen & Virgo, 1993). Additionally, among Hispanics, Roman Catholic views about divorce may prompt some hesitation about remarriage. Remarriage is also far less common for women who divorced when over 40 (Ahlburg & De Vita, 1992; Coleman & Ganong, 1990). This may be because such women are con-sidered less attractive as prospective spouses than are their younger counterparts.

Thus, therapists are most likely to hear about contemplated remarriage from White clients—men throughout the age spectrum, and women under 40. Regarding motives, men may be desperate for the nurturance they see women as providing (Kissman & Allen, 1993). Women with children may be tempted to remarry to improve their financial situation (Coleman & Ganong, 1990; Ganong & Coleman, 1994); in fact, remarriage gener-ally improves the financial situation of a woman in Janet's circumstances somewhat, although it generally does not restore her predivorce standard of living (Morgan, 1991). Sometimes, an adult whose ex-spouse has remarried, consciously or unconsciously considers remarriage "to show him (or her)," and "keep even" in an immature, competitive way. Of course, other motives more conducive to marital longevity can play a part when remarriage is considered, too. Because remarriages have high disruption rates, yet offer opportunities for improved life satisfaction after divorce (Kelley, 1992; Visher & Visher, 1988), therapists must help clients carefully consider their reasons for remarriage, as well as the effect of possible remarriage on offspring.

Remarriage of Ex-Spouse.

As indicated, for an unremarried divorced person, the remarriage of an ex-spouse can be traumatic. If a rejected divorced person like Victoria yearns for reconciliation, her ex-husband's remarriage dashes her hopes. Generally, depression ensues, and a re-encounter with the mourning process commonly—and sometimes incompletely—experienced during the divorce transition is likely. Even if one initiated the divorce, or came to accept it, the finality of the ex-spouse's remarriage can evoke some reworking of the mourning process. Because men remarry more frequently and more quickly (Cherlin, 1992; Ganong & Coleman, 1994), unremarried women are the ones most likely to be in this position. Therapists may find that when ex-husbands remarry, women who are generally doing well experience temporary setbacks in vocational, parental, and/or social spheres.

The Aging of Children and Grandparents.

During the postdivorce phase, children who were of middle-school age or younger during the divorce transition become less dependent on the custodial parent (usually the mother), and more involved with their teachers and peers. Although usually happy to watch this growth, custodial mothers may also feel some anxiety as their children come to need them less (Bogolub, 1984). Consciously or unconsciously, the increased emotional separation may evoke the loss of closeness experienced during the marital rupture. In these cases, the promotion of offspring independence can become difficult.

Similarly, parents of children who were preadolescent and adolescent during the divorce transition face the challenge of youth who now "leave the nest." Accustomed to long-term offspring presence and assistance, these parents may find it harder to let go of grown children than parents who did so during the divorce transition, when everything was in flux. Although a son or daughter may continue helping from a new location, emotionally, a parent during the postdivorce phase may still experience loss, as Victoria's lament illustrates. Such difficulties in letting go are most prevalent among White families, as three- and four-generational living is so common among Blacks and Hispanics that an empty nest is far less likely (Del Carmen & Virgo, 1993).

Additionally, during the postdivorce phase, noncustodial parents sometimes experience offspring rejection (Greif & Kristall, 1993). As previously noted, offspring rejection may occur because of a noncustodial parent's behavior, or a custodial parent's brainwashing. But offspring rejection may occur for more nebulous reasons, too. For example, when parents live apart, a self-involved young adult may simply let one relationship slide. Alternately, a young adult's unconscious psychological distortions may generate rejection of a parent. Since offspring tend to stay in touch with the custodial parent (Aquilino, 1994), a noncustodial parent who has done nothing to offend sometimes suffers. In these cases, the rejected parent may remain involved (e.g., send holiday cards, attend performances) long into the postdivorce phase, in the hope that offspring will eventually appreciate parental love (Greif & Kristall, 1993). Because most noncustodial parents are fathers who lose contact with offspring over time (Ahlburg & De Vita, 1992; Booth & Amato, 1994; Seltzer, 1991), such cases are relatively rare. Still, because of their desire for help, these unfairly rejected noncustodial parents—both mothers and fathers—may seek therapy out of proportion to their numbers.

Finally, as divorced adults age, their parents do too. Elderly parents may fear that their adult children's divorces will deplete the ability to assist them (Bogolub, 1989); the reality is that particularly for daughters, divorce does not interfere with elder care (Spitze et al., 1994). However, when providing this care during the postdivorce phase, the middle-aged divorced person may feel more burdened than her married counterpart. In part, this burden stems from the isolation as a single person that Victoria has described. It also stems from the gradual loss of grandparental support in childrearing duties, which may be more keenly felt by single parents than by married parents. During the postdivorce phase, grandparental support is frequently for older offspring (e.g., participation in a youngster's visits home from college, assistance with emergencies), and less constant than support to younger grandchildren, but appreciated nonetheless. In Black, Hispanic, and Soviet emigrant families, and in other families with extended networks, both the isolation and the loss of child-care assistance are diluted as others fill in, and the divorced person's sense of elder care burden is decreased.

Deterioration during the Postdivorce Phase

During the postdivorce phase, the majority of divorced adults do well, facing as matters of course the remarriage of self and spouse, and changing coparental and intergenerational relationships. However, a minority of adults—most frequently women (Chiriboga et al., 1991; Kitson, 1992)—find that life after divorce gets harder and harder.

Younger Divorced Parents with Childrearing Difficulties.

Some custodial parents find childrearing during the postdivorce phase an impossible strain, rather than a challenge that can be mastered (Richards & Schmlege, 1993). One reason for postdivorce dysfunctional parenting is a chronic psychological problem, such as disorganization, fragility, impulse-ridden behavior, or excessive narcissism. Most divorced parents troubled by such conditions are mothers with default custody. For such a woman, unless the marriage was marked by violence or substance abuse, the financial and social support it provided, while imperfect, comprised some protection against the financial and emotional overload of solo mothering present during the postdivorce phase. With this buffer gone, and a decreased standard of living ever present, a mother who could previously provide minimally may no longer be able to do so.

Another reason for postdivorce dysfunctional parenting is social isolation, which can cut across ethnic lines. Even though Black and Hispanic families tend to have strong extended family helping networks, these are not ubiquitous. Poor Black mothers in neighborhoods where people fear going out can be very much alone (Cherlin, 1992), as can recently emigrated Hispanic women separated from kin (Chillman, 1993), or women of any ethnicity whose divorce has engendered kin rejection. Finally, both custodial mothers and custodial fathers sometimes find that the onset of adolescence makes it harder to parent effectively (Richards & Schmlege, 1993). Overall, emotional disturbance, material poverty, lack of social support, and offspring lifestage can create serious parenting problems during the postdivorce phase.

Middle-Aged and Older Divorced Women with Depression.

Chief among the numerous difficulties facing middle-aged and older divorced women are loss of children who move out, loss of other social supports (e.g., friends known while married, sisters who die), difficulty obtaining well-paying employment, permanently diminished standard of living, elder-care burdens, and decreased opportunity for remarriage. We recall that most middle-aged women recover from divorce (Kitson, 1992), and are able to remedy some of these difficulties, while many older women derive solace from memories (Weingarten, 1988). Nonetheless, there is a subgroup of middle-aged and older women who, because of temperament or circumstances, do not encapsulate their grief or build skills to cope with difficulties during the divorce transition. These women continue to be depressed during the postdivorce phase. If their husbands have left them, they may remain obsessed with sexual jealousy (Wallerstein, 1994). Like Victoria, these women feel they have nothing to look forward to. For them, the divorce transition was not a time of progress, and there are few gains, or none at all, to consolidate during the postdivorce phase. Because of strong cultural imperatives for independence, it is likely that African American and Soviet emigrant women are underrepresented in this population of depressed women.

THE POSTDIVORCE PHASE: ISSUES OF CHILDREN ADOLESCENTS, AND YOUNG ADULTS

During the divorce transition period described in part II, sons and daughters usually resided with a custodial mother. They faced loss of contact with the noncustodial father, temporarily diminished parenting in the custodial mother, decreased standard of living, and, often, physical relocation. Children living in paternal custody or joint residential custody fared better regarding father contact and standard of living. We recall that although sons and daughters who experience parental divorce are generally quite upset during the divorce transition, they are not likely to encounter more problems in later life than are their counterparts from intact families (Cherlin, 1992).

Later Life Experience of Children of Divorce

Even though people who experience parental divorce during childhood or adolescence should not be thought of as bound for inevitable trouble, their life experience during the postdivorce phase has unique features. First, many youngsters who experience parental divorce grow up to be self-sufficient and capable (Kissman & Allen, 1993). From a young age, they have experienced a good deal of household responsibility, and, most likely, the reality that they will have to support themselves financially as adults (Aquilino, 1994). If they lived with custodial mothers, they may have also experienced a healthy sense of responsibility to these sometimes-dependent women, and learned to integrate caretaking with their own blossoming independence. Among females growing up with parental divorce, Soviet emigrants and African Americans may experience the strongest independence messages, as their upbringing is not likely to be diluted by mixed messages about the merits of paid employment for women.

    Second, children who were very young at the time of the divorce, and are school-age or adolescent during the postdivorce phase, tend not to remember the intact family (Wallerstein, 1984), and may simply accept the single-parent household as a given rather than a deviation from the norm. Third, unlike people who grew up with happily married parents, adult children of divorce tend to keep in touch with only one parent (Aquilino, 1994). Overwhelmingly, this parent is the custodial mother. Since there is no evidence that decreased contact with a noncustodial father interferes with child or adolescent development (Ihinger-Tallman et al., 1993; King, 1994; Maccoby & Mnookin, 1992), we likewise view the parent contact experiences of these adult children of divorce as different, but not deprived. In fact, their voluntary contact with custodial mothers, which may involve caretaking as well as affection, is perhaps the strongest testimony we have of divorced women's abilities to raise their children (Aquilino, 1994), who could simply turn away from them when adulthood is reached. Overall, during the postdivorce phase, people who experienced parental divorce while growing up seem to accept the single-parent household, and the demands for independence and responsibility that it creates.

Of course, as they mature, children of divorce may feel the impact of their parents' split on a deeper level, even if they are autonomous and unashamed of their parents' marital dissolution. For example, if they are of impressionable temperament, adolescents and young adults may fear that their own marriages, like those of their parents, will disrupt. Young women are particularly likely to have this fear, as people tend to identify with the same-sex parent, and most children of divorce were raised in mother-custody homes (Beal & Hochman, 1991). On the other hand, Black youth may be less likely to have this fear: Marriage is less common among Blacks than among Whites (Bulcroft & Bulcroft, 1993; Cherlin, 1992; Taylor et al., 1990; Williams et al., 1992), and also less central to a sense of personal fulfillment and life satisfaction (Bulcroft & Bulcroft, 1993; Cherlin, 1992; Fine et al., 1992).

Likewise, some young people may fear that they will follow in their parents' footsteps when they themselves become parents, and inflict an upsetting experience on their future children. Young women raised in father-custody homes and young men raised in mother-custody homes may have an additional fear about the ability to be a good parent, because they lacked a full-time same-gender parental role model (Beal & Hochman, 1991).

But all children receive food for thought from their developmental experiences, and children of unhappily married couples may be even more worried than children of divorce about their future functioning as spouses and parents. Children of divorce may have characteristic struggles, as do people from any background, but this does not mean that they have been damaged by their upbringing, or that their struggles cannot be resolved.

The Dilemmas of Stepchildren

Like their parents, sons and daughters who enter stepfamilies during the postdivorce phase face particular dilemmas. For example, a school-age parentified son who was "the man of the house" during the postdivorce transition is likely to resent his new live-in stepfather (Ganong & Coleman, 1994; Visher & Visher, 1988). Teenaged stepdaughters and their new stepfathers often encounter difficulty interacting (Bee, 1994; Cherlin, 1992; Pasley et al., 1993), perhaps because of inevitable, subtle-or-not-so-subtle sexualization. Teenaged stepsiblings newly under the same roof may be uncomfortable for the same reason, while younger children mourn the loss of closeness with the formerly single custodial parent (Visher & Visher, 1988). Since stepfamilies are most prevalent among White people, it is White children and youth—rather than their Black and Hispanic counterparts—who are most likely to experience these relational complexities.

Like the difficulties children and adolescents encounter during the divorce transition, the difficulties they encounter in new stepfamilies are borne of short-term upheaval, and can usually be resolved over time (Whitsett & Land, 1992). This, however, is if the stepfamily lasts. We recall that the redivorce rate exceeds the divorce rate, and nearly 50% of children entering remarried families experience a second divorce within 10 years (Bumpass, cited in Ganong & Coleman, 1994); it appears that no research has yet been done on these twice-disrupted offspring.

Offspring Problems Originating in Divorce

On occasion, long-range problems do unfold in the aftermath of parental divorce during childhood. Sometimes, youth do not gain self-sufficiency, or come to accept divorce simply as one fact of life among many. For example, school age children in maternal or paternal custody arrangements occasionally remain consumed with feelings of longing for and anger at the noncustodial parent. This is most likely when the noncustodial parent handles support payments or visitation in an erratic manner. Children who move to a new, poorer neighborhood may never get over it; physical deprivation dovetailed with other feelings of deprivation can result in chronic depression. As previously noted, angry or depressed children may act out their unhappiness in a variety of ways (e.g., belligerence with peers or diminished school performance).

Likewise, during the postdivorce phase, some adolescents and young adults manifest chronic feelings of inadequacy and insecurity. Rather than successfully negotiating the formation of their own identities, they remain governed by a sense that they matter little, because they fell through the cracks of their parents' lives, or missed a happy childhood. These troubled young people sometimes find the struggles that are competently managed by so many sons and daughters of divorce to be overwhelming. For example, most offspring of divorce will be able, ultimately, to overcome fear of failing in marriage; if they so choose, they attempt long-term sexual closeness, either in marriage, or in heterosexual or homosexual cohabitation. But a minority among offspring of divorce remain immersed in their parents' unhappy marriages, and need to repeat them. These young people attract unloving people, or reject those with more to offer (Wallerstein & Blakeslee, 1989).

Similarly, a minority among offspring of divorce grow up bitter about the sharp drop in material circumstances which beset them when their parents separated (Wallerstein & Blakeslee, 1989). As late adolescents and young adults, they express their simmering anger in a passive-aggressive way, and simply drift (Wallerstein & Blakeslee, 1989), rather than focusing on financial self-support. A 19-year-old who manifested this pattern announced in treatment that he was "on strike against life."

Finally, some youngsters may be seriously held back by feelings of responsibility for divorced parents (usually mothers) who are not doing well. For example, a young adult may refrain from adult commitments, feeling consciously or unconsciously that these may deplete financial or emotional resources needed by an isolated, dependent mother. Since it is possible for most offspring of divorce to balance individuation and the needs of dependent parents, these feelings of guilt and excessive responsibility are often a smokescreen for deeper feelings of inadequacy vis-à-vis the challenges of late adolescence and young adulthood. As part of a self-destructive, floundering, or constricted lifestyle, it is common for these young people to abuse alcohol or other drugs. These substances numb anxiety, anger, fear, and other feelings that have generally diminished among sons and daughters by the postdivorce phase of the divorce cycle.

The Reasons for Problems.

Overall, then, among offspring of divorce, emotional status ranges from self-sufficient to insecure, and the ability to master conflicts sometimes generated by divorce ranges from strong to nonexistent. What accounts for this variety? Probably, one factor is the nature of the parental divorce itself; this includes the intensity of the preseparation disagreements, the way divorce was explained, how the parents got along after marital rupture, the custodial parent's ability to respond to the children, the extent of financial decline, and allied matters. The uglier the divorce, the more the son or daughter has to overcome throughout the developmental process.

Temperament, siblings, and extended family can also influence the amount of individual upheaval experienced. We have seen how each can buffer or heighten divorce impact during the preseparation phase and the divorce transition, and each operates during the postdivorce phase as well. Other relevant factors are experiences related to ethnicity, and the socioeconomic level of the youngster during the postdivorce years.

Case Example: A Combination of Reasons.

Consider John, an African-American male, age 20, whose parents went their own ways when he was 8 years old. Temperamentally, John has always been very sensitive to the interactions around him; as a young man, he vividly recalls his parents' quarrels many years ago. After the separation, John's father did not stay in touch with him, and did not pay child support. His mother was never able to provide for John above the near-poverty level. She wanted John to be "tough," and rarely discussed feelings with him. John was an only child, and received little additional attention from extended family; he was "the quiet one," and more attention was paid to those in more obvious need. After John graduated high school, he did not look for a job. Currently, he has no friends, and spends most of his time watching TV. His mother despairs to a therapist that "my son is doing nothing and wasting his life." She suspects drug involvement, and wants to know if John can be helped.

Although the difficulty of John's parents' divorce, his own sensitivity, and the paucity of family support play a part in his emotional paralysis, other factors contribute too. The schools in the poor urban neighborhood where John grew up are characterized by danger, truancy, and low expectations for students; pushed along from grade to grade because he never "got in trouble," John graduated high school barely knowing how to read. Additionally, as a Black male he is likely to encounter discrimination if he seeks employment. John's situation illustrates how poverty and prejudice can compound the effects of marital dissolution, and contribute to a poor young adult outcome that more fortunate offspring of divorce may escape.

NOTES

1. A strength of the study by Kitson (1992) and the study by Maccoby and Mnookin (1992) is that both utilized nonclinical samples (i.e., samples not composed exclusively of people seeking professional mental health help). Kitson's sample was diverse with regard to age, gender, and ethnicity. However, it was not diverse with regard to income, since it targeted upper middle-class, middle-class, and working-class communities, and did not generally include the poor. Maccoby and Mnookin's sample was diverse with regard to income, gender, and ethnicity. However, it was not diverse with regard to age, since it focused on parents of children under 16. In the absence of studies with more inclusive samples, we must frame our discussion of "long-haul" postdivorce adjustment with these two complementary studies, based on "almost-inclusive" samples.

2. Remarriage constitutes a major topic in its own right, separate from divorce. No attempt is made here to provide complete coverage of remarriage, as this book emphasizes only those aspects which overlap with divorce. These include, for example, the divorced person's anticipation of stepfamily life, the divorced person's reaction to ex-spousal remarriage, and offspring reaction to the newly formed stepfamily.

Chapter 10

The Mental Health Professional's Postdivorce Role

We have seen that although most adults and offspring do well during the postdivorce phase, they face predictable challenges. Among clients who seek help at this time, then, the therapist is likely to meet adults and offspring who function adequately, but need help in handling particular dilemmas. Less frequently, during the postdivorce phase, the therapist meets with people who have more serious problems, and are exceptions to the norm of postdivorce well-being.

Whether the client's dilemma is encapsulated or more serious, it is often a result, variation, or continuation of a divorce transition issue. So, the four goals that guided treatment during the divorce transition—improvement of the emotional status of individuals, improvement of financial and social support for the custodial parent, improvement of the relationship between offspring and the custodial parent, improved relationship between ex-spouses—remain relevant during the postdivorce phase. In fact, now that emotions have cooled and concrete stresses have diminished, it may be possible to help clients achieve these goals to a greater extent than previously.

Similarly, many strategies suggested for the divorce transition phase apply during the postdivorce phase. For example, if a custodial mother encounters difficulty in letting go of growing offspring, many of the techniques used to strengthen the single parent, and help her become aware of her children's needs would now be relevant. Likewise, when strong feelings between former spouses prevent cooperation during the divorce transition and then diminish during the postdivorce phase (Maccoby & Mnookin, 1992), previously described techniques to help couples develop businesslike, child-oriented relationships are useful.

During the postdivorce phase, therapists generally must give careful consideration to treatment duration. During the preseparation phase and the divorce transition, divorce-related struggles usually have "built-in" beginnings, middles, and ends, and treatment duration follows accordingly. For example, a young woman grapples with a decision to leave her husband, a rejected ex-husband mourns the loss of his marriage, a middle-aged woman seeks a job and a new social life; in each case, a sense of closure (e.g., finalized separation decision, securing of a job) experienced by therapist and client helps determine when treatment ends. This sense of closure may evolve after periods as divergent as a month, 5 months, or a year.

For people who seek professional help during the more stable, open-ended postdivorce phase, on the other hand, there is less feeling of issues running their course, so the therapist must make more deliberate decisions about treatment duration. People with encapsulated problems who are generally doing well may receive sufficient help via short-term treatment, usually planned for 8 to 12 weeks (Parad & Parad, 1990). These clients have many strengths, and previously described techniques are often used within a time-limited framework. These techniques take hold more quickly than during the divorce transition because the clients are not overwhelmed by recent—or current—massive losses and changes. In contrast, for the minority of clients who deteriorate during the postdivorce phase, open-ended treatment with a strong supportive element becomes one option among several which may help.

A SHORT-TERM, FOCUSSED APPROACH
TO THE PREDICTABLE CHALLENGES
OF THE POSTDIVORCE PHASE

As indicated, the prospects for treating the predictable challenges of the postdivorce phase, both among the divorced and their offspring, are generally favorable. The therapist employs a short-term, focussed stance that allows for selective use of techniques that are also used during the divorce transition.

First, the therapist attends to the uniqueness of the client's postdivorce distress, and inquires about the divorce experience. During this process, the therapist generally normalizes the client's presenting problem (e.g., contemplation of remarriage, changing relationship with son or daughter) as typical of people who have weathered divorce. Aware that premature normalization may cause clients to feel that their problems have been trivialized, or that they are not being heard in depth, the therapist is careful not to normalize too quickly. With proper timing, though, normalization reassures clients who are generally doing well that their postdivorce improvement is not threatened by the problem that causes them to seek professional help. (Normalization is used less frequently during the preseparation phase and the divorce transition, when it is likely to cause a highly distressed client to feel trivialized no matter how much has been disclosed.) Then, enlisting the client's strengths, the therapist selectively draws on goals and strategies that are also relevant to divorce transition clients.

Case Example: Emotional Smothering of a Youngster

When Luisa, a 32-year-old Hispanic woman, divorced 5 years ago, she and Alicia, her 6-year-old daughter, moved in with Luisa's parents. Luisa began working as a saleswoman in a department store, her first full-time job. Luisa's parents felt they had to take their daughter and granddaughter in, but as traditional, Roman Catholic Hispanics they were ashamed of the divorce and Luisa's employment. Luisa escaped their criticism by busying herself with Alicia. When Alicia began first grade, the little girl developed school phobia, and Luisa sought professional help.

In the initial sessions, 6-year-old Alicia sat on her mother's lap, as if she were much younger. The therapist, named Elaine, quickly gleaned that, as in most cases of school phobia, Alicia was responding to her mother's feeling that the physical and emotional separation school entailed were "bad." Since Luisa seemed to be the reason for the school phobia, Elaine did not see Alicia after the first two sessions. Through gentle yet specific questions, Elaine helped Luisa conclude that "after all I've been through, I don't want to let my baby go." Elaine then commented that such clinging is common among divorced mothers. This comment helped Luisa become less defensive and more relaxed during the treatment process.

The following dialogue illustrates how Elaine utilized Luisa's strengths to help her to get past the divorce-engendered need to keep Alicia a baby.

Luisa: I know I should encourage her to grow up, like you've been saying. But sometimes I don't want to.

Elaine: You say you still don't want her to grow up.

Luisa: No, I guess I don't. I like being her whole world. I won't know what to do with myself on the weekends if she's busy with friends and homework.

Elaine: You won't know what to do.

Luisa: Right.

Elaine: Well, do you think you could figure out how to enjoy your free time without Alicia? *(Elaine introduces the topics of pleasure and self-nurturance as relevant to Luisa as a single parent.)*

Luisa: I guess, I don't know.

Elaine: You sound uncertain.

Luisa: Well . . . I'll be all alone with my folks, and they're always mad at me. I won't be in the mood for fun.

Elaine *(after exploring Luisa's relationship with her parents)*: Have you talked to your parents about how you've been getting along lately? *(Although she has been guided thus far by the goal of improving the relationship between the custodial mother and her child, Elaine now realizes that the goal of improving social support for the custodial parent is also relevant. She introduces the idea of working with extended family.)*

Luisa: What good will that do?

Elaine: If you think a minute, are there any ideas *you* get about good that might come from talking to your folks?

Luisa *(pause)*: Not really.

Elaine: You sound skeptical about the point of discussing things, and that's natural. But talking to them might get them thinking about your side of things.

Luisa: There's two of them, and only one of me. What if they start picking on me?

Elaine *(after exploring how the parents could pick on Luisa, and other fears Luisa has)*: Does that mean you don't want to talk to them?

Luisa: No. But it's hard to start.

Elaine *(after exploring what the difficulties in starting the discussion might be)*: Haven't you ever done anything hard before? *(Here Elaine encourages Luisa to think about her strengths.)*

Luisa: Well, I left my ex-husband.

Elaine: And you started working in the department store. *(Elaine continues to point out Luisa's strengths.)*

Luisa: Well, I could try. But what if no good comes of it? *(Luisa seems to be asking for encouragement).*

Elaine: If no good comes of it, you're no worse off than you are now. Or, you might want to bring your folks to an appointment here. Then, I could help keep things on track when you talk to each other. I wouldn't just take your side. I'd try to see things from their side too. But first let's discuss how you might talk about things at home. *(Elaine presents herself as a flexible therapist who works with various components of the extended family system. Viewing her client as an adult with strengths, she does not infantilize Luisa by insisting that family work under her guidance is the only way to address Luisa's stress.)*

The Short-Term, Focussed Approach with Families, Couples, Individual, and Groups

Therapists can use this same approach (in-depth exploration, normalization of postdivorce phase issues, utilization of strengths, selective use of divorce transition treatment goals and strategies) with most encapsulated postdivorce phase concerns. In cases like Luisa's, or in cases of ex-spousal conflict, close relationships need to be reworked, and family or conjoint work makes sense.

In contrast, it makes sense to see adolescents and young adults in short-term individual treatment, or in time-limited, focussed groups composed of people in their own age group. This is because the postdivorce phase concerns of these young people (viz., feared tainting of their future role performances as spouses and parents) dovetail with age-specific identity struggles (Zastrow & Kirst-Ashman, 1990), which are generally addressed individually or in peer groups; by definition, the formation of identity involves emotional separation from parents (or parent figures), and therapists generally rely on treatment modalities reflecting this reality.

For youth who are members of close extended families with members living with or near each other, interesting variations occur. Such youth may be African American, Hispanic, Soviet Jewish emigrant, or Orthodox Jewish. Although individual or group sessions guided by the goal of improved emotional status for individuals still make sense, therapists working with youth reared with ethnic values of intergenerational loyalty and helping must be careful not to suggest (overtly or covertly) that individuation has to do with the rejection of one's roots. For example, a 19-year-old daughter of a divorced Hispanic woman may decide in treatment that both a close and loving marriage for herself and loyalty to her divorced mother are personal goals.

Although older adolescents and young adults generally benefit from individual or group sessions, exceptions occur when a divorced parent contemplates remarriage; here, offspring may need to do some anticipatory problem solving with the biological parent and the prospective stepparent. These sessions are most important when remarriage is contemplated by the residential parent, rather than the nonresidential parent.

When Short-term, Focussed Work Leads to Long-term Treatment

During the divorce transition, most clients lack the inclination to introspect about their longstanding patterns in living, because "getting through the day" and "taking care of business" consume most available time and energy. In contrast, during the postdivorce phase, if they are psychologically oriented, clients often use their current concerns as entry points or "doorways" to deeper issues.

For example, George, a noncustodial father divorced for 5 years, sought treatment when his 17-year-old son, Pete, decided he wanted nothing to do with his father. George was particularly upset because he had been consistently responsible regarding support payments and visitation. Problem solving around the possible renewal of the father-son relationship eventually led to George's acknowledgment that rejection "has always been a touchy issue for me." When George realized that Pete's rejection re-evoked the pain of the rejection by his ex-wife Sally, the treatment emphasis shifted from the father-son relationship to the ex-spousal relationship.

With his therapist's help, George conducted a "marital autopsy" (Rice & Rice, 1986b). Using this process, still relevant today, people transcend a blaming mentality and obtain a rational understanding of the marital demise. Blaming can be a powerful tie, and understanding helps people free themselves from it. Concurring with the Rices, I believe that a marital autopsy is best conducted during the postdivorce phase, when rationality is more attainable than during the highly emotional divorce transition.

In this case, George, who had a lifelong struggle with alcohol, examined his idea that Sally had been "cruel" in "not giving me another chance." In treatment, George concluded that he married Sally as a mother figure they both hoped would rescue him; Sally left when she tired of this role. Via the marital autopsy, George realized he had to take responsibility for his drinking. He stopped fixating on rejection by his ex-wife and son, and began to consider what it would mean to seek professional help for his alcohol problem.

WORKING WITH THE MORE SERIOUS PROBLEMS OF THE POSTDIVORCE PHASE

Higher functioning clients often obtain help from planned short-term treatment, but the small minority of clients with more serious problems are likely to benefit from other approaches.

Assisting Younger Parents with Childrearing Difficulties

Emotionally Disturbed Parents.

During the postdivorce phase, flawed parenting is generally not caused by the divorce process per se, but rather by such factors as chronic emotional disturbance or social isolation. Even among the emotionally disturbed, the waning of overwhelming losses and changes during the divorce transition may improve parental functioning (see chapter 7), but this trend will not continue during the relatively stable postdivorce phase. Given the stability of circumstances during the postdivorce phase—as well as the ongoing needs of children and adolescents living at home— treatment of emotionally troubled custodial parents at this time is often long term, with a strong supportive element. Such treatment helps insure that youngsters will get as much as their parents can possibly give over a long period of time.

When working with these very limited clients, the therapist addresses basic, everyday matters. She helps them handle children's bedtimes, homework, chores, discipline, and arguments. She also helps clients handle their own temper, confusion, and lethargy. Although the therapist attempts to help the client translate skills from one situation to another (e.g., "Is there anything we figured out before that might work here?''), she does not expect that much generalization will occur—although sometimes it does. Usually, individual and family techniques described as applicable for seriously disturbed parents during the divorce transition (i.e., specific education on children's needs, modelling of parenting skills, presentation of legal abuse and neglect standards) all apply, but the possibility of using these techniques in a time-limited context is much less likely.

Additionally, during the postdivorce phase, the therapist may draw upon extended family, if available, to help the emotionally disturbed custodial mother. (Custodial mothers comprise the majority of emotionally disturbed custodial parents; as previously indicated, custodial fathers, as a group, are high functioning [Downey, 1994; Greif & DeMaris, 1990]). In contrast to extended family situations involving non-disturbed divorced mothers (see chapter 8), it may make sense for a therapist to help a maternal grandmother, godmother, or other relative assume a dominant role with the offspring of a severely limited divorced mother; relatives living nearby as well as those living with the mother may assist. To dispel any ideas about maternal laziness, selfishness, and the like, the therapist must sometimes discuss the mother's condition with the mother-substitute. Simultaneously, the therapist strengthens and encourages any limited capacities the mother does have. This approach preserves the family unit, and allows children to maintain contact with their mother.

As previously noted, such extended family assistance is most likely to be available and nonconflictual among Black, Hispanic, (Del Carmen & Virgo, 1993) and Soviet Jewish emigrant families. When the custodial mother is emotionally disturbed, some of the typical intergenerational problems in these ethnic groups are diminished. For example, conflict between a Black grandmother and a mentally ill Black mother over who is in charge may be minimized, as the mother may be relieved rather than angered by her mother's dominant role. Likewise, a mentally ill Hispanic woman is less likely to be employed than her mentally healthier counterpart, and is thus less likely to incur the criticism of relatives who believe that the place of the Hispanic woman is in the home. When work with extended family of the mentally ill custodial mother is attempted during the postdivorce phase, these trends may improve therapeutic outcomes.

As during the divorce transition, the therapist may rely on modified goals because of the level of client disturbance. For example, once an emotionally limited parent reaches a minimum childrearing level, prevention of further deterioration in the parent–child relationship (rather than improvement in the parent–child relationship) may become the goal. If a custodial mother seems to be doing particularly well, the therapist may encourage her to experiment with independent living without treatment for a while, particularly if she has a supportive extended family. The option of returning to therapy should problems erupt is made explicit.

If frustration and impatience about limited movement enter the countertransference, the therapist may find it useful to rely on the conceptualization of clients as basically either "growth" or "maintenance". In contrast to growth cases, maintenance cases require the therapist to use all energy to simply keep the client stable, oriented, and functioning. This dichotomy helps the therapist honor rather than undervalue her own work, and take seriously such accomplishments as prevention of parental hospitalization and prevention of placement of sons and daughters.

Socially Isolated Parents.

Social isolation is another cause of flawed parenting during the postdivorce phase. Occasionally (see chapter 8), treatment can help overcome social isolation stemming from rejection by relatives. But clinical sessions do not help when custodial mothers are isolated because they or potentially helpful kin fear travel in dangerous neighborhoods, or because they have no kin. Clients isolated for these reasons can be helped immeasurably by mutual assistance groups, which may be either professionally led groups or self-help (Kissman & Allen, 1993). (Again, we emphasize custodial mothers; custodial fathers tend to be a financially advantaged, educated population [Depner, 1993; Downey, 1994], unlikely to live in dangerous neighborhoods and unlikely to be without social support [Guttmann, 1993].) In dangerous neighborhoods, a daytime weekend meeting with child care provided is apt to be much more helpful for employed divorced mothers than an evening meeting. Because African American and Hispanic women are often overrepresented among the poor women who live in such neighborhoods, they are quite likely to be among those using these groups.

In these groups, the women become resources for each other, sharing ideas about single parenting, and providing moral support around role overload and allied matters. They can also invent strategies for less burdened extended family members to make safe trips to the neighborhood. If politically inclined, they may even work together for measures such as improved police protection. During the postdivorce phase, such action is more likely than during the divorce transition, when concrete life changes and emotional upheaval sap most energy.

For recently emigrated divorced Hispanic women with no extended family (Chillman, 1993), or other divorced women who are similarly isolated, the new connections made in self-help groups sometimes become family substitutes. Depending on their ages, group members may act as surrogate sisters or mothers for each other. In addition to providing services such as ideas, child care, and help with errands, these newfound social networks may decrease loneliness. They also improve the depleted self-esteem of divorced women, who learn that others can gain from them.

Assisting Depressed Middle-Aged and Older Women

While chronically troubled divorced parents who have children and adolescents living with them often benefit from long-term, supportive treatment during the postdivorce phase, chronically depressed middle-aged and older women do not necessarily require such treatment at this time. True, for some of these women, long-term supportive treatment may prevent further deterioration, as it does in their younger counterparts. On the other hand, since minor children are not involved, therapists in both private and agency practice will feel less urgency about such preventive work, and be more willing to experiment with alternate modalities.

For these discouraged clients, who often face economic and social obstacles not of their own making, warmth and support are clearly important, but most effective when used in concert with efforts to "shake up" clients, or provide them with new experiences. For example, clients who are politically oriented may be encouraged to participate in an action group.

Consider Margaret, age 55, and Sally, age 48. Both women had sought treatment because of chronic listlessness and malaise, and both were employed at jobs providing a hand-to-mouth existence. Margaret, who had not been employed outside the home before the divorce, suffered a distressing income drop when her husband left her; with her therapist's encouragement, she joined a women's organization working to expand alimony possibilities in her state's divorce laws. Sally was a survivor of her ex-husband's physical abuse; with her therapist's encouragement, she joined an organization that advocated for more aggressive police involvement in battering incidents. Both women attended monthly evening meetings, and did committee work as they were able.

In each case, the therapist was concerned with the treatment goal of improving the client's emotional status, and operated on the premise that sometimes, changes in feeling state follow changes in behavior, rather than vice versa. Ultimately, neither Margaret nor Sally could be described as completely satisfied with her life. But, in finding constructive outlets for their chronic and understandable anger, each moved from a victim stance to a proactive stance, experienced some lifting of her depression, and learned "to view the glass as half full," rather than "half empty."

When clients are not politically oriented, therapists must find other strategies to provide new experiences. For example, some clients who were too depressed and self-absorbed during the divorce transition to join issue-oriented groups on topics such as vocational development, or social skills and social opportunities for the divorced, may be ready for such groups at this time.

Sometimes, with depressed clients, a therapist will encounter negativism. That is, the client provides no responses to open-ended questions geared to elicit ideas on possible new experiences, and opposes everything the therapist suggests. Aware that the client is displacing all anger over the divorce onto the therapist and putting much energy into defeating her, the therapist stops pulling for the client's ideas, and stops making suggestions. The therapist may then try a paradoxical approach, and wonder with the client what is really wrong with the status quo. Feeling no pressure to do what the therapist wants (viz., answer questions, or take action), the client may develop her own ideas for shifting her circumstances.

Finally, when clients have good reason to be depressed, the therapist never pressures them to "get over" their depressions. While encouraging new activity in direct or subtle ways, the therapist is also sensitive to ongoing financial and sexual deprivation that are unlikely to dissipate. For instance, the therapist may tell her clients that occasional bouts of "the blues" signify that they are sensitive people. When depressed clients are given permission to express their pain from time to time during the postdivorce phase, they have more energy to use in positive endeavors.

With middle-aged and older women, long-term treatment with an emphasis on understanding patterns in living is generally not recommended, as severely depressed clients may not have the energy for an endeavor offering few immediate benefits. For example, a 50-year-old divorced client once blurted in session, "You want to me to think about what happened 40 years ago? I'm so miserable I have to use all my strength to drag myself out of bed every day. I can't even decide what to wear to work. How can I remember the past?"

Assisting Troubled Younger Children

We recall that during the postdivorce phase, a small proportion of offspring manifest serious problems. For example, children consumed with longing for noncustodial parents may perform poorly in school over a long period, while adolescents and young adults who feel pervasively insecure or inadequate may flounder in work and relationships.

The treatment of disturbed children during the postdivorce phase parallels their treatment during the preseparation period and the divorce transition. To review, individual treatment for youngsters can promote expression and integration of divorce-engendered feelings, talking out rather than acting out of negative emotion, connection to age-appropriate activities, and mastery of self-destructive impulses that might otherwise result in substance abuse, suicidal gestures and/or attempts, or other manifestations.

Along with individual treatment, parental involvement is a must. Frequently, by the time of the postdivorce phase, the father is not involved, and only a custodial mother is available for treatment. Less frequently available for treatment at this time are noncustodial fathers, custodial fathers, noncustodial mothers, and joint residential parents.

During the postdivorce phase, the therapist has a distinct orientation toward parents. First, much is expected of them. Generally, the therapist accepts parents' self-absorption as a given during the preseparation phase and the divorce transition. But, guided by the goal of improving the relationship between offspring and the custodial parent, the therapist can be more challenging with parents in the postdivorce phase. For example, if a custodial mother was rejected by her ex-husband, the therapist might be less gentle during the postdivorce phase than during the divorce transition regarding the effect of the woman's depression on her son.

Second, if both parents are involved, the complications created by the ongoing physical separation must be addressed. Guided by the goal of improving the relationship between separated spouses, the therapist relies on techniques for helping separated spouses achieve a cooperative coparental relationship (see chapter 8), anticipating more success during the postdivorce phase than during the divorce transition. Accomplishment of this goal is more likely, not just because of the cooling of divorce transition emotions (Maccoby & Mnookin, 1992), but also because of the incentive for parental problem solving provided by a child who is more than transiently troubled. As during the divorce transition, the therapist refrains from meeting with both parents and children together, to avoid stimulating children's reconciliation fantasies. However, sessions including individual parents and their children are common.

Sometimes, when individual offspring treatment is effective and parents finally learn to attend seriously to their children, child disturbance abates, and the therapist can bow out, having reconnected the family in a new, healthy way. Treatment involving disturbed children during the postdivorce phase becomes long term only when

1. adults cannot improve their parenting skills,
2. ex-spouses cannot improve their coparental relationships (as in the case of chronically disputing couples [Johnston, 1993]), or

3. children do not respond to improved parenting or an improved coparental relationship.

In the latter case, work with the parents acquires a new emphasis; the therapist supports parental changes, which are not easily come by, and reminds parents that their behavior, while important, is not the only variable that affects child mental health. Then, divorced parents can continue as allies in the treatment of the youngster without undue guilt about the long-term effects of the dissolution of their marriage.

For single parents in the postdivorce phase, the experience of long-term problems in their children can be quite troublesome. The possibility of ongoing care of a troubled child can disrupt hard-won peace of mind, and seem overwhelming to someone who has just weathered the divorce transition. In such a case, the therapist must help parents conserve some time and energy for their own needs. She must also help them learn to live with the uncertainty regarding therapeutic outcome of a son or daughter. For divorced parents who place a high premium on independence for self and offspring (e.g., African American and Soviet Jewish emigrant parents), the possibility of a youngster's long-term dependence may be particularly upsetting. With these parents, the therapist may give extra attention to the working through of feelings of guilt and failure. She may also highlight the strengths of a limited child, if parents can view these as examples of independence.

Assisting Troubled Adolescents and Young Adults

We recall that short-term individual or group treatment during the postdivorce phase often makes sense for well-functioning adolescents and young adults who have experienced their parents' marital dissolution, and who have resultant encapsulated fears about adulthood. Adolescents and young adults who are more troubled, however, may need long-term treatment at this time. This treatment has a thrust similar to that conducted with younger children of divorce: integration of feelings, connection to age-appropriate activities, mastery of impulses. Although treatment of younger children of divorce generally involves regular parental involvement, treatment of older offspring generally does not, so the client sometimes develops strong feelings toward the therapist as a parental figure.

The reason for such attachment is that unhappy, low-functioning young people whose parents have divorced sometimes feel that they grew up almost unnoticed; unlike their psychologically healthier counterparts, these young people may want their therapists to "re-raise" them, although they simultaneously fear this. Among Black youth, who frequently present a "tough" or "cool" veneer (Gibbs, 1989), these feelings may be masked, but they are still present. Among Soviet emigrant youth, feelings may also be masked. If these youngsters grew up overseas, they were raised in a culture where the whole idea of voluntarily discussing personal problems with a professional stranger was totally alien (Brodsky, 1988; Castex, 1992); if they are referred for mental health services after parental divorce, their bewilderment over the nature of therapy may temporarily dominate any other emotions. In contrast, mainstream Jewish youth were often raised in a culture where consultation with mental health experts is common; these youth may be more in touch with their feelings, and ready to discuss them (Hines et al., 1992).

In a subtle way, the desire for parental nurturance is expressed by adolescents and young adults who devote themselves excessively to the care of a dependent divorced parent, and ignore themselves; these young people give others what they dare not admit they need. Of course, similar longings for nurturance develop among offspring of lasting marriages, but the public nature of divorce and the actual physical split may give longing among offspring of the divorced a particular intensity.

Thus, in addition to competence with all the usual skills employed with troubled youth (e.g., developing alternate ways of handling feelings that lead to self-destructive behavior, facilitating negotiation of life-stage tasks such as employment and relationships), the therapist working with youth during the postdivorce phase pays special attention to clues pertaining to the need for parenting. For example, when a youngster arrives for an appointment drunk or "high," she may be asking for the therapist to reach out like a good, loving parent, find out what is bothering her, and make demands for appropriate behavior.

On the other hand, because of the nature of the clinical relationship, therapists cannot always fill a youngster's need to have a parent "be there." For example, a therapist cannot take a client's phone call immediately after a job interview, or provide tutoring to a teenager who did not graduate from high school, and wants to attain a graduate equivalency diploma (GED). With psychologically sophisticated youth, there may ensue a discussion of the longing for parenting, the need to accept that it may never be there exactly as desired, and the approximations of parental nurturance that do exist. Those unable to conceptualize such matters may have to learn experientially to let go of anger, and be satisfied with the surrogate parenting they can get. As nurturance is accepted and anger abates, real growth can occur.

In addition to providing some re-parenting, and some perspective on the need for parenting, therapists working with adolescents and young adults who have experienced parental divorce may also provide individual or couple sessions for the divorced parents, and family sessions. In contrast to work with younger offspring, work with older offspring generally uses these parent and family sessions sparingly, since older offspring are moving toward independence. In these cases, parent and family sessions tend to be focussed on what parents can offer in specific situations, ranging from college planning to offspring drug addiction; unless divorced parents are unusually accessible, therapists would not broach a more general reworking of the parent–youngster relationship. However, if a son's or daughter's unmet needs do erupt in family sessions during the postdivorce phase, they should be addressed in these sessions as well as in individual offspring sessions. In contrast to the family sessions for younger children, family sessions with older offspring may include both parents, as the ability to grasp reality will generally prevent any reconciliation fantasies stimulated among these older offspring from getting out of hand.

Case Example: Culturally Sensitive, Therapeutic Reparenting.

Twenty-year-old Anna K. contacted a community mental health clinic at the urging of her mother Irena, age 45. Anna resided with Irena and her brother, Alex, age 15. Irena was concerned about Anna because Anna refused to attend college, despite her above average high school performance. Additionally, Anna was employed far below her capacity in a fast-food restaurant, and associated with young people who Irena feared were drug users. The whole idea of seeking mental health services was utterly foreign to both Irena and Anna (Brodsky, 1988; Castex, 1992), and the treatment application was a sign of Irena's desperation and feeling of failure regarding her daughter.

Irena and her ex-husband Leonid, both physicians in the former Soviet Union, had divorced 6 years ago, when Anna was 14. At that time, the K. family had been in the United States for 3 years. The marital disengagement was marked by stony silence rather than violent arguments, and the divorce was never explained to the children; Leonid simply moved out. As is typical of women and men in Soviet emigrant families (Castex, 1992; Drachman & Shen-Ryan, 1991), Irena adjusted more readily to the nursing positions available to Soviet emigrant physicians that did Leonid. However, Irena found it difficult to maintain authority with her adolescent daughter in her new country; Anna's freedom in the United States contrasted with the regimentation of the former Soviet Union (Belozersky, 1990), and Anna spoke English better than her mother. A depressed, defeated man, Leonid paid child support. He had almost nothing to do with Irena, maintained regular but perfunctory contact with his daughter and son, and was not involved in their lives. The therapist, Ed, a White male born in the United States, had a working knowledge of the help-seeking attitudes of various ethnic groups. Ed noted that Anna's stiff, constricted presentation reflected the reluctance of most Soviet emigrants to share any emotion with a stranger (Castex, 1992). Ed also noted a typically Soviet distrust of anyone who seemed to be a bureaucrat. Finally, Ed noted Anna's genuine confusion about a mental health service based on discussion of feelings, rather than on medicine administered by a psychiatrist. Ed reflected that this confusion was typical of emigrants accustomed to the health care system in the former Soviet Union; there, patients generally do not have choices, but rather are told exactly what to do (Belozersky, 1990; Brodsky, 1988). Nonetheless, underneath Anna's multifaceted and quite understandable distance from him, Ed sensed a young woman sorely in need of parenting.

To form a relationship with Anna, Ed was more formal than with other clients; his purpose was to give Anna some continuation of her former health care experiences. He was also more concrete; his purpose was to avoid an emphasis on emotions that would upset Anna. Thus, Ed carefully explained that the purpose of sessions was to make sure Anna's life was the way she wanted it to be, and initially explored facts and patterns of daily living more than emotions. To avoid the impression of intruding into the life of an understandably distrustful young woman, he spoke in a slow, matter-of-fact way, and interspersed questions about Anna's life with more general discussion of the differences between the United States and the former Soviet Union, where Anna had lived until she was 11.

Deep down, Anna appreciated Ed's low-key yet parental approach. Anna had never really experienced an adult who was in command, and had been on her own far too soon. Her parents' divorce and the disruption of her family contributed to the sense of being alone, adrift, and angry, as did the emigration experience, which entailed the loss of everything familiar.

Ed carefully refrained from telling Anna what to do, although he expressed interest in her past (e.g., her parent's divorce, the transition to life in the United States) and present (e.g., her job and her social life). When Anna missed appointments from time to time, Ed called her at home. Because of her father's unavailability, the nonsexual attention of a male had particular meaning. Eventually, some of Anna's angry acting-out began to subside.

Ed also met every other week with Irena. Leonid refused contact. Irena was receptive to Ed's ideas about retreating from her current pushy, ineffectual behavior with Anna. Although Irena was not always able to put these ideas into action, she did grasp Ed's message that at age 20, Anna had to make her own choices. Because she was also raising an adolescent son, Irena was interested in looking further at her maternal behavior. She learned that emigration and her divorce had sapped much energy that could have gone into raising Anna, and that she had been unable to help her then teenaged daughter negotiate a culture she herself did not understand. Irena felt that with Ed's guidance, as well as time elapsed and knowledge gained since emigration and divorce, she would be able to give more guidance, limits, and involvement to Alex.

Part V

EPILOGUE

Chapter 11

Additional Areas of Interest for Therapists

Many adults, adolescents, and children from all walks of life are drastically influenced by the divorce process. At the outset, this volume put forth a particular orientation for the therapist helping these people. The focal points in this orientation are

1. ongoing attention (not just lip service) to client's age, ethnicity, gender, and income,
2. awareness of issues characteristic of each stage in the divorce process (preseparation phase, divorce transition, postdivorce phase),
3. impressions of the level of ego functioning and coping skills of each family member,
4. an eclectic orientation encouraging use of various treatment modalities (e.g., crisis intervention, structural family treatment, support groups, long-term individual therapy),
5. reference to specific goals in the planning of treatment strategies,
6. awareness that goals can sometimes be attained only to a limited extent, and
7. vigilance regarding countertransference and the maintenance of therapeutic optimism.

The preceding chapters have demonstrated the utility of this orientation. They have also demonstrated that although treatment during each stage of the divorce process is important, the lion's share of work, for clients and therapists, occurs during the divorce transition. At this time, the immediacy of the actual physical separation, and the interpersonal complexities facing former spouses and their children lead to wrenching tangible and emotional upheaval extending over several years. This upheaval occurs in both individual lives and families, and the work for the therapist is correspondingly emotionally charged and multifaceted.

Finally, the preceding chapters suggest that the therapist working with divorcing and divorced families take an interest not just in the treatment room, but also in the real world. For example, therapists assisting maritally disrupted families from varied socioeconomic and ethnic backgrounds are likely to care not only about their own clients, but also about the availability of divorce-related services to a broad range of potential clients. Additionally, these therapists are generally concerned with public policy and legal matters that affect their clients' lives. And, to refine their clinical work, effective therapists are eager for new research findings on the impact of divorce on adults, adolescents, and children.

Thus, the preceding chapters imply the need for therapists to be aware of the broader context of their work, with regard to family life education (FLE) programs, social policies, legal issues, and social science research. Therapists with a political or research bent may actually work to promote or influence projects they view as beneficial.

FAMILY LIFE EDUCATION (FLE) PROGRAMS

Family Life Education Programs for the Divorced

This volume has stressed clinical work with individuals and families who experience divorce. Family life education (FLE) programs, particularly those for divorced parents, are a complementary way of helping the same population. FLE programs are generally short term (one to six sessions), and utilize videotapes, lectures, discussion, role play, and experiential exercises. They provide information (e.g., how to apply for child support), develop attitudes (e.g., decreased concern about household neatness for employed divorced mothers), and teach specific interpersonal skills (e.g., separating feelings from behavior) (Buehler, Betz, Ryan, Legg, & Trotter, 1992). Because some courts require participation in divorce-related FLE (Garber, 1994; Kramer & Washo, 1993), clients may be either mandated or voluntary. One complication is that ''voluntary'' clients may be present at the advice of attorneys, who want litigating clients to appear concerned and responsible (Buehler et al., 1992).

Therapists working with divorcing and divorced families generally view FLE programs favorably, because they can improve parenting skills and parental confidence among divorced mothers and fathers. Additionally, these programs reach many people that therapy does not. This broad scope of contact is due to (a) mandated participation, (b) the participation of people who seek a short-term service without extensive personal disclosure, and (c) the greater likelihood of a fee waiver (Devlin, Brown, Beebe, & Parulis, 1992).

The Benefit to Underserved Minorities.

Additionally, FLE programs can bring divorce-related services to underserved minorities. As previously noted, the divorce rates among African Americans (Bumpass et al., 1989, 1991; Moore & Schwebel, 1993; Heaton & Jacobson, 1994) and Hispanics (Chillman, 1993; Family and household structure, 1992; Vega, 1990) are high. Yet, both African Americans (Jackson, 1991) and Hispanics (Carrasquillo, 1991) underuse formal mental health services. An FLE program given in an African American church, or in a Hispanic neighborhood organization does more than help those who attend; the program leader can refer to therapy those who might not otherwise contact mental health services perceived as foreign and unhelpful. Attention to culturally relevant topics (e.g., grandparents as resources for children of divorce) in the FLE programs improves their success and also establishes rapport with minority individuals and families who might be referred to clinical services.

The Benefit to Divorced Fathers.

Family Life Education programs can also reach divorced fathers. As previously noted, divorced men are much less likely to apply for divorce-related therapy than are their female counterparts (Cohen & Lowenberg, 1994; Myers, 1989). I speculate that this is not just because of a general male reluctance to seek therapy (Meth & Passick, 1990), but also because of child support arrears. These debts are far more common among fathers than mothers (Depner, 1993), and it is likely that most men thus indebted will vigorously avoid any situation—including therapy—where the topic will be raised. (See chapter 8 for ideas on how therapists can address this obstacle in outreach to individual fathers, and in clinical sessions.) In FLE programs, the arrears of any one participant will most likely go undiscussed, so the seeking of help is less threatening. Ultimately, the consciousness-raising that FLE programs promote may lead to more responsible payment behavior (Devlin et al., 1992).

Divorced fathers may benefit from gender-mixed FLE programs or from FLE programs designed specifically for fathers (Devlin et al., 1992; Schwebel, Fine, & Moreland, 1988). The latter accommodate both custodial and noncustodial fathers, often feature male leaders, and stress problem areas common among males in this society, such as awareness of feelings (Devlin et al., 1992; Downey, 1994; Schwebel et al., 1988), communication skills (Devlin et al., 1992; Downey, 1994; Schwebel et al., 1988), and maintaining or strengthening family ties (Cooney, 1994). As men become more comfortable with feelings, and better able to get along with their children and extended families (e.g., childrens' maternal grandparents), they become more aware of their importance as fathers, and are likely to increase involvement with their children. Although this volume has stressed that a positive relationship with the custodial parent (usually the mother) is sufficient to rear a youngster to adulthood, I concur with Furstenberg and Cherlin (1991) that paternal involvement is desirable, as it can engender benefits to children that go beyond the "good-enough" parenting provided by custodial mothers (Devlin et al., 1992).

Other FLE Programs

Although programs for parents are among the most common and significant FLE programs for the divorced, other FLE programs make contributions as well. For example, school-based programs aim to prevent divorce-related problems among children (Grych & Fincham, 1992) and programs for those contemplating or entering remarriage highlight appropriate interpersonal expectations and potential areas of role strain (Kaplan & Hennon, 1992). Overall, therapists working with the divorced should promote these programs, both as resources in their own right, and as a way of encouraging people who need further therapy to seek it.

SOCIAL POLICY

It has long been recognized (e.g., Emery, 1988; Rice & Rice, 1986b; Straus, 1988) that if a social policy helps families or the poor, it helps divorced families even more. That is, any publicly funded or publicly mandated improvement in life circumstances is felt particularly keenly by financially stressed, overworked, single parents, whose support systems are almost always in need of strengthening. A brief overview of some of the most basic needed policy initiatives for American society today follows.

Needed Policy Initiatives in Three Areas

Education.

Currently, public education, particularly in our inner cities and other poor neighborhoods, often takes place in old, unsafe buildings. Books and other materials are out-of-date, teachers are overworked, and classes are too big. As a result, many youth drop out, while others graduate from high school functionally illiterate, unprepared for employment. Frequently, these undereducated youth are African American or Hispanic.

Increased aid for public education (Williams, 1994), and use of state or national standards for student achievement could do much to increase the possibilities for young people entering the adult world. For those whose parents are divorced, education has particular meaning, as the need for economic self-support is greater than among those who grew up in intact families (Aquilino, 1994).

Employment-Related Issues.

An increase in the minimum wage, which does not currently support a full-time working mother and her family (Kissman & Allen, 1993; Riessman, 1990), would greatly benefit divorced custodial parents, by allowing them to choose labor force participation over AFDC. If health insurance for all Americans becomes mandatory, custodial parents will not have to choose between AFDC and Medicaid health insurance on the one hand, and employment without health insurance on the other. Also relevant to working parents are accessible, affordable, high-quality child care (Acock & Demo, 1994; Grych & Fincham, 1992; Zigler & Gilman, 1990), flex-time jobs (Acock & Demo, 1994; Ahlburg & DeVita, 1992) and closing of the gender wage gap (Kissman & Allen, 1993).

For custodial mothers, the benefit of social policy changes facilitating employment goes far beyond the improvement of material circumstances. Labor force participation of these women often improves emotional status as well as finances, resulting in improved parenting (Acock

& Demo, 1994). For custodial fathers and joint custody parents, implementation of these policy changes would probably also be beneficial on both material and emotional levels. However, the benefits would be less dramatic, given the higher baseline levels of income and social support in both of these groups (Downey, 1994; Guttmann, 1993).

Public Assistance.

Among women who apply for AFDC benefits, 45% do so because of separation or divorce (DeParle, 1994). Generally, applicants are women who cannot find jobs, or those with very young children. While they receive AFDC, the poverty for themselves and their children is grinding; over the last two decades, the actual cash value of the monthly welfare check and food stamps such a woman receives has eroded about 25% (DeParle, 1994).

Most of these women prefer employment, and will be off AFDC within 2 years (DeParle, 1994). What can be done to make the time-limited welfare experience more humane? As Chillman (1993) suggests, the basic answer is to raise the monthly grants to a level where a simple but adequate life can occur. Food stamp allowances might be enlarged, and the quality and circumstances of Medicaid health services improved (Chillman, 1993); current services are severely limited, and lengthy waiting room stints routinely beset mothers and children needing to see physicians.

Social Policy: The Current Climate

As Zigler and Gilman pointed out in 1990, knowledge about policy initiatives that can support American parents—divorced and otherwise—in raising their children is readily available; the initiatives sketched above are examples of such common knowledge, and probably quite familiar to the reader. The question that follows is: What causes Americans to refrain from acting on what they know? One answer seems to be a long standing reluctance to see society as a unified whole, with government responsible for promoting quality of life for all of the members of that society. For example, one obstacle to achieving the public assistance improvements depicted above is a public mentality viewing aid programs for families and children as charity for which recipients should be grateful, rather than as an entitlement which society makes available to members who are temporarily unable to sustain themselves. The "AFDC as charity" mentality is in marked contrast to attitudes in other industrialized nations, such as Sweden, France, and England (Fine & Fine, 1994).

Ironically, the inability to view members of society as interconnected may eventually backfire on those who eschew an increased role for government in human lives as mere "bleeding heart" altruism. The failure to invest in today's children (e.g., their education, their care while their mothers work, the life quality they receive while on public assistance) will raise inescapable costs for taxpayers 20 years from now; when people are not raised to a competent, self-sufficient adulthood, incarceration and public assistance costs inevitably skyrocket.

As this book goes to press, American public policy is in flux. For example, Congress is considering revision of AFDC benefits; therapists concerned about the financial circumstances of their poor or potentially poor clients (divorced and otherwise) may find this a critical time to speak up. Likewise, health insurance, for a time, held center stage in congressional debate; politically oriented therapists may find it important to remain vigilant regarding a propitious moment for renewal of national level health insurance discussion.

LEGAL ISSUES

The therapist who addresses marital disruption needs to follow changing divorce laws, and influence them insofar as possible. Additionally, when indicated, the therapist needs to understand divorce laws as entry points either to policy issues or to related legal matters which are not divorce-specific, but influence the divorced. The following brief overview identifies areas of divorce law which need change. It also demonstrates links of divorce law to social policy or to other areas of the law.

Custody

As outlined in chapter 4, custody laws in most states have evolved during this century. To review, these laws have successively viewed children as their fathers' property, as better off in the care of their mothers, and, most recently, as better off when both parents have joint custody (Downey & Powell, 1993; Fine & Fine, 1994; Guttmann, 1993). These laws can encourage but not require a particular form of custody. As previously noted, despite the current fashion of joint custody, the vast majority of divorces involving children result in sole custody mothers (Maccoby et al., 1993). Since it appears that we cannot legislate who takes care of children, the key custody issue for therapists is not to advocate for legal changes. Rather, it is to advocate for policy changes that will enhance the lives of (generally female) custodial parents, (e.g., improved child-care facilities, larger grants for AFDC families).

Child Support

In contrast, in the area of child support, there have been meaningful legal changes. As of 1988, federal law requires states to establish guidelines for judges to use when awarding child support. As of 1994, federal law requires mandatory withholding of all support payments from obligors' paychecks. Taken together, these two laws help accomplish (a) uniform award sizes, uninfluenced by the biases of individual judges, (b) award adequacy, and (c) obligor compliance (Fine & Fine, 1994). As a result, the life quality of many divorced families (generally mother headed) has been enhanced.

In the area of child support, then, strengthened divorce laws improve human lives. Therapists interested in strengthening these laws further might advocate for any of several current noncompeting ideas. Previously, I proposed an idea that would benefit AFDC families (Bogolub, 1994): Child support collected from an ex-spouse owing an AFDC family might accrue to the family. AFDC families now receive only $50 from child support payments per month, no matter how much is collected, with the remainder going to recoup taxes spent on AFDC payments. The proposed arrangement would eliminate a double standard, and enable AFDC families to benefit in the same way as other families. Given the child support amounts owed, the possibility of AFDC families receiving so much that the custodial parent's incentive to work is lost is very slim.

Other ideas are proposed by major scholars in the area of divorce. Cherlin (1993) suggests that the current state-based system be replaced by a federal clearinghouse that would collect and distribute all support payments withheld from paychecks. This would increase collection rates from husbands who cross state lines to avoid payments, and cut down on the need for custodial parents (generally mothers) to use costly private collection agencies to obtain what is due them (Lewin, 1994). Garfinkel (1992) argues for an assured child support benefit. Since even mandatory withholding and federal administration will not ensure that all support payments are made, the federal government would pay custodial parents the support they are owed, even if it has not been collected from the nonresidential parent. A program similar to the one Garfinkel proposes already operates in Sweden (Fine & Fine, 1994). Garfinkel also argues for larger awards, citing empirical research indicating that nonresidential fathers can afford to pay more (Garfinkel, 1992; McDonald, Moran, & Garfinkel, 1990).

Such divorce law changes would improve the incomes of custodial parents and their children, but therapists need to see the child support issue in a broader context. For example, a circumscribed focus on the compliance of indebted fathers, who are often low income (Peterson & Nord, 1990; Seltzer, 1991; Arditti & Keith, 1993), obscures the more fundamental problem of an economy in which both men and women can work hard, earn little, and find it difficult to part with money (Bogolub, 1994; Williams, 1994). In fact, particularly among African Americans, Hispanics and other groups where low incomes are prevalent, a narrow focus on child support enforcement creates an artificial enmity between men who owe and women who are owed (D. L. Franklin, 1992). Compliance is important, but even when child support is paid regularly, it does not provide a major change in income level for divorced families. Only improved wages for custodial parents (overwhelmingly female) can do that. This realization brings therapists with an activist bent back to the employment-related policy issues raised above, as a complement to advocacy for changes in child support laws.

Alimony

Alimony, or spousal support, is also an area where divorce laws need strengthening. In the vast majority of cases, ex-husbands make payments to ex-wives rather than vice versa. As previously indicated, alimony rarely lasts more than 2 years (Zastrow & Kirst-Ashman, 1990), accrues to only about 15% of divorced women (Fine & Fine, 1994; Zastrow & Kirst-Ashman, 1990), and, in most states, is viewed as rehabilitation, that is, preparation for financial independence (Fine & Fine, 1994).

However, rehabilitation for some middle-aged women is simply not possible. Throughout this volume, we have seen that divorced former middle- and upper middle-class homemakers generally cannot develop marketable skills that will support a lifestyle anywhere near what they experienced while married. As Weitzman (1988) points out, these women often raised children and devoted themselves to husbands' careers with the expectation that these services would be exchanged for lifelong financial stability. When divorce occurs, men change the unspoken rules of the game, and middle-aged ex-wives are too old to benefit much from new rules requiring that they find employment (Weitzman, 1988). For older women who are not employable at all, the problems are even worse.

Certainly, the majority of women who divorce are not leaving marriages of this type. Yet, former middle- and upper middle-class homemakers deserve attention too. When such women are middle-aged, long-term alimony as a supplement to their own postdivorce wages makes sense, if ex-husbands are at their earning peak and capable of providing it. For unemployable older women, the amounts would have to be larger, if ex-husbands could afford it; the aim of new alimony-related legislation would be to equalize income in the postdivorce households (Weitzman, 1988).

Long-term alimony may also make sense for blue-collar middle-aged women who are unable to elevate postdivorce incomes through improved employment situations. If children are grown and ex-husbands do not pay child support, these men can afford to contribute to alimony the amount they previously paid (or would have paid) as child support. Because of blue-collar ex-husbands' income levels, the alimony amounts would be considerably smaller than those received by women with more prosperous ex-husbands.

Thus, therapists with an interest in middle-aged and older divorced women may want to work for laws promoting long-term spousal support as an alimony option. In a related vein, through their professional organizations, such therapists may also become involved in obtaining and presenting data documenting wage and hiring discrimination against middle-aged women. Such documentation would facilitate better enforcement of extant laws prohibiting age discrimination. Progress in fighting age discrimination against middle-aged women will not end the need for long-term alimony, which will still be relevant in some cases (e.g., older women, middle-aged women earning fair but meager wages), but it will decrease the need for this proposed form of spousal support.

RESEARCH

Extant research in the area of divorce has undergirded this volume, and has much to offer. The differential effects of divorce on women of various ages, the impact of divorce on the income of women and children, the postdivorce evolution of ties between ex-spouses, reasons for custodial fatherhood, visitation behavior of nonresidential parents—these are but examples from a wide range of research topics where knowledge has developed steadily. Still, there are several aspects of divorce research in which growth is critical.

Needed: Research on Divorce and Ethnicity

Although most divorce research has focused on White people, the trend has begun to shift in the last decade. Most often, research on divorce and ethnicity has compared the divorce experience of Blacks and Whites. For example, Fine et al. (1992), Fine and Schwebel (1987), Gove and Shin (1989), and Kitson (1992) all found that divorce is easier for Blacks, although the finding is limited to Black females in the work of Gove and Shin, and Kitson. Explanations for the ease of Black divorce adaptation generally refer to African American culture, and cite extended family network (Fine & Schwebel, 1987), value placed on all children, regardless of parents' marital status (Fine & Schwebel, 1987), and lack of stigma associated with divorce (Kitson, 1992). A smaller amount of comparative divorce research focusses on Hispanics. For example, Wagner (1987) found that relative to White divorced mothers, Mexican American divorced mothers receive less support from extended family because Catholicism, which is the prevalent religion among Mexican Americans, views divorce negatively.

In the future, research on divorce and ethnicity might develop beyond this comparative mode, and focus on building more detailed knowledge about specific groups. For example, Black women's ease of adaptation to divorce might be further scrutinized, in light of the tendency of Black women to be stoic (McGoldrick et al., 1991) and underrate the complexity of their experience (P. M. Hines, personal communication, November 19, 1990). On the other hand, where little or no research is available, comparative studies are needed as a first step. The divorce experience of Soviet Jewish emigrants or Orthodox Jews might be compared to that of mainstream American Jews, or to that of Whites in general.

New research on divorce in any ethnic group might also address variables modulating divorce experience within that group. These include socioeconomic level (Fine et al., 1992) and subculture (Fine et al., 1992; Del Carmen & Virgo, 1993; Mirande, 1991). This volume has demonstrated the effect of subculture on divorce through reference to Orthodox Jews, mainstream American Jews, and Soviet emigrant Jews. Future authors might examine divorce among Blacks of West Indian descent and Blacks of African descent, or divorce among Cuban Americans and Mexican Americans. Another variable that can influence divorce among emigrants (e.g., Soviet Jewish emigrants, emigrants from Central America) is number of years away from country of origin.

In general, more research regarding ethnicity and divorce is clearly needed (e.g., Moore & Schwebel, 1993; Neff & Schluter, 1993). Just as extant findings have shaped the ethnic-specific techniques presented in this volume, new findings will provided the basis for modifying and improving these techniques. Finally, remember that ethnic groups discussed in this volume were chosen to be representative rather than exhaustive. Study of the divorce process in ethnic groups not discussed here (e.g., Asian, European, Native American) is of utmost importance.

Needed: Research on Divorce, Family Process, and Family Structure

Chapter 1 indicated that for quite some time, the dominant question in research on children of divorce was how these children fared in the long run compared with their counterparts from intact families. Currently, Acock and Demo (1994), Allen (1993), and Demo (1993) opine that this question is becoming obsolete. These authors suggest that variables more proximate to children's lives than parental marital status have greater effect. Such variables include the value adults place on children, household income, amount of discord between parents, and parents' social support. Noting that awareness of these more influential variables is longstanding (see chapter 1), I concur with their conclusion. Furthermore, setting up a battle about which family type is best, as was done in much prior research (e.g., Amato & Keith, 1991b), is an oversimplification. The "battle mentality" also reflects a need to win a not-so-subtle contest, currently framed in the language as "family values" versus "cultural diversity."

Acock and Demo (1994) suggest that future research focus on processes (e.g., parental conflict, income decline) that occur across a variety of family structures (e.g., married parents, divorced parents), and bypass altogether the question of which structure (married or divorced) is "better." Like research that examines the complexity of divorced families of varied ethnicity, research that pinpoints reactions of adults, adolescents, and children to critical family processes will be of particular use to the therapist who wants not to judge, but to decide when and how to intervene.

On the other hand, it is important to pursue research on the complexities of various divorced family structures. For example, the dramatic increase in homes headed by custodial fathers (Downey, 1994; Meyer & Garasky, 1993) suggests the need for more studies in this area; contributions such as Greif's work on custodial fathers' role adjustment (e.g., Greif & DeMaris, 1990) and Downey's work (1994) on custodial fathers' impact on children's school performance represent a beginning. One area where new work might occur is the relationship between custodial fathers' economic status and paternal functioning. Although the economic status of custodial fathers is generally far better than that of custodial mothers (Downey, 1994; Meyer & Garasky, 1993), a portion of custodial father families are poor or near poor (Meyer & Garasky, 1993). In what ways are their role performances similar to or different from that of their poor or near poor female counterparts? Findings would guide therapists assessing and treating both male and female custodial parents.

Additionally, research on particular divorced family structures should pinpoint strengths. For example, Acock and Demo (1994) note that in mother-headed divorced families, some women demonstrate particular competence and mastery, or an ability to carry out multiple roles. Findings about strengths are important to therapists who must sometimes elicit hidden strengths in order to build client self-esteem. These findings are also important for planning goals that troubled clients might achieve.

Emergent Research Topics

To remain current, research should monitor the experience of divorced people who feel the effects of recent changes in social policy and divorce laws. For example, as this book goes to press, the 1993 Family and Medical Leave Act (FMLA), intended to enable employees to take unpaid leave to care for children or elderly parents (Noble, 1994b), has been in operation for about 2 years; analyses after one year indicated FMLA was being used as intended (Noble, 1994b). But, relative to married mothers, can divorced mothers afford to use FMLA's unpaid leave? As previously noted, Spitze et al. (1994) found that divorce does not compromise women's ability to care for elderly parents; it remains to be seen if today's divorced women will be "superwomen" (i.e., work full time and provide care), or if they will lighten their employment load with FMLA leaves. The answer will help advocates for the divorced in the political arena, by letting them know if FMLA is relevant to their constituency.

Likewise, mandatory withholding of child support from the paychecks of obligors (overwhelmingly nonresidential fathers) began in 1994. As this book goes to press, hard data are as yet unavailable, but the measure will probably increase collection rates for child support. The questions then arise: Will increased child support payment rates increase visitation and other forms of nonpayment contact with children? If so, will this contact between nonresidential fathers and children differ in its impact in any way from the contact that is not stimulated by forced payment? The answers will not be particularly useful when therapists assist nonresidential fathers who would have paid support without the garnishing of their checks, but the answers will be very useful when planning ways to reach out to nonresidential fathers whose support payments are forced.

Overall, empirical research helps therapists assisting today's diverse divorcing and divorced families anticipate client issues and plan intervention strategies. These therapists should not rely in a static fashion on the orientation presented in this volume, but should be open to refining and modifying this orientation on the basis of new findings that research provides.

REFERENCES

Acock, A. C., & Demo, D. H. (1994). *Family diversity and well-being.* Newbury Park, CA: Sage.

Ahlburg, D. A., & DeVita, C. J. (1992). New realities of the American family [entire issue]. *Population Bulletin, 47* (2).

Ahrons, C. R., & Miller, R. B. (1993). The effect of the postdivorce relationship on paternal involvement: A longitudinal analysis. *American Journal of Orthopsychiatry, 63,* 441–450.

Ahrons, C. R., & Rodgers, R. (1987). *Divorced families: A multidisciplinary developmental view.* New York: W. W. Norton.

Allen, K. R. (1993). The dispassionate discourse of children's adjustment to divorce. *Journal of Marriage and the Family, 55,* 46–49.

Amato, P. (1993). Children's adjustment to divorce: Theories, hypotheses, empirical support. *Journal of Marriage and the Family, 55,* 23–38.

Amato, P. R., & Keith, B. (1991a). Parental divorce and adult well-being: A meta-analysis. *Journal of Marriage and the Family, 53,* 43–58.

Amato, P. R., & Keith, B. (1991b). Parental divorce and the well-being of children: A meta-analysis. *Psychological Bulletin, 110,* 26–46.

Aquilino, W. S. (1994). Impact of childhood family disruption on young adults' relationships with parents. *Journal of Marriage and the Family, 56,* 295–313.

Arditti, J. A. (1991). Child support noncompliance and divorced fathers: Rethinking the role of paternal involvement. *Journal of Divorce and Remarriage, 14,* 107–119.

Arditti, J. A. (1992). Differences between fathers with joint custody and noncustodial fathers. *American Journal of Orthopsychiatry, 62,* 186–195.

Arditti, J. A., & Keith, T. Z. (1993). Visitation frequency, child support payment, and the father-child relationship postdivorce. *Journal of Marriage and the Family, 55,* 699–712.

Asmussen, L. & Larson, R. (1991). Young adolescents in single-parent and married-parent families. *Journal of Marriage and the Family, 53*, 1021–1030.

Axelrod, R. (1994, July 1–7). Abusers among us. *Jewish Week*, pp. 16–17.

Barber, B. L., & Eccles, J. S. (1992). Long-term influence of divorce and single parenting on adolescent family- and work-related values, behaviors, and aspirations. *Psychological Bulletin, 111*, 108–126.

Baucom, D. H., & Epstein, N. (1990). *Cognitive behavioral marital therapy*. New York: Brunner Mazel.

Bayme, S. (1990). The Jewish family in American culture. In D. Blankenhorn, S. Bayme, & J. B. Elshtain (Eds.), *Rebuilding the nest: A new commitment to the American family* (pp. 149–160). Milwaukee: Family Service Association.

Bayme, S. (1994). Changing perceptions of divorce. *Journal of Jewish Communal Service, 70*, 120–126.

Beal, E. W. & Hochman, G. (1991). *Adult children of divorce*. New York: Delta.

Bee, H. (1994). *Lifespan development*. New York: Harper Collins.

Belozersky, I. (1990). New beginning, old problems: Psychocultural frame of reference and family dynamics during the adjustment period. *Journal of Jewish Communal Service, 67*, 124–130.

Berg, I. K., & Miller, S. D. (1992). Working with Asian American clients: One person at a time. *Families in Society, 73*, 356–363.

Bertoia, C. & Dakich, J. (1993). The fathers' rights movement: Contradictions in rhetoric and practice. *Journal of Family Issues, 14*, 592–615.

Besharov, D. J. (1990). The feminization of poverty: Has legal services failed to respond? *Clearinghouse Review, 24*, 210–218.

Birns, B. & ben–Ner, N. (1988). Psychoanalysis constructs motherhood. In B. Birns & D. F. Hay (Eds.), *The different faces of motherhood* (pp. 47–72). New York: Plenum.

Bogolub, E. (1984). Symbiotic mothers and infantilized only children: A subtype of single-parent family. *Child and Adolescent Social Work Journal, 1*, 89–101.

Bogolub, E. (1989). Families of divorce: A three-generational perspective. *Social Work, 34*, 375–376.

Bogolub, E. (1991). Women and mid-life divorce: Some practice issues. *Social Work, 36*, 428–433.

Bogolub, E. (1994). Child support: Help to women and children, or government revenue? *Social Work, 39*, 487–489.

Bohannon, P. (1970). The six stations of divorce. In P. Bohannon (Ed.), *Divorce and after* (pp. 29–55). Garden City, NY: Doubleday.

Bonkowski, S. (1989). Lingering sadness: Young adults' response to parental divorce. *Social Casework, 70,* 219–223.

Booth, A., & Amato, P. R. (1994). Parental marital quality, parental divorce, and relations with parents. *Journal of Marriage and the Family, 56,* 21–34.

Booth, A., & Edwards, J. N. (1989). Transmission of marital and family quality over the generations: The effect of parental divorce and unhappiness. *Journal of Divorce, 13,* 41–58.

Bowman, P. J. (1993). The impact of economic marginality among African American husbands and fathers. In H. P. McAdoo (Ed.), *Family ethnicity: Strength in diversity* (pp. 120–137). Newbury Park, CA: Sage.

Boyd–Franklin, N. (1989). *Black families in therapy: A multi-systems approach.* New York: Guilford.

Bray, J. H., & Berger, S. H. (1993). Nonresidential parent-child relationship following divorce and remarriage: A longitudinal perspective. In C. E. Depner & J. H. Bray (Eds.), *Nonresidential parenting* (pp. 156–181). Newbury Park, CA: Sage.

Bray, J. H., & Depner, C. E. (1993). Perspectives on nonresidential parenting. In C. E. Depner & J. H. Bray (Eds.), *Nonresidential parenting* (pp. 3–12). Newbury Park, CA: Sage.

Breitowitz, I. A. (1994). A primer on Jewish divorce: A guide for the Jewish communal professional. *Journal of Jewish Communal Service, 70,* 145–153.

Brodsky, B. (1988). Mental health attitudes and practices of Soviet Jewish immigrants. *Health and Social Work, 13,* 130–136.

Brody, J. (1992, March 18). When love turns violent: The roots of abuse. *The New York Times,* p. C12.

Brown, F. H. (1989). The postdivorce family. In B. Carter & M. McGoldrick (Eds.), *The changing family life cycle* (pp. 371–398). Boston: Allyn and Bacon.

Buehler, C., Betz, P., Ryan, C. M., Legg, B. H., & Trotter, B. B. (1992). Description and evaluation of the orientation for divorcing parents: Implications for postdivorce prevention programs. *Family Relations, 41,* 154–162.

Bulcroft, R. A., & Bulcroft, K. A. (1993). Race differences in attitudinal and motivational factors in the decision to marry. *Journal of Marriage and the Family, 55,* 338–355.

Bumpass, L. L., Martin, T. C., & Sweet, J. A. (1989). Background and early marital factors in marital disruption (National Survey of Families and Households Working Paper No. 14). Madison: Center for Demography and Ecology, University of Wisconsin–Madison.

Bumpass, L. L., Martin, T. C., & Sweet, J. A. (1991). The impact of family background and early marital factors on marital disruption. *Journal of Family Issues, 12,* 22–42.

Byrne, R. C. (1990). The effectiveness of the beginning experience workshop: A paraprofessional group marathon workshop for divorce adjustment. *Journal of Divorce, 13,* 101–120.

Cain, B. S. (1988). Divorce among elderly women: A growing social phenomenon. *Social Casework, 69,* 563–568.

Cain, B. S. (1989). Parental divorce during the college years. *Psychiatry, 52,* 135–146.

Canter, C. (1990, July 1). More women over 40 getting divorces on L. I. *The New York Times* (Long Island section), pp. 6–7.

Caplan, G. (1990). The prevention of psychological disorder in children of divorce. In H. J. Parad & L. G. Parad (Eds.), *Crisis intervention book 2: The practitioner's sourcebook for brief therapy* (pp. 331–358). Milwaukee: Family Service Association.

Carrasquillo, A. L. (1991). *Hispanic children and youth in the United States.* New York: Garland.

Castex, G. M. (1992). Soviet refugee children: The dynamic of migration and school practice. *Social Work in Education, 14,* 141–151.

Castex, G. M. (1994). Providing services to Hispanic/Latino populations: Profiles in diversity. *Social Work, 39,* 288–296.

Chan, L. Y., & Heaton, T. B. (1989). Demographic determinants of delayed divorce. *Journal of Divorce, 13,* 97–112.

Chase–Lansdale, P. L., & Hetherington, E. M. (1990). The impact of divorce on life–span development: Short- and long–term effects. In D. L. Featherman & R. M. Lerner (Eds.), *Life–span development and behavior* (Vol. 10, pp. 118–135). Hillsdale, NJ: Erlbaum.

Cherlin, A. (1992). *Marriage, divorce, remarriage.* Cambridge: Harvard University Press.

Cherlin, A. (1993, December 30). Making deadbeats pay up at work. *The New York Times,* p. A19.

Chess, S., Thomas, A., Korn, S., Mittelman, M., & Cohen, J. (1983). Early parental attitudes, divorce and separation, and young adult outcome: Findings of a longitudinal study. *Journal of the American Academy of Child Psychiatry, 22,* 47–51.

Chillman, C. S. (1993). Hispanic families in the United States: Research perspectives. In H. P. McAdoo (Ed.), *Family ethnicity: Strength in diversity* (pp. 141–163). Newbury Park, CA: Sage.

Chira, S. (1993, October 21). Fathers who want time off for families face uphill battle. *The New York Times,* p. C6.

Chira, S. (1994, April 6). Hispanic families use alternatives to day care, study finds. *The New York Times*, p. A19.

Chiriboga, D. (1982). Adaptation to marital separation in earlier and later life. *Journal of Gerontology, 37,* 109–114.

Chiriboga, D. A., Catron, L. S., & Associates. (1991). *Divorce: Crisis, challenge, or relief.* New York: New York University Press.

Cohen, O. & Lowenberg, M. (1994). Support systems in the divorce transition. *Journal of Jewish Communal Service,* 168–174.

Coleman, M., & Ganong, L. H. (1990). Remarriage and stepfamily research in the 1980's: Increased interest in an old family form. *Journal of Marriage and the Family, 52,* 925–940.

Combrinck–Graham, L. (1988). When parents separate or divorce: The sibling system. In M. D. Kahn & K. G. Lewis (Eds.), *Siblings in therapy: Lifespan and clinical issues* (pp. 190–208). New York: W. W. Norton.

Constantino, C. (1981). Intervention with battered women: The lawyer-social worker team. *Social Work, 26,* 456–461.

Cooney, T. M. (1994). Young adults' relations with parents: The influence of recent parental divorce. *Journal of Marriage and the Family, 56,* 45–56.

Cooney, T. M., Smyer, M. A., Hagestad, G. O., & Klock, R. (1986). Parental divorce in young adulthood: Some preliminary findings. *American Journal of Orthopsychiatry, 56,* 470–477.

Counts, R., & Sacks, A. (1985). The need for crisis intervention during marital separation. *Social Work, 30,* 146–150.

Darnton, N. (1992, April 13). A split verdict on America's marital future. *Newsweek,* p. 52.

Davis, L., & Hagen, J. (1992). The problem of wife abuse: The interrelationship of social policy and social work practice. *Social Work, 37,* 15–20.

DeFrain, J., LeMasters, E. E., & Schroff, J. A. (1991). Environment and fatherhood: Rural and urban influences. In F. M. Bozett & S. M. H. Hanson (Eds.), *Fatherhood and families in cultural context* (pp. 162–186). New York: Springer.

Del Carmen, R., & Virgo, G. N. (1993). Marital disruption and nonresidential parenting: A multicultural perspective. In C. E. Depner & J. H. Bray (Eds.), *Nonresidential parenting* (pp. 13–36). Newbury Park, CA: Sage.

Dell, P. F., & Applebaum, A. S. (1977). Trigenerational enmeshment: Unresolved ties of single-parents to family of origin. *American Journal of Orthopsychiatry, 47,* 52–59.

Demo, D. H. (1992). Parent-child relations: Assessing recent changes. *Journal of Marriage and the Family, 54*, 104–117.

Demo, D. H. (1993). The relentless search for effects of divorce: Forging new trails or tumbling down the beaten path. *Journal of Marriage and the Family, 55*, 42–45.

Demo, D. H., & Acock, A. C. (1988). The impact of divorce on children. *Journal of Marriage and the Family, 50*, 619–648.

DeParle, J. (1994, June 19). Welfare as we've known it. *The New York Times* (News of the Week in Review), p. 4.

Depner, C. E. (1993). Parental role reversal: Mothers as nonresidential parents. In C. E. Depner & J. H. Bray (Eds.), *Nonresidential parenting* (pp. 37–57). Newbury Park, CA: Sage.

Despert, J. L. (1953). *Children of divorce.* Garden City, NY: Doubleday.

Devlin, A. S., Brown, E. H., Beebe, J., & Parulis, E. (1992). Parent education for divorced fathers. *Family Relations, 41*, 290–296.

Devore, W., & London, H. (1993). Ethnic sensitivity for practitioners: A practice model. In H. P. McAdoo (Ed.), *Family ethnicity: Strength in diversity* (pp. 317–331). Newbury Park, CA: Sage.

Diedrick, P. (1991). Gender differences in divorce adjustment. *Journal of Divorce and Remarriage, 14*, 33–45.

Donnelly, D., & Finkelhor, D. (1992). Does equity in custody arrangements improve the parent-child relationship? *Journal of Marriage and the Family, 54*, 837–845.

Douglas, H. (1991). Assessing violent couples. *Families in Society, 72*, 525–533.

Downey, D. B. (1994). The school performance of children from single-mother and single-father families: Economic or interpersonal deprivation? *Journal of Family Issues, 15*, 129–147.

Downey, D. B., & Powell, B. (1993). Do children in single-parent households fare better living with same-sex parents? *Journal of Marriage and the Family, 55*, 55–71.

Drachman, D., & Shen-Ryan, A. (1991). Immigrants and refugees. In A. Gitterman (Ed.), *Handbook of social work practice with vulnerable populations* (pp. 618–646). New York: Columbia University Press.

Dutton, D. G., & Painter, S. (1993). The battered woman syndrome: Effects of severity and intermittency of abuse. *American Journal of Orthopsychiatry, 63*, 614–622.

Eckholm, E. (1992, July 20). Fathers find that child support means owing more than money. *The New York Times*, pp. A1, A13.

Emery, R. E. (1988). *Marriage, divorce, and children's adjustment.* Newbury Park, CA: Sage.

Everett, C. A., & Volgy, S. S. (1991). Treating divorce in family therapy practice. In A. S. Gurman & D. P. Kniskern (Eds.), *Handbook of family therapy* (Vol. 2, pp. 508–524). New York: Brunner Mazel.

Facundo, A. (1991). Sensitive mental health services for low income Puerto Rican families. In M. Sotomayor (Ed.), *Empowering Hispanic Families* (pp. 121–139). Milwaukee: Family Service Association.

Family and household structure. (1992). In P. Ries & A. J. Stone (Eds.), *The new American woman 1992–93* (pp. 244–262). New York: W. W. Norton.

Farmer, S., & Galaris, D. (1993). Support groups for children of divorce. *The American Journal of Family Therapy, 21,* 40–50.

Farnsworth, J., Pett, M. A., & Lund, D. A. (1989). Predictors of loss management and well–being in later life widowhood and divorce. *Journal of Family Issues, 10,* 102–121.

Fine, M. A., & Fine, D. R. (1994). An examination and evaluation of recent changes in divorce laws in five Western countries: The critical role of values. *Journal of Marriage and the Family, 56,* 249–264.

Fine, M. A., McKenry, P. C., & Chung, H. (1992). Post–divorce adjustment of Black and White single parents. *Journal of Divorce and Remarriage, 17,* 121–134.

Fine, M. A., & Schwebel, A. I. (1987). An emergent explanation of differing racial reactions to single parenthood. *Journal of Divorce and Remarriage, 11,* 1–15.

Fishman, S. B. (1989). Marginal no more: Jewish and single in the 1980s. *Journal of Jewish Communal Service, 65,* 328–331.

Fossett, M. A., & Kiecolt, K. J. (1993). Mate availability and family structure among African Americans in U.S. metropolitan areas. *Journal of Marriage and the Family, 55,* 288–302.

Frankel, A. (1991). The dynamics of day care. *Families in Society, 72,* 3–10.

Franklin, A. J. (1992). Therapy with African American men. *Families in Society, 73,* 350–355.

Franklin, D. L. (1992). Feminization of poverty and African-American families: Illusions and realities. *Affilia, 7,* 142–155.

Friedman, N. (1994). The Jewish factor in remarriage and stepparenting. *Journal of Jewish Communal Service, 70,* 134–144.

Fulmer, R. (1989). Lower–income and professional families: A comparison of structure and life cycle process. In B. Carter & M. McGoldrick (Eds.), *The changing family life cycle* (pp. 545–578). Boston: Allyn and Bacon.

Furstenberg, F., & Cherlin, A. (1991). *Divided families: What happens to children when parents part.* Cambridge: Harvard University Press.

Furstenberg, F., Morgan, S. P., & Allison, P. D. (1987). Paternal participation and children's well–being after marital dissolution. *American Sociological Review*, *52*, 695–701.

Furstenberg, F., & Teitler, J. O. (1994). Reconsidering the effects of marital disruption: What happens to children of divorce in early adulthood? *Journal of Family Issues*, *15*, 173–190.

Ganong, L. H., & Coleman, M. (1994). *Remarried family relationships*. Newbury Park, CA: Sage.

Garber, B. D. (1994). Practical limitations in considering psychotherapy with children of separation and divorce. *Psychotherapy*, *31*, 254–261.

Gardner, R. A. (1976). *Psychotherapy with children of divorce*. New York: Jason Aronson.

Gardner, R. A. (1990). Childhood stress due to parental divorce. In J. D. Noshpitz & R. D. Coddington (Eds.), *Stressors and the adjustment disorders* (pp. 43–59). New York: Wiley.

Garfinkel, I. (1992). *Assuring child support: An extension of social security*. New York: Russell Sage Foundation.

Garfinkel, I., & McLanahan, S. (1990). The effects of the child support provisions of the Family Support Act of 1988 on child well–being. *Population Research and Policy Review*, *9*, 205–234.

Garfinkel, I., Meyer, D. R., & Sandefur, G. D. (1992). The effects of alternative child support systems on Blacks, Hispanics, and non-Hispanic Whites. *Social Service Review*, *66*, 505–523.

Gelles, R. J., & Cornell, C. P. (1990). *Intimate violence in families*. Newbury Park, CA: Sage.

Germain, C. B. (1991). *Human behavior in the social environment*. New York: Columbia University Press.

Gerstel, N., Riessman, C. K., & Rosenfield, S. (1985). Explaining the symptomatology of separated and divorced women and men: The role of material conditions and social networks. *Social Forces*, *64*, 84–101.

Gibbs, J. T. (1989). Black American adolescents. In J. T. Gibbs, L. N. Huang, & Associates (Authors), *Children of color* (pp. 179–223). San Francisco: Jossey Bass.

Glass, B. L. (1990). Child support enforcement: An implementation analysis. *Social Service Review*, *64*, 542–558.

Glick, P., & Lin, S. (1986). Recent changes in divorce and remarriage. *Journal of Marriage and the Family*, *48*, 737–747.

Goode, W. J. (1956). *After divorce*. Glencoe, Ill.: Free Press.

Gove, W. R., & Shin, H. (1989). The psychological well-being of divorced and widowed men and women. *Journal of Family Issues*, *10*, 122–144.

Greenstein, T. N. (1990). Marital disruption and the employment of married women. *Journal of Marriage and the Family*, *52*, 657–676.

Greenstein, T. N. (1993). Maternal employment and child behavioral outcomes. *Journal of Family Issues*, *14*, 323–354.

Greif, G. L. (1987). Mothers without custody. *Social Work*, *32*, 11–16.

Greif, G. L. (1992). [Review of *Joint custody and shared parenting*]. *Journal of Marriage and the Family*, *54*, 470.

Greif, G. L., & DeMaris, A. (1990). Single fathers with custody. *Families in Society*, *71*, 259–266.

Greif, G. L., & Kristall, J. (1993). Common themes in a group for noncustodial parents. *Families in Society*, *74*, 240–245.

Grych, J. H., & Fincham, F. D. (1992). Interventions for children of divorce: Toward greater integration of research and action. *Psychological Bulletin*, *111*, 434–454.

Guterman, N. (1993). Confronting the unknowns in Jewish family violence: A call for knowledge development. *Journal of Jewish Communal Service*, *70*, 26–33.

Guttmann, J. (1993). *Divorce in psychosocial perspective: Theory and research*. Hillsdale, NJ: Erlbaum.

Haffey, M., & Cohen, P. M. (1992). Treatment issues for divorcing women. *Families in Society*, *73*, 142–148.

Hall, R. E. (1992). Bias among African-Americans regarding skin color: Implications for social work practice. *Research on Social Work Practice*, *2*, 479–486.

Handelman, M., & Miller, A. P. (1990). Vocational services in Soviet Jewish resettlement: The challenge for the nineties. *Journal of Jewish Communal Service*, *67*, 108–113.

Hatchett, S. J., & Jackson, J. S. (1993). African American extended kin systems: An assessment. In H. P. McAdoo (Ed.), *Family ethnicity: Strength in diversity* (pp. 90–108). Newbury Park, CA: Sage.

Heaton, T. B., & Jacobson, C. K. (1994). Race differences in changing family demographics in the 1980s. *Journal of Family Issues*, *15*, 290–308.

Heitler, S. (1990). *From conflict to resolution*. New York: W. W. Norton.

Herzog, E., & Sudia, C. E. (1973). Children in fatherless homes. In B. M. Caldwell & H. N. Riciuti (Eds.), *Review of child development research* (Vol. 3, pp. 141–232). Chicago: University of Chicago Press.

Heschel, S. (1991). Jewish feminism and women's identity. In R. J. Siegel & E. Cole (Eds.), *Jewish women in therapy* (pp. 31–39). New York: Harrington Park Press.

Hetherington, E. M., & Clingempeel, W. G. (1992). Coping with marital transitions: A family systems perspective. *Monographs of the Society for Research in Child Development, 57* (2–3, Serial No. 227).

Hetherington, E. M., Cox, M., & Cox, R. (1978). The aftermath of divorce. In J. H. Stevens, Jr., & M. Matthews (Eds.), *Mother-child, father-child relationships* (pp. 149–176). Washington, DC: National Association for the Education of Young Children.

Hetherington, E. M., & Tryon, A. (1989). His and her divorces. *The Family Therapy Networker, 13*(6), 58–61.

Hicks, S., & Anderson, C. (1989). Women on their own. In M. McGoldrick, C. Anderson, & F. Walsh (Eds.), *Women in families* (pp. 308–333). New York: W. W. Norton.

Hines, P. M. (1989). The family life cycle of poor Black families. In B. Carter & M. McGoldrick (Eds.), *The changing family life cycle* (pp. 545–578). Boston: Allyn and Bacon.

Hines, P. M. (1990). African American mothers. *Journal of Feminist Family Therapy, 2*, 23–32.

Hines, P. M., Preto, N. G., McGoldrick, M., Almeida, R., & Weltman, S. (1992). Intergenerational issues across cultures. *Families in Society, 73*, 323–338.

Ho, M. K. (1987). *Family therapy with ethnic minorities.* Newbury Park, CA: Sage.

Ho, M. K. (1992). *Minority children and adolescents in therapy.* Newbury Park, CA: Sage.

Hochschild, A. (1989). *The second shift.* New York: Avon.

Hodges, W. F. (1991). *Interventions for children of divorce.* New York: Wiley.

Holdnack, J. A. (1992). The long-term effects of parental divorce on family relationships and the effects on adult children's self-concept. *Journal of Divorce and Remarriage, 18*, 137–155.

Holmes, T. R., & Rahe, R. H. (1967). The social readjustment rating scale. *The Journal of Psychosomatic Research, 11*, 213–218.

Howe, M. (1991, August 25). Battered alien spouses find a way to escape an immigration trap. *The New York Times*, p. 40.

Hulewat, P., & Levine, M. W. (1994). The center for divorcing families: Breaching the barriers to service. *Journal of Jewish Communal Service, 70*, 154–159.

Ihinger-Tallman, M., Pasley, K., & Buehler, C. (1993). Developing a middle-range theory of father involvement postdivorce. *Journal of Family Issues, 14*, 550–571.

Isaacs, M. B., Montalvo, B., & Abelsohn, D. (1986). *The difficult divorce.* New York: Basic Books.

Jackson, J. S. (1991). Introduction. In J. S. Jackson, (Ed.), *Life in Black America* (pp. 1–12). New York: Sage.

Jacobs, L., & Dimarsky, S. B. (1991/1992). Jewish domestic abuse: Realities and responses. *Journal of Jewish Communal Service, 68,* 94–113.

Jacobson, G. (1983). *The multiple crises of marital separation and divorce.* New York: Grune and Stratton.

Jendrek, M. P. (1993). Grandparents who parent their grandchildren: Effects on lifestyle. *Journal of Marriage and the Family, 55,* 609–622.

Johnson, D. (1993, August 31). More and more, the single parent is Dad. *The New York Times,* pp. A1, A15.

Johnson, I. M. (1992). Economic, situational, and psychological correlates of the decision–making process of battered women. *Families in Society, 73,* 168–176.

Johnson, S. M. (1977). *First person singular: Living the good life alone.* Philadelphia: Lippincott.

Johnston, J. R. (1993). Children of divorce who refuse visitation. In C. E. Depner & J. H. Bray (Eds.), *Nonresidential parenting* (pp. 109–135). Newbury Park, CA: Sage.

Johnston, J. R., & Campbell, L. E. G. (1993). A clinical typology of interparental violence in disputed–custody divorces. *American Journal of Orthopsychiatry, 63,* 190–199.

Jones, S. L., & Jones, P. K. (1993). The role of adult children in their parent's divorce. *Journal of Divorce and Remarriage, 21,* 55–71.

Kagan, J. (1984). *The nature of the child.* New York: Basic Books.

Kahn, J. R., & London, K. A. (1991). Premarital sex and the risk of divorce. *Journal of Marriage and the Family, 53,* 845–855.

Kalter, N. (1990). *Growing up with divorce.* New York: Free Press.

Kamerman, S. B., & Kahn, A. J. (1988). U.S. issues in international perspective. In A. J. Kahn & S. B. Kamerman (Eds.), *Child support: From debt collection to social policy* (pp. 350–376). Newbury Park, CA: Sage.

Kaplan, L., & Hennon, C. B. (1992). Remarriage education: The personal reflections program. *Family Relations, 41,* 127–134.

Kaplan, L., Hennon, C. B., & Ade-Ridder, L. (1993). Splitting custody of children between parents: Impact on the sibling system. *Families in Society, 74,* 131–143.

Kaslow, F. W., & Schwartz, L. L. (1987). *The dynamics of divorce: A life cycle perspective.* New York: Brunner Mazel.

Katzev, A. R., Warner, R. L., & Acock, A. C. (1994). Girls or boys?

relationship of child gender to marital instability. *Journal of Marriage and the Family, 56,* 89–100.

Kaufmann, K. S. (1988). *Reworking the relationship: College students and their divorcing parents* (Work in Progress: Stone Center for Developmental Services and Studies). Wellesley, MA: Wellesley College.

Kaye/Kantrowitz, M. (1991). The issue is power: Some notes on Jewish women and therapy. In R. J. Siegel & E. Cole (Eds.), *Jewish women in therapy* (pp. 7–18). New York: Harrington Park Press.

Kelley, P. (1992). Healthy stepfamily functioning. *Families in Society, 73,* 579–587.

Kelly, J. B. (1993). Developing and implementing post-divorce parenting plans: Does the forum make a difference? In C. E. Depner & J. H. Bray (Eds.), *Nonresidential parenting* (pp.136–155). Newbury Park, CA: Sage.

Kelly, J., & Wallerstein, J. (1977). Brief interventions with children in divorcing families. *American Journal of Orthopsychiatry, 47,* 23–39.

Kenemore, T. K., & Wineberg, L. D. (1984). The tie that binds: A clinical perspective on divorced mothers and adolescent sons. *Clinical Social Work Journal, 12,* 332–346.

Kersten, K. K. (1990). The process of marital disaffection: Interventions at various stages. *Family Relations, 39,* 257–265.

Keysar, A. (1994). Single-parent families' participation in the Jewish community. *Journal of Jewish Communal Service, 70,* 127–133.

Kilborn, P. T. (1992, July 7). Lives of unexpected poverty in a land of plenty. *The New York Times,* pp. A1, A14.

King, V. (1994). Non–resident father involvement and child well-being: Can dads make a difference? *Journal of Family Issues, 15,* 78–96.

Kissman, K. (1991). Feminist–based social work with single-parent families. *Families in Society, 72,* 23–28.

Kissman, K., & Allen, J. (1993). *Single-parent families.* Newbury Park, CA: Sage.

Kitson, G. C. (1992). *Portrait of divorce.* New York: Guilford.

Koel, A., Clark, S. C., Straus, R. B., Whitney, R. R., & Hauser, B. B. (1994). Patterns of relitigation in the postdivorce family. *Journal of Marriage and the Family, 56,* 265–277.

Koff, G. J. (1989). *Love and the law.* New York: Simon & Schuster.

Kramer, L., & Washo, C. A. (1993). Evaluation of a court-mandated prevention program for divorcing parents: The children first program. *Family Relations, 42,* 179–186.

Krantz, S. (1988). Divorce and children. In S. M. Dornbusch & M. H.

Strober (Eds.), *Feminism, children, and the new families* (pp. 249–273). New York: Guilford.

Krantzler, M. (1974). *Creative divorce*. New York: M. Evans.

Kressel, K., & Deutsch, M. (1977). Divorce therapy: An in-depth survey of therapists' views. *Family Process, 16,* 413–443.

Kristall, J. B., & Greif, G. L. (1994). Meeting the needs of noncustodial parents in the Jewish community. *Journal of Jewish Communal Service, 70,* 160–167.

Kruk, E. (1994). The disengaged noncustodial father: Implications for social work practice with the divorced family. *Social Work, 39,* 15–25.

Kubler-Ross, E. (1969). *On death and dying*. New York: Macmillan.

Kurdek, L. (1989). Children's adjustment. In M. R. Textor (Ed.), *The divorce and divorce therapy handbook* (pp. 77–102). Northvale, NJ: Jason Aronson.

Lawson, C. A. (1992, August 6). Violence at home: "They don't want anyone to know." *The New York Times,* pp. C1, C6.

Leon, I. (1992). Perinatal loss: Choreographing grief on the obstetrics unit. *American Journal of Orthopsychiatry, 62,* 7–8.

Lewin, T. (1994, May 21). Private firms help single parents get what's due. *The New York Times,* pp. 1, 9.

Longres, J. F. (1990). *Human behavior in the social environment*. Itasca, IL: Peacock.

Lowery, C. R. (1989). Psychotherapy with children of divorced families. In M. R. Textor (Ed.), *The divorce and divorce therapy handbook* (pp. 225–241). Northvale, NJ: Jason Aronson.

Maccoby, E. E., Buchanan, C. M., Mnookin, R. H., & Dornbusch, S. M. (1993). Postdivorce roles of mothers and fathers in the lives of their children. *Family Psychology, 7,* 24–38.

Maccoby, E. E., Depner, C. E., & Mnookin, R. H. (1990). Coparenting in the second year after divorce. *Journal of Marriage and the Family, 52,* 141–155.

Maccoby, E. E., & Mnookin, R. H. (1992). *Dividing the child: Social and legal dilemmas of custody*. Cambridge: Harvard University Press.

Mack, R. N. (1989). Spouse abuse—a dyadic approach. In G. R. Weeks (Ed.), *Treating couples: The intersystem model of the Marriage Council of Philadelphia* (pp. 191–214). New York: Brunner Mazel.

Marek, T. (1989). Separation and divorce therapy—a struggle to grow for clients and therapists. In G. R. Weeks (Ed.), *Treating couples: The intersystem model of the Marriage Council of Philadelphia* (pp. 215–235). New York: Brunner Mazel.

Marshall, R. (1991). *The state of families, 3*. Milwaukee: Family Service America.

Masheter, C. (1991). Postdivorce relationships between ex-spouses: The roles of attachment and interpersonal conflict. *Journal of Marriage and the Family, 53*, 103–110.

Mauldin, T. A. (1991). Economic consequences of divorce or separation among women in poverty. *Journal of Divorce, 14*, 163–177.

McAdoo, H. (1990). A portrait of African American families in the United States. In S. E. Rix (Ed.), *The American woman 1990–91: A status report* (pp. 71–93). New York: W. W. Norton.

McDonald, T. P., Moran, J. R., & Garfinkel, I. (1990). Absent fathers' ability to pay more child support. *Journal of Social Service Research, 13*, 1–18.

McGoldrick, M., Preto, N. G., Hines, P. M., & Lee, E. (1989). Ethnicity and women. In M. McGoldrick, C. Anderson, & F. Walsh (Eds.), *Women in families* (pp. 169–199). New York: W. W. Norton.

McGoldrick, M., Preto, N. G., Hines, P. M., & Lee, E. (1991). Ethnicity and family therapy. In A. S. Gurman & D. P. Kniskern (Eds.), *Handbook of family therapy* (Vol. 2, pp. 546–582). New York: Brunner Mazel.

McLanahan, S., & Bumpass, L. L. (1988). Intergenerational consequences of family disruption. *American Journal of Sociology, 94*, 130–152.

Meth, R. L., & Passick, R. S. (1990). *Men in therapy: The challenge of change*. New York: Guilford.

Meyer, D. R., & Garasky, S. (1993). Custodial fathers: Myths, realities, and child support policy. *Journal of Marriage and the Family, 55*, 73–89.

Milne, A. (1992). Divorce mediation: An application of social work skills and techniques. In C. W. LeCroy (Ed.), *Case studies in social work practice* (pp. 154–160). Belmont, CA: Wadsworth.

Minkler, M., Roe, K. M., & Robertson-Beckley, R. J. (1994). Raising grandchildren from crack-cocaine households: Effects on family and friendship ties of African-American women. *American Journal of Orthopsychiatry, 64*, 20–29.

Mirande, A. (1991). Ethnicity and fatherhood. In F. M. Bozett & S. M. H. Hanson (Eds.), *Fatherhood and families in cultural context* (pp. 53–82). New York: Springer.

Mitchell-Flynn, C., & Hutchinson, R. L. (1993). A longitudinal study of the problems and concerns of urban divorced men. *Journal of Divorce and Remarriage, 20*, 161–182.

Montalvo, F. F. (1991). Phenotyping acculturation and biracial assimilation of Mexican Americans. In M. Sotomayor (Ed.), *Empowering Hispanic Families* (pp. 97–119). Milwaukee: Family Service Association.

Moore, V. I., & Schwebel, A. I. (1993). Factors contributing to divorce: A study of race differences. *Journal of Divorce and Remarriage, 20*, 123–135.

Morgan, L. A. (1991). *After marriage ends: Economic consequences for midlife women*. Newbury Park, CA: Sage.

Morgan, S. P., Lye, D. N., & Condran, G. A. (1988). Sons, daughters, and the risk of marital disruption. *American Journal of Sociology, 94*, 110–129.

Mott, F. L. (1994). Sons, daughters and fathers' absence: Differentials in father–leaving probabilities and in home environments. *Journal of Family Issues, 15*, 97–128.

Myers, M. (1989). *Men and divorce*. New York: Guilford.

Neff, J. A., & Schluter, T. D. (1993). Marital status and depressive symptoms: The role of race/ethnicity and sex. *Journal of Divorce and Remarriage, 20*, 137–160.

Noble, B. N. (1994a, February 13). After the divorce, the deluge. *The New York Times* (Business section), p. 25.

Noble, B. N. (1994b, July 31). Making family leave a reality. *The New York Times* (Business section), p. 19.

Olson, M. R., & Haynes, J. A. (1993). Successful single parents. *Families in Society, 74*, 259–267.

Paasch, K. M., & Teachman, J. D. (1991). Gender of children and receipt of assistance from absent fathers. *Journal of Family Issues, 12*, 450–466.

Parad, H. J., & Parad, L. G. (1990). Crisis intervention: An introductory overview. In H. J. Parad and L. G. Parad (Eds.), *Crisis intervention book 2: The practitioner's sourcebook for brief therapy* (pp. 3–66). Milwaukee: Family Service Association.

Pasley, K., Dollahite, D. C., & Ihinger-Tallman, M. (1993). Clinical applications of research findings on the spouse and stepparent roles in remarriage. *Family Relations, 42*, 315–322.

Pear, R. (1993, January 15). Poverty termed a divorce factor. *The New York Times*, p. A10.

Pearson, J. & Thoennes, N. (1990). Custody after divorce: Demographic and attitudinal patterns. *American Journal of Orthopsychiatry, 60*, 233–249.

Peck, J. S., & Manocherian, J. (1989). Divorce and the changing family life cycle. In B. Carter & M. McGoldrick (Eds.), *The changing family life cycle* (pp. 335–369). Boston: Allyn and Bacon.

Peterson, J. L., & Nord, C. W. (1990). The regular receipt of child support: A multistep process. *Journal of Marriage and the Family*, 52, 539–551.

Peterson, R. R. (1989). *Women, work, and divorce*. Albany, NY: State University of New York Press.

Pope, H., & Mueller, C. W. (1976). The intergenerational transmission of marital instability: Comparisons by race and sex. *Journal of Social Issues*, 32, 49–66.

Price, S. J. & McKenry, P. C. (1988). *Divorce*. Newbury Park, CA: Sage.

Rather, J. (1994, June 12). Court orders in abuse cases often fail to deter violence. *The New York Times* (Long Island section), p. 24.

Rayman, P. (1987). Women and unemployment. *Social Research*, 54, 355–376.

Reisman, B. (1994). A preferred family policy for the American Jewish community. *Journal of Jewish Communal Service*, 70, 109–114.

Rice, D. G., & Rice, J. K. (1986a). Separation and divorce therapy. In N. S. Jacobson and A. S. Gurman (Eds.), *Clinical handbook of marital therapy* (pp. 279–299). New York: Guilford.

Rice, J. K., & Rice, D. G. (1986b). *Living through divorce*. New York: Guilford.

Richards, L. N., & Schmlege, C. J. (1993). Problems and strengths of single-parent families: Implications for practice and policy. *Family Relations*, 42, 277–285.

Riessman, C. K. (1990). *Divorce talk: Women and men make sense of personal relationships*. New Brunswick, NJ: Rutgers University Press.

Ross, C. E., Mirowsky, J., & Goldsteen, K. (1990). The impact of the family on health: The decade in review. *Journal of Marriage and the Family*, 52, 1059–1070.

Rubin, L. (1979). *Women of a certain age: The midlife search for self*. New York: Harper and Row.

Rubin, L. (1992). *Worlds of pain*. New York: Basic Books.

Sakai, C. E. (1991). Group intervention strategies with domestic abusers. *Families in Society*, 72, 536–542.

Sands, R., & Richardson, V. (1986). Clinical practice with women in their middle years. *Social Work*, 31, 36–43.

Schlesinger, R. A. (1991). Midlife transitions among Jewish women: Counseling issues. In R. J. Siegel & E. Cole (Eds.), *Jewish women in therapy* (pp. 91–100). New York: Harrington Park Press.

Schwebel, A. I., Fine, M., & Moreland, J. R. (1988). Clinical work with divorced and widowed fathers: The adjusting family model. In

P. Bronstein & C. P. Cowan (Eds.), *Fatherhood today: Men's chang-ing role in the family* (pp. 291–319). New York: Wiley.

Scott, C. (1990, November 7). As baby boomers age, fewer couples untie the knot. *The Wall Street Journal*, pp. B1, B6.

Seltzer, J. A. (1991). Relationships between fathers and children who live apart: The father's role after separation. *Journal of Marriage and the Family, 53,* 79–101.

Seltzer, J. A., & Brandreth. Y. (1994). What fathers say about involve-ment with children after separation. *Journal of Family Issues, 15,* 49–77.

Seltzer, J. A., & Garfinkel, I. (1990). Inequality in divorce settlements: An investigation of property settlements and child support awards. *Social Science Research, 19,* 82–111.

Shapira, E., & Tiell, J. F. (1994). Career and economic implications of divorce within the Jewish community. *Journal of Jewish Communal Service, 70,* 175–178.

Sidel, R. (1990). *On her own: Growing up in the shadow of the American dream.* New York: Penguin.

Silverstein, L. B. (1991). Transforming the debate about child care and maternal employment. *American Psychologist, 46,* 1025–1032.

Simons, R., Whitbeck, L. B., Beaman, J., & Conger, R. D. (1994). The impact of mothers' parenting, involvement by nonresidential fa-thers, and parental conflict on the adjustment of adolescent children. *Journal of Marriage and the Family, 56,* 356–374.

Slonim, M. B. (1991). *Children, culture, and ethnicity.* New York: Garland.

Soifer, S. (1991). Infusing content on Jews and the problem of anti–Semitism into social work curricula. *Journal of Social Work Educa-tion, 27,* 156–167.

Soldano, K. W. (1990). Divorce: Clinical implications for treatment of children. In B. D. Garfinkel, G. A. Carlson, & E. B. Weller (Eds.), *Psychiatric disorders in children and adolescents* (pp. 392–409). Phil-adelphia: Saunders.

Spitze, G., Logan, J. R., Deane, G., & Zerger, S. (1994). Adult chil-dren's divorce and intergenerational relationships. *Journal of Mar-riage and the Family, 56,* 279–294.

Sprenkle, D. H. (1989). The clinical practice of divorce therapy. In M. Textor (Ed.), *The divorce and divorce therapy handbook* (pp. 171–195). Northvale, NJ: Jason Aronson.

Springer, C. (1991). Clinical work with adolescents and their parents during family transition: Transference and countertransference issues. *Clinical Social Work Journal, 19,* 405–415.

Stack, C. (1974). *All our kin: Strategies for survival in a Black community*. New York: Harper and Row.

Straus, M. B. (1988). Divorced mothers. In B. Birns & D. F. Hay (Eds.), *The different faces of motherhood* (pp. 215–238). New York: Plenum Press.

Tavris, C. (1989, February 26). A remedy but not a cure. [Review of *Second chances*]. *New York Times Book Review*, 13–14.

Taylor, R. J., Chatters, L. M., Tucker, M. B., & Lewis, E. (1990). Developments in research on black families: A decade review. *Journal of Marriage and the Family*, *52*, 993–1014.

Teachman, J. D. (1991). Who pays? Receipt of child support in the United States. *Journal of Marriage and the Family*, *53*, 759–772.

Teachman, J. D. & Paasch, K. (1993). The economics of parenting apart. In C. E. Depner & J. H. Bray (Eds.), *Nonresidential parenting* (pp. 61–86). Newbury Park, CA: Sage.

Textor, M. (1989). The divorce transition. In M. Textor (Ed.), *The divorce and divorce therapy handbook* (pp. 3–44). Northvale, NJ: Jason Aronson.

Thomson, E., & Colella, U. (1992). Cohabitation and marital stability. *Journal of Marriage and the Family*, *54*, 259–267.

Thomson, E., McLanahan, S., & Curtin, R. B. (1992). Family structure, gender, and parental socialization. *Journal of Marriage and the Family*, *54*, 368–378.

Thweatt, R. W. (1980). Divorce: Crisis intervention guided by attachment theory. *American Journal of Psychotherapy*, *34*, 240–245.

Timberlake, E. M., & Chipungu, S. S. (1992). Grandmotherhood: Contemporary meaning among African-American middle-class grandmothers. *Social Work*, *37*, 216–222.

Tolman, R. M., & Bennett, L. (1992). Group work with men who batter. In C. W. LeCroy (Ed.), *Case studies in social work practice* (pp. 206–213). Belmont, CA: Wadsworth.

Toner, R. (1992, July 5). New politics of welfare focuses on its flaws. *The New York Times*, pp. 1, 16.

Tschann, J. M., Johnston, J. R., Kline, M., & Wallerstein, J. S. (1989). Family process and children's functioning during divorce. *Journal of Marriage and the Family*, *51*, 431–444.

Tschann, J. M., Johnston, J. R., Kline, M., & Wallerstein, J. S. (1990). Conflict, loss, change and parent-child relationships: Predicting children's adjustment during divorce. *Journal of Divorce*, *13*, 1–22.

Tucker, M. B., & Taylor, R. J. (1989). Demographic correlates of relationship status among Black Americans. *Journal of Marriage and the Family*, *51*, 655–665.

Uhlenberg, P., Cooney, T., & Boyd, R. (1990). Divorce for women after midlife. *Journal of Gerontology: Social Sciences*, *45*, S3–S11.

Umberson, D., & Williams, C. L. (1993). Divorced fathers: Parental role strain and psychological distress. *Journal of Family Issues*, *14*, 378–400.

Vega, W. A. (1990). Hispanic families in the 1980s: A decade of research. *Journal of Marriage and the Family*, *52*, 1015–1024.

Visher, E. B., & Visher, J. S. (1988). *Old loyalties, new ties: Therapeutic strategies with stepfamilies*. New York: Brunner Mazel.

Wagner, R. M. (1987). Changes in extended family relationships for Mexican American and Anglo single mothers. *Journal of Divorce and Remarriage*, *11*, 69–87.

Wagner, R. M. (1993). Psychosocial adjustments during the first year of parenthood: A comparison of Mexican–American and Anglo women. *Journal of Divorce and Remarriage*, *19*, 121–142.

Wallace, J. B. (1992). Reconsidering the life review: The social construction of talk about the past. *The Gerontologist*, *32*, 120–125.

Wallerstein, J. (1984). Children of divorce: Preliminary report of a ten-year follow-up of young children. *American Journal of Orthopsychiatry*, *54*, 444–458.

Wallerstein, J. (1986). Women after divorce: Preliminary report from a ten-year follow-up. *American Journal of Orthopsychiatry*, *56*, 65–77.

Wallerstein, J. (1989, January 22). Children after divorce: Wounds that don't heal. *The New York Times* (Magazine section), pp. 18–21, 41–44.

Wallerstein, J. (1990). Transference and countertransference in clinical intervention with divorcing families. *American Journal of Orthopsychiatry*, *60*, 337–345.

Wallerstein, J. (1993, December 14). *Three sisters revisited* [lecture and discussion]. Twelfth Peter Blos Biennial Lecture. The Martha K. Selig Educational Institute and Jewish Board of Family and Children's Services. New York: New York University Medical Center, Farkas Auditorium.

Wallerstein, J. (1994). Children of divorce: Challenge for the 1990's. *Journal of Jewish Communal Service*, *70*, 100–108.

Wallerstein, J., & Blakeslee, S. (1989). *Second chances*. New York: Ticknor and Fields.

Wallerstein, J., & Kelly, J. (1977). Divorce counseling: A community service for families in the midst of divorce. *American Journal of Orthopsychiatry*, *47*, 4–22.

Wallerstein, J., & Kelly, J. (1980). *Surviving the breakup*. New York: Basic Books.

Walsh, F. (1991). Promoting healthy functioning in divorced and remarried families. In A. S. Gurman & D. P. Kniskern (Eds.), *Handbook of family therapy* (Vol. 2, pp. 525–545). New York: Brunner Mazel.

Weingarten, H. (1988). The impact of late life divorce: A conceptual and empirical study. *Journal of Divorce, 12*, 21–39.

Weiss, R. (1975). *Marital separation.* New York: Basic Books.

Weitzman, L. (1988). Women and children last: The social and economic consequences of divorce law reforms. In S. M. Dornbusch & M. H. Strober (Eds.), *Feminism, children, and the new families* (pp. 212–248). New York: Guilford.

West, B., & Kissman, K. (1991). Mothers without custody: Treatment issues. In C. A. Everett (Ed.), *The consequences of divorce* (pp. 229–338). New York: Haworth.

Whitbeck, L. B., Hoyt, D. R., & Huck, S. M. (1993). Family relationship history, contemporary parent-grandparent relationship quality, and the grandparent-grandchild relationship. *Journal of Marriage and the Family, 55*, 1025–1036.

White, L. K. (1990). Determinants of divorce: A review of research in the eighties. *Journal of Marriage and the Family, 52*, 904–912.

Whitsett, D., & Land, H. (1992). The development of a role strain index for stepparents. *Families in Society, 73*, 14–22.

Williams, B. (1994). Reflections on family poverty. *Families in Society, 75*, 47–50.

Williams, D. R., Takeuchi, D. T., & Adair, R. K. (1992). Marital status and psychiatric disorders among Blacks and Whites. *Journal of Health and Social Behavior, 33*, 140–157.

Wiseman, R. (1975). Crisis theory and the process of divorce. *Social Casework, 56*, 205–212.

Yu, M. (1993). Divorce and culturally different older women: Issues of strategies and interventions. *Journal of Divorce and Remarriage, 21*, 41–54.

Zastrow, C. & Kirst-Ashman, K. (1990). *Understanding human behavior and the social environment.* Chicago: Nelson Hall.

Zigler, E. F., & Gilman, E. P. (1990). An agenda for the 1990's: Supporting families. In D. Blankenhorn, S. Bayme, & J. B. Elshtain (Eds.), *Rebuilding the nest: A new commitment to the American family* (pp. 237–250). Milwaukee, WI: Family Service Association.

INDEX

A

Abuse and neglect of children, 95
  case example of, 136–137
Abused women. *See* Battered
  women
Adolescents. *See* Age; Children;
  Divorce transition stage;
  Postdivorce stage; Predivorce
  stage
Adults. *See* Custodial fathers;
  Custodial mothers; Custody;
  Divorce transition stage;
  Employment; Postdivorce
  stage; Predivorce stage
AFDC. *See* Aid to Families with
  Dependent Children (AFDC)
African Americans
  abuse, ambivalence about facing
    and, 50–51
  adult children of divorce, 186
    case example of, 189
  anger ventilation of, 131
  attitude toward therapy among,
    133–134, 204, 213
  church and community support for,
    107
    case example of, 173–174
  discipline among, 129
  discrimination against, 13, 50, 74,
    118
  divorce rates of, 7, 8, 13–14, 213
  elder care and, 102, 183
  employment attitudes of women,
    66, 101, 118

extended family
  assistance from, 14, 44–45, 64,
    96–97, 102, 168–169
  conflicts and, 45, 97, 168–169
  emotionally disturbed parents
    and, 198
  relationships, case example of,
    173–174
Family Life Education programs
  and, 213
independence for women
  case example of, 74–76
  cultural emphasis on, 14, 41, 66,
    90, 118, 184, 203
male/female ratio among, 13–14
marriage as a value among, 14,
  186
maternal role as a value among,
  51, 111, 131
mourning among, 111
noncustodial parent, loss of, 103
postdivorce dating by, 121
public education of, 13, 215
  case example of, 189
remarriage by, 14, 181
scapegoating of offspring among,
  149
social isolation of, 184, 199
Age
  of offspring and changes in
    custody, support, and
    visitation arrangements, 180
  divorce rates affected by, 6
  and impact of divorce on children,
    43, 106

245

Springer Publishing Company

BEYOND THE TRADITIONAL FAMILY
Voices of Diversity

Betty Polisar Reigot and **Rita K. Spina**, PhD

In this innovative text, the authors present original qualitative research based on personal interviews with selected modern families. These interviews reveal the new variety of domestic relationships that are emerging today, including single mothers by choice, adolescent mothers, fathers as caretakers, homosexual parents, grandparents as parents, and parents by technology. The stories carry important implications for social policy and provide insightful qualitative materials for professionals including sociologists, family therapists and academics in social work and psychology.

Contents:

1995   224pp   0-8261-9030-8   hardcover

536 Broadway, New York, NY 10012-3955 • (212) 431-4370 • Fax (212) 941-7842

Springer Publishing Company

LOGOTHERAPY FOR THE HELPING PROFESSIONAL
Meaningful Social Work

David Guttmann, DSW

In this helpful guide, the author explains the pioneering work of Dr. Viktor Frankl and his theories of logotherapy. This volume will enable helping professionals to supplement traditional methods of psychotherapy with logotherapy techniques in order to improve their effectiveness through clearer understanding of their clients' problems. Professionals can then derive greater personal meaning and satisfaction from their work, thereby lessening the potential for stress and burnout. This volume addresses therapists, clinical social workers, and counselors.

Contents:

I: Major Concepts in Logotherapy. The Development of Logotherapy • Logotherapy and Psychoanalysis: Similarities and Differences • The Noetic or Spiritual Dimension • The "Tragic Triad": Logotherapy's Attitude to Guilt, Suffering, and Death

II: Logotherapeutic Treatment and Application. Paradoxical Intention as a Special Logotherapeutic Technique • "Dereflection" as Counteracting Behavior • Other Logotherapeutic Techniques • The "Socratic Dialogue" Logotherapy's Main Tool in Helping Seekers Search for Meaning

III. Research in the Service of Logotherapy. Research on Major Logotherapeutic Concepts • Further Developments in Logotherapeutic Research

1995   320pp   0-8261-9020-0   hardcover

536 Broadway, New York, NY 10012-3955 • (212) 431-4370 • Fax (212) 941-7842

S *Springer Publishing Company*

TREATING ATTACHMENT ABUSE
A Compassionate Approach

Steven Stosny, PhD

Attachment abuse can involve both physical and emotional violence between people in close relationships, which includes couples, parents and their children, and adult children and their aging parents, among others. Attachment abusers blame their victims for their own feelings of shame, inadequacy, or inability to love. Dr. Stosny's innovative and integrative approach to the treatment of attachment abuse emphasizes the importance of compassion for both the abused and the abuser. This hands-on manual provides a series of treatment modules designed to teach the perpetrators and the victims how to cope with their feelings and to end attachment abuse.

Contents:

The Role of Attachment in Abuse. Beginnings: Self-Building, Abuse, and Treatment • Attachment • Attachment Abuse: Why We Hurt the Ones We Love • Pathways to Abuse: Deficits in Attachment Skills and Affect-Regulation • A New Response for Clinicians in the Prevention of Emotional Abuse and Violence • Compassion and Therapeutic Morality

Treating Attachment Abuse. The Compassion Workshop • Healing • Dramatic Compassion • Self-Empowerment • Empowerment of Loved Ones • Negotiating Attachment Relationships • Moving Toward the Future

1995 304pp 0-8261-8960-1 hard $44.95 (outside US $49.80)

536 Broadway, New York, NY 10012-3955 • (212) 431-4370 • Fax (212) 941-7842

Springer Publishing Company

COUNSELING ADULTS IN TRANSITION
Linking Practice with Theory

Nancy K. Schlossberg, EdD
Elinor B. Waters, EdD, and
Jane Goodman, PhD

In this updated edition of a highly successful text, the authors expand on their transition model, which offers effective adult counseling through the integration of empirical knowledge and theory with practice. The authors combine an understanding of adult development with practical strategies for counseling clients in personal and professional transition. A framework is provided for individual, group, and work settings. The final chapter goes beyond intervention to discuss issues such as consulting and advocacy.

Contents:

Contributions of Adult Development Theories to the Transition Framework • The Transition Framework • A Framework for Helping: Factors that Influence Negotiating the Transition • What Counselors Hear About Individual Transitions • What Counselors Hear About Relationship Transitions • What Counselors Hear About Work Transitions • What Can Counselors Do To Help Individuals in Transition? • What Can Counselors Do in Groups to Help Adults in Transition? • Group Counseling Practice

1995   320pp   0-8261-4231-1   hardcover

536 Broadway, New York, NY 10012-3955 • (212) 431-4370 • Fax (212) 941-7842